Emmanuel Joseph Sieyès

POLITICAL WRITINGS

Emmanuel Joseph Sieyès

POLITICAL WRITINGS

Including the Debate between
Sieyès and Tom Paine in 1791

EDITED, WITH AN INTRODUCTION
AND TRANSLATION OF
What Is the Third Estate?
BY MICHAEL SONENSCHER

Hackett Publishing Company, Inc.
Indianapolis/Cambridge

Printed in the United States of America

14 13 12 11 2 3 4 5 6 7

For further information, please address:

Hackett Publishing Company, Inc.
P.O. Box 44937
Indianapolis, IN 46244-0937

www.hackettpublishing.com

Cover design by Listenberger Design & Associates
Interior design by Jennifer Plumley
Composition by Professional Book Compositors, Inc.
Printed at Edwards Brothers, Inc.

Library of Congress Cataloging-in-Publication Data

Sieyès, Emmanuel Joseph, comte, 1748–1836.
Political writings: including the debate between Sieyès and Tom Paine in 1791 / Emmanuel Joseph Sieyès; edited, with an introduction and translation of What is the Third Estate?, by Michael Sonenscher.
p. cm.
Includes bibliographical references and index.
ISBN 0-87220-431-6 — ISBN 0-87220-430-8 (pbk.)
1. Political science. 2. State, The. I. Sonenscher, Michael. II. Title.

JC179.S53 2003
320.1—dc21 2003047178

ISBN-13: 978-0-87220-431-7 (cloth)
ISBN-13: 978-0-87220-430-0 (pbk.)

The paper used in this publication meets the minimum requirements of American National Standard for Information Sciences—Permanence of Paper for Printed Library Materials, ANSI Z39.48-1984

Contents

ACKNOWLEDGMENTS

I am grateful to the Provost and Fellows of King's College, Cambridge for their support and encouragement, and to the British Academy for a grant to enable me to study Sieyès' papers in the Archives Nationales in Paris. I owe a great deal to John Dunn, Biancamaria Fontana, and Pasquale Pasquino for organizing a seminar series at King's College in 1989–1990 that first showed me why Sieyès' political thought is worth trying to understand. I have an even bigger debt to Istvan Hont for his unfailing intellectual generosity and constant willingness to give me the benefit of his own understanding of eighteenth-century political thought. I am grateful, too, to Elizabeth Allen, Richard Bourke, Colin Jones, and Miles Taylor for their comments on earlier drafts of the Introduction. I am particularly indebted to Brian Rak and his colleagues at Hackett for their skill, patience, and kindness. I am also most grateful to the anonymous reader asked by Hackett to comment on an earlier version of the Introduction. The extensive comments that he or she wrote went well beyond the ordinary call of duty and were a genuine model of constructive criticism. If I have fallen short of the advice I was given, the fault is certainly mine.

Introduction

Emmanuel Joseph Sieyès and the Idea of Representative Government

The idea of representative government has a somewhat deceptive simplicity. At its most straightforward it looks as if it is simply democracy at one remove, a set of elected representatives making decisions that, on a smaller, more manageable scale, we might have been able to make for ourselves. But it is not quite the case that we pay taxes to the people we elect, or expect them to pay us the welfare benefits to which we may sometimes be entitled. Nor is it quite the case that we enlist in armies, navies or air forces belonging to our elected representatives. Instead we pay state or federal taxes, just as we sometimes receive state or federal benefits or decide to enlist in the French army, the German air force, or the United States navy. We do so, moreover, irrespective of which particular political party we may have decided to support or whether we actually voted for or against the government of the day. Representative governments rule us all, whatever the size of their electoral majorities and whatever the kind of mandate they might have been given on the day that the polls closed. Representative governments also represent us all, especially where matters of foreign policy are concerned, although it is not entirely clear whether this makes us all responsible for any, or every, act of government carried out in our name. But even if we are responsible for all of our representatives' acts, it is still not the case that they are responsible for all of ours. This applies not only to the choices that we make from day to day, but above all to our freedom to choose representatives of our own, not those nominated by the government of the day. Yet even though we do, in some sense, choose our representatives, we usually vote for political parties and not for the individual members of a government themselves. And however we do choose them, we still do not owe them much allegiance because we can, and may well, elect a different government in four or five years time. Nor do our representatives owe much allegiance to us, because the oaths that they swear are not oaths of allegiance to us but to the national or federal constitutions from which their rights and powers derive. It is, in short, not entirely clear whether a representative government represents us or represents a state. It may be the case that it does both. But it is not entirely clear why it should, or how it actually does.

These uncertainties and ambiguities are all good reasons for reading the work of the abbé Emmanuel Joseph Sieyès (1748–1836), because these are the theoretical problems that Sieyès addressed. They are the theoretical problems underlying modern democracy and the sometimes perplexing combination of sovereign states, majority rule, competitive markets, and individual liberty that modern democracy is usually taken to be. Sieyès thought about these problems for most of his adult life, well before the publication of *What is the Third Estate?* (*Qu'est ce qu'est le tiers état?*), the pamphlet that established his reputation as the theoretical architect of the French Revolution of 1789, and long after the coup d'état of 18 Brumaire of the Year VIII (9 November 1799), the military coup that brought Napoleon Bonaparte to power, in which Sieyès himself played a major part. He took great care to preserve his manuscript notes and drafts, taking them with him to Brussels when he went into exile in 1815 and bringing them back to France when the July Revolution of 1830 allowed him to return. Some of these papers go back to the late 1760s and early 1770s. Others, although not dated, were certainly written in the first or second decades of the nineteenth century. In 1770, at the age of twenty-two, he made a list of the books that he would like to have bought if, as he noted, he had ever had enough money to afford them all.[1] He may not have read every one, but his extensive notes and comments (including comments on English-language works), show that he did read a great deal during the following years. Sieyès insisted quite frequently that well before 1789 he had thought of everything to be found in the relatively small number of pamphlets that he wrote, all published during the period of the French Revolution. He even drafted his own review of *What is the Third Estate?* to highlight his conviction that, although it might look like a work of circumstance, it was, as he put it, the product of years of silent study of "moral theory appropriate to a whole society" (*la grande morale sociale*) and of "the true science of the social order" (*la véritable science de l'ordre social*).[2] He sometimes railed privately against the Revolution ("that detestable revolution") for robbing him of the time he needed to read and write, not just on politics but also on moral theory,

---

[1] Archives Nationales, Paris (henceforth A. N.) 284 AP 1, dossier 3. I have tried to use Sieyès' papers extensively in this introduction, partly because of the light they throw on the more elaborately structured arguments of his published works and partly because of the many terminological innovations that they contain. References to secondary authorities have been limited mainly to the sources of factual information mentioned in the text. A guide to further reading can be found below, pp. 181–2.

[2] A. N. 284 AP 4, dossier 8. The full text of this draft has been published by Pasquale Pasquino in his *Sieyès et l'invention de la constitution en France* (Paris, Odile Jacob,1998), pp. 166–70.

the theory of knowledge and political economy, the subject for which he became responsible when he was elected to the French *Institut* in 1795.[3] Yet even in exile he wrote nothing systematic. The frequent but usually minor revisions he made to his published works suggest a preoccupation with linguistic precision bordering on the compulsive.[4] His unpublished papers reveal a recurrent dissatisfaction with his own terminology and a constant uneasiness about the arbitrary potential of any conceptual language once some particular choice of terms had been selected from the boundless possibilities of what he called "the lingual world." In extremis he sometimes had to dictate what he thought. The only surviving record of his version of the French republican constitution of the Year VIII, the constitution established after the coup d'état by Napoleon Bonaparte in 1799, was produced in this way.[5]

Much of this restless intelligence was applied to the creation of a new conceptual vocabulary for analyzing and describing political society. Although some of his innovations appeared in his published work, many others were left unpublished and have begun to come to light only since 1967 when his papers were acquired by the French Archives Nationales.[6] The term "social science" (*science sociale*), for example, made a first, short-lived appearance in the earliest edition of *What is the Third Estate?* before being replaced by what, to his contemporaries, was the more recognizable "science of the social art" (*science de l'art social*) in the four subsequent editions of the pamphlet, published during his lifetime.[7] Alongside "so-

---

[3] Looking back at a draft of a work on human needs and the means they have to meet them (*Des besoins de l'homme et de ses moyens*) that he had started in 1775, he commented, "I had so much material. Why did that detestable revolution divert me from my work!" ("J'avais tant de matières. Pourquoi cette détestable révolution m'a-t-elle détourné de mes travaux!"). A. N. 284 AP 5, dossier 3[1].

[4] See the note on the difference between being distinguished *by* and distinguished *from* someone, in the *Essay on Privileges*, below p. 74, for an example of the use to which this interest in precision could be put.

[5] Antoine-Jacques-Claude-Joseph Boulay de la Meurthe, *Théorie constitutionnelle de Sieyès* (Paris, 1836).

[6] There are now two valuable collections of extracts from these papers: Christine Fauré, Jacques Guilhaumou, and Jacques Valier (eds.), *Des Manuscrits de Sieyès 1773–1799* (Paris, Honoré Champion, 1999) and Roberto Zapperi, *Emmanuel Joseph Sieyès: Ecrits Politiques* (Montreux, Editions des Archives contemporaines, 1998). Many quotations from Sieyès' papers can be found in English translation in Murray Forsyth, *Reason and Revolution: The Political Thought of the abbé Sieyes* (Leicester (UK), Leicester University Press, 1987), a very fine work which has not, perhaps, been given the recognition that it deserves.

[7] The most extensive examination of the origins of the phrase remains Brian W. Head, "The Origins of 'La Science Sociale' in France," *Australian Journal of French Studies*, 19 (1982), pp. 115–32. Georges Gusdorf, *Les sciences humaines et la pensée occidentale, vol. 8. La*

cial science" Sieyès also contemplated a treatise on sociology (*De la sociologie*) as the basis of a system of government variously called "sociocracy" (*sociocratie*), "legiocracy" (*légiocratie*), "natiocracy" (*natiocratie*), or "humanocracy" (*homo-cratie*).[8] This impersonal system of rule would be based on what Sieyès called an "*electual* system," "*electorality*," or "*electicism*."[9] Its integrative principle would not be patriotism, but *adunation,* or the use of a hierarchy of representative institutions to turn the many different interests making up a large and populous society into a single nation. Its moral counterpart would be *assimilation,* or the values that the members of a nation would come to share. "*Assimilation,*" Sieyès noted, "is to manners (*mœurs*) as *adunation* is to interests."[10] The combination of the two, he speculated, would give rise to an *ethocracy,* or the rule of morality. It would not replace politics but would set moral authority alongside the exercise of political power, starting with the moral choices involved in individual self-government and running, "if it ever happens one day," to the "government of the human race, following the cosmopolitan law made by the deputies of nations."[11] He also toyed with the idea of a "Treatise on socialism" (*Traité du socialisme*) or, more elaborately, a "Treatise on socialism, or on the *goal* given by man to himself in society and of the *means* he has to attain it" (*Traité du socialisme, ou du but que se propose l'homme en société et des moyens qu'il a d'y parvenir*).[12]

The date of this particular piece of terminological experimentation cannot be inferred from the manuscript on which it appears. Nor is it particularly important, because "socialism" was not a term that Sieyès himself actually coined. Until the early nineteenth century the words "socialism" and "socialist" were used (mainly pejoratively) to refer to the followers of Samuel Pufendorf, the author of one of the seventeenth-century's major works of natural jurisprudence, *The Law of Nature and of Nations* (*De Iuri Naturali et Gentium*), published first in 1672 and translated into French by the Huguenot exile Jean Barbeyrac in 1706. As the

---

Conscience révolutionnaire Les Idéologues (Paris, Payot, 1978), p. 394, claimed that the term was used in 1786 in the entry "science" in the *Encyclopédie méthodique. Logique, Métaphysique et Morale,* ed. Pierre-Louis Lacretelle, 4 vols. (Paris, 1786–1791), vol. 4, p. 750, but did not notice that the fourth volume was published only in 1791.

[8] A. N. 284 AP 3, dossier 1[3].

[9] A. N. 284 AP 4, dossier 7; Fauré, Guilhaumou and Valier (eds.), *Des Manuscrits de Sieyès 1773–1799,* p. 460.

[10] A. N. 284 AP 4, dossier 11.

[11] A. N. 284 AP 5, dossier 1[11] (*Ethocratie*).

[12] A. N. 284 AP 3, dossier 1[3].

French historian, philosopher, and political economist Joseph Xavier Droz noted in his *De la philosophie morale* (*Moral Philosophy*) of 1823,

> A philosopher who is very little read nowadays, but whose writings advanced civilization in Europe, namely Pufendorf, thought that man is a moral being only because he is a sociable being, and since his duties cannot be accomplished or even exist other than in society, they all derive from a single obligation, namely, to preserve, improve, and embellish social life.

This, Droz explained, was why the "disciples" of his "wise doctrine" were known as "*socialists*."[13] A decade or so later, however, "socialism" was beginning to mean several somewhat different things. In one sense, it was used, as in an article by the French journalist Louis Reybaud published in the *Revue des Deux Mondes* in 1836, significantly entitled "Modern Socialists" to refer (again somewhat disparagingly) to the advocates of "industrialism," or the various political and economic systems set out in the works of Claude-Henri de Saint-Simon, Jean-Baptiste Say, Charles Comte, and Charles Dunoyer, published in the first quarter of the nineteenth century. In another sense, however, it was also used, as in a series of articles in the *Revue encyclopédique* by the French political philosopher Pierre Leroux between 1832 and 1834, to refer (also disparagingly) to those who advocated setting social limits on the right to private property in the way that the Jacobin leader, Maximilien Robespierre, had done in the draft of the Declaration of the Rights of Man that he had presented to the French Republican Convention in the spring of 1793 and that both the French *Society of the Rights of Man* and the English *National Union of the Working Classes and Others* had incorporated into their founding articles in 1830.[14]

---

[13] Joseph Droz, *De la philosophie morale, ou des différens systèmes sur la science de la vie* (Paris, 1823), pp. 37–8. It was undoubtedly with this sense in mind that a reviewer of a treatise on property (*De la propriété*) by a Picard magistrate named Etienne Géry Lenglet, published in 1798 and reissued in 1801, described Lenglet as someone with "sympathies for the socialists." The remark was cited by Edgard Allix, "La rivalité entre la propriété foncière et la fortune mobilière sous la révolution," *Revue d' Histoire Economique et Sociale,* 6 (1913), pp. 297–348 (p. 332, n. 3) as having been published in vol. V of the *Magasin encyclopédique* of 1801. Frustratingly (but not uncharacteristically) Allix misdescribed his source. Although the *Magasin encyclopédique* did review Lenglet's treatise in 1801, the review does not have the phrase he cites. Since Allix simply cited the phrase without comment, it is probable that it was used in another contemporary review, but I have not been able to find the correct source.

[14] On the early history of the word "socialism" see Giorgio Spini, "Sulle origini dei termini 'socialista' e 'socialismo'," *Rivista Storica Italiana,* 105 (1993), pp. 679–97 and Franco Venturi, *Italy and the Enlightenment. Studies in a Cosmopolitan Century* (London, Longman, 1972), pp. 52–62.

Sieyès' "socialism" lay at the confluence of these different conceptions of human association. It could be connected to the idea of the state as an artificial moral person, responsible in the last instance for upholding justice in human affairs, as with Pufendorf and the first "socialists."[15] It could also be connected to the idea of industry as the underlying principle of human association, as with "socialism" in its second incarnation as the "industrialism" of Jean Baptiste Say or the "transcendental industrialism" of the German idealist philosopher Johann Gottlieb Fichte.[16] It could even (as the French political economist André Morellet indicated in a hostile set of annotations to an edition of *What is the Third Estate?* published, without Sieyès'authorization, in 1822) be connected to a failure or refusal to endorse a fully individuated system of private property, as with "socialism" in its third incarnation, or socialism, as it has come to be known.[17] Each of these renditions captures something of the theory of human association that Sieyès called "the representative system" or "the system of representative government."[18] But none of them corresponds fully to the way of thinking about the relationship between politics, industry, and property that Sieyès himself devised.

The term "representative government" was not itself an innovation. It featured prominently in late-eighteenth-century discussions of the future constitution of the United States of America and concurrent arguments over British parliamentary reform.[19] From this perspective, Sieyès' politi-

---

[15] For concise descriptions of Pufendorf's "socialism," see Istvan Hont and Michael Ignatieff, "Needs and Justice in the *Wealth of Nations*: An Introductory Essay" in Istvan Hont and Michael Ignatieff (eds.), *Wealth and Virtue. The Shaping of Political Economy in the Scottish Enlightenment* (Cambridge, 1983), pp. 1–44 (30–5) and Istvan Hont, "The Language of Sociability and Commerce: Samuel Pufendorf and the Theoretical Foundations of the 'Four-Stages Theory,'" in Anthony Pagden (ed.), *The Languages of Political Theory in Early-Modern Europe* (Cambridge, 1987), pp. 253–76.

[16] The phrase "transcendental industrialism" appears in an article by the royalist political philosopher Ferdinand, baron d'Eckstein, "De l'industrialisme" in *Le Catholique,* vol. 5 (1827), p. 241, as a description of Fichte's *Der geschlossene Handelstaat* (*The Closed Commercial State*) [Stuttgart, 1800], by way of contrast to the "industrialisme de l'aune et de la toise" (p. 232) of the Saint-Simonians, Say and Comte.

[17] This edition of *Qu'est-ce qu'est le tiers état?* was published in 1822, four years after Morellet's death in 1819. See, for example, the notes at pp. 85 and 173 for examples of Morellet's objections to what he took to be Sieyès' perfunctory gestures towards giving property theoretical legitimacy.

[18] Emmanuel Joseph Sieyès, *Instruction donnée par S. A. S. Monseigneur le duc d' Orléans à ses représentans aux bailliages* (n. p. 1789), p. 73.

[19] The phrase was used specifically to refer to the difference between the democracies of the ancient world and the government of a large territorial republic like the United States. "For," as the authors of *The Federalist* put it in 1788, "it cannot be believed that any form of representative government could have succeeded within the narrow limits occupied

cal thought was connected both to a long tradition of investigation into the constitutions of free states or commonwealths and to more recent discussions in Europe and the United States of the extent to which long-established analytical distinctions between monarchies and republics could still be applied to the property-based societies of the eighteenth century and the industry and trade that they housed. Republics standardly elected their rulers, but sometimes paid a price for doing so, in political dissension and executive weakness. Monarchies standardly inherited their rulers, but sometimes paid a price for doing so, in complicated systems of administration and the absence of any obvious mechanism for legitimating legislation. One major strand of eighteenth-century thought centered upon the question as to how far the two systems of rule could be combined. In France, the marquis d' Argenson's *Considerations on the Present and Former Government of France,* posthumously published in 1764, but written in the late 1730s, set out a model of what d'Argenson called a "royal democracy," or a "republican monarchy," as the basis of a reformed royal government with a largely elected administrative base.[20] But if democracy could be used to make monarchies more like republics, it could also be refined and used to make republics more like monarchies. "In a large government, which is modelled with masterly skill," wrote the Scottish philosopher David Hume in his essay on *The Idea of a Perfect Commonwealth* (first published in 1752), "there is compass and room enough to refine the democracy, from the lower people, who may be admitted into the first elections or first concoction of the commonwealth, to the higher magistrates, who direct all the movements."[21] A generation later, the American Federalist James Madison also commended "the policy of refining the popular appointments by successive filtrations" to produce the bicameral federal legislature and the indirectly elected executive President, which were to become the most permanent features of the constitution of the United States.[22] Sieyès' political thought shared the same concerns. Whatever else it was, his theory of representative govern-

---

by the democracies of Greece:" *The Federalist,* 63 [1788], ed. Terence Ball (Cambridge, U.K., Cambridge University Press, 2003, p. 309. More generally, see Bernard Manin, *The Principles of Representative Government* (Cambridge, U.K., Cambridge University Press, 1997) and, in the context of eighteenth-century France, Keith Michael Baker, *Inventing the French Revolution* (Cambridge, U.K., Cambridge University Press, 1990).

[20] René Louis de Voyer de Paulmy, marquis d'Argenson, *Considérations sur le gouvernement ancien et présent de la France* (Amsterdam, 1764).

[21] David Hume, *Essays,* ed. E. F. Miller (Indianapolis, Liberty Press, 1987), p. 528.

[22] James Madison, *The Papers of James Madison,* vol. 10 (Chicago, University of Chicago Press, 1977), p. 19. On Hume and Madison, see most recently the *Forum* on "The Madisonian Moment," *The William and Mary Quarterly,* 59 (2002), issue no. 4.

ment was designed to put an end to having to choose between a republic and a monarchy.

But Sieyès' theory also went more emphatically beyond established usage by referring to something systemic in human association and, more specifically, to the idea that any durable and extensive human association involves two quite different kinds of representation that together add up to a single system. This, in Sieyès' terminology, was why the idea of representative government appeared as either "the system of representative government" or, more usually, "the representative system" and why its theoretical basis could be described as "social science," rather than the more obviously applied "science of the social art." It was a theory of representation with both a political and a nonpolitical dimension that, as even some of Sieyès' strongest political opponents acknowledged, could be detached quite readily from the events of the French Revolution itself.[23] The fact that it could be detached in this way may also help to explain the persistent tension between the system's theoretical ambition and a certain amount of cloudiness in the accompanying details of its constitutional design. Sieyès himself was quite explicit in acknowledging the problems his theory would face. The task of the philosopher, he wrote in the carefully crafted epigraph that he put at the beginning of *What is the Third Estate?*, was to reach his intellectual goal. It was up to the administrator to take the practical steps involved in getting there. He repeated the claim quite frequently (see below, pp. 7, 160). Constitutional theory was simply a part, although an important part, of the wider representative system. Accordingly, the kind of constitution that Sieyès thought suitable for a free state in the modern world was, in generic terms, quite similar to the kind of not-quite republican, but not-quite royal constitution which the authors of *The Federalist* advocated for the United States of America.

---

[23] "Sieyès combines a rare sagacity and a fertile imagination with shafts of luminous intelligence, with precision in terminology, and, above all, with that language of the soul that the majority of sophists of that school [of social-contract theorists] simply do not have. Theory, for him, is something serious. He believes in it in good faith. Accept the premises on which his reasoning is based, and his logic is invigorating, irresistible. All these qualities make Sieyès' writings so dangerous and seductive that it is certain that they have had more effect and done more harm than all the others. . . . Endowed with an unusual talent, an ability to see things very precisely, and great intellectual energy, Sieyès could have done as much good as he has done harm. If he had been willing to adopt those true principles to which he often came very close, he would have been the most vigorous and most eloquent defender of monarchy": Karl Ludwig von Haller [Charles Louis de Haller], *Restauration de la Science Politique, ou Théorie de l'état social naturel opposée à la fiction d'un état civil factice,* 5 vols. (Lyon and Paris, 1824–1875), vol. 1, pp. 72, 76 (the whole passage, pp. 70–6, is an interesting, if hostile, assessment of Sieyès' thought and its relationship to the tradition of modern natural jurisprudence).

But it was based on a concept of representation that was both more systematic and more general in its applicability than anything to be found in *The Federalist* or its intellectual forebears.

One kind of representation, Sieyès claimed, was to be found in all the nonpolitical activities involved in everyday life. The other kind of representation was the kind to be found in a political society. Maintaining the representative system meant ensuring that neither of these two kinds of representation could replace the other. If either were to disappear, the system itself would no longer exist. Both kinds of representation, Sieyès argued, had their origins in human needs and the means that humans used to meet those needs (the theme of needs and means was a recurrent feature of the titles of the many works that he planned, but never wrote). But they were still fundamentally different, because the kind of representation involved in daily life was essentially plural while the kind of representation involved in political life was essentially singular. Both, nonetheless, belonged to a single system, because both kinds of representation served to meet the same fundamental purpose. Anyone acting as somebody's representative could enable that person to do something else. Almost every aspect of human culture, Sieyès observed, was connected to that fact. The arts, the sciences, and almost everything involved in any durable human association were related to people's ability to find ways to reduce the amount of effort involved in meeting their needs and, by doing so, to increase the enjoyment of the lives that they lived. It was this ability, he noted, that set humans apart from other living beings.[24] This simple idea lay at the core of Sieyès' theory of representative government.

---

[24] "In nature, everything that has needs (and every living being has needs) has the right to satisfy them and, consequently, rights to the essential means to do so. Every living combination is a system that devours (devouring what is appropriable to its nature). The one lives off the other so that, by way of this sort of attraction, or rather *appropriation,* every living being sorts things out as best it can. This is what the state of isolation, improperly described as the natural state (although it is no more than its first premise), amounts to . . . .

"Among those systems related in kind I would single out the human race, by virtue of the superiority of its reason and its ability to will, as having its own proper rule of conduct. Devouring this internal rule of conduct amounts to devouring the system. Appealing to it, understanding it, adapting to it, sorting things out by way of exchange, finding ways to assist one another to meet mutual needs, is a good deal better than devouring one another. Appropriation by means of using the will of the individual by whom one seeks to appropriate something is what best serves the purpose of proposing to appropriate something. Thus human needs do not give rise to the right to devour one another but to assist one another. The essential dividing line between man and other animals is the existence in each individual human being of this inner property, this will, with which one can reach an understanding or an agreement. The rights of men over other men do not have any full or sufficient equivalent in human relations with the other species. They remain in *a state of natural war*

Sieyès, it was said in 1797, had a portrait of Voltaire hanging in his room.[25] It was an image that fitted the idea of representative government as a work of human art. The historically contingent character of the arts and sciences; their place in embellishing human life, morally as well as materially; and the ever-present possibility that human presumptuousness might wreck them forever were among the abiding themes of Voltaire's many works. But Sieyès brought a degree of analytical rigour that was absent from Voltaire to what he, like many of his contemporaries, called "the science of the social art" (the phrase he used in the second and subsequent editions of *What is the Third Estate?*). By doing so, he was able to give his first abbreviated coinage, "social science," the kind of foundational status previously associated with claims about natural law and natural jurisprudence. Humans, he argued, use various means to meet their several needs, but some means are intrinsically different from others. The need for security, for example, may give rise to the establishment of a political society, with laws and a more-or-less complicated system of government and administration amounting, as Sieyès usually put it, to a permanent "public" or "representative establishment." But a political society is not like most of the other means that humans may choose. Most of these are fairly easy to substitute for one another. Choosing between them usually involves no more than a change of allegiance, like switching from one bank to another to find a more efficient way of transferring money. This is the kind of choice involved in a market and is the kind of choice that Sieyès took as the simplest basis of human association. It did not, he noted, even need exchange to get started, however much the faculty of exchange might subsequently serve to maintain and stimulate it very powerfully. All it needed was human judgment and the ability to see that doing something jointly might be a better way to get something done.[26] This, Sieyès argued, was why representation was built into the way that human societies work. But the kind of representation involved in ordinary life is not quite the same as the kind involved in a political society, because at any one place or time there is usually only one of the latter on offer, and if there was more than one, with two sets of laws and

---

with them. The rights of a man over a man derive from the same source, from needs. But they are no more than an exchange. They can be reduced to one single right: not to use force on someone else, to leave him free, to determine his will by offering him something that he will prefer to what you ask of him. Thus the rights of man amount to the *equality* which allows the two *bargainers* to agree freely (the social state guarantees that equality)." A. N. 284 AP 5, dossier 1, no. 5 (sheet headed "Droits de l'homme").

[25] Forsyth, *Reason and Revolution*, pp. 58, 228, n. 52.

[26] A. N. 284 AP 3, dossier 11.

two sorts of government, it would not be the right kind of means to meet the need for which it was established. (The component parts of a federal system, it might be noted, can be separated functionally to fit the same analytical model.) Some of the means that individuals use are therefore essentially different from others. Some can be changed quite easily, like switching from one bank to another, without involving any change in how either might actually work. Others, however, offer something unique and can be changed only from within. Sieyès' idea was that to be able to survive and prosper, every human association had to have both.

This implied that the two parts of any human association were made up of different kinds of means. One part was made up of the means individuals use to meet their individual needs. The other was made up of the means individuals use to meet their common needs. One set of means consisted of those used severally by the individual members of the association; the other consisted of those used by the association itself. Sieyès was reluctant to reduce this distinction to one between economics and politics, noting in the early nineteenth century that the word *onéologie* coined by the political economist Jean Baptiste Say was a better term to use to analyze all the nonpolitical aspects of human life, not just those with a market price.[27] But the distinction between the two was the reason why, Sieyès argued, a political society had to have what he called "a representative establishment based on individual liberty" and why that representative (or public) establishment had to be kept quite separate from individual liberty.[28] "Thus," he wrote,

> you should not think of regarding all the work carried out in society as part of the public establishment. You should not arrange it, command it, direct it or pay for it as if it is a public function; you should not organize one corporation for agricultural producers and another for wheelwrights, joiners, smiths, masons, tailors, carters, etc. That kind of social organization would no longer be the kind of social state that was established to protect and perfect *individual liberty*.[29]

This strong emphasis upon individual liberty was based upon a radical rejection of any kind of similarity between the mechanisms involved in making moral choices and those involved in understanding the physical world. "Beware," Sieyès wrote, "of the idea, disseminated all-too-widely by modern scholars, that morality, like physics, can be given a foundation

---

[27] A. N. 284 AP 5, dossier 3^2.

[28] A. N. 284 AP 5, dossier 1^2 (sheet entitled, "Besoin de la société = respect de la liberté individuelle").

[29] A. N. 284 AP 5, dossier 1^2 (sheet entitled, "Besoin de la société = respect de la liberté individuelle").

based on experience" (below, p. 16). However much it had to have real purchase on experience of every kind (it involved "combinations of facts," not "combinations of chimeras"), morality was the work of the synthesizing power of the human mind, not the "simple observation" that was the basis of understanding the external world (pp. 15–16). Political society had, therefore, to be envisaged as a set of artificial devices (Sieyès' favorite analogy was with the design of a machine) whose purpose, in the first instance, was to prevent the individual capacity for moral choice from becoming entangled in anything extraneous to its own rationality. (It was probably this that lay behind the considerable following that Sieyès attracted in the German-speaking world, especially among admirers of the Prussian philosopher Immanuel Kant.)[30] Individuals, Sieyès noted, "for whose benefit everything exists," had to be left to "their desires, their tastes, their industry, and their aptitudes" because these human qualities were necessarily individuated and were, therefore, the starting points of individual rationality. Since no set of laws could be "extra- or supra- or ultra-natural," political society had to coexist with what was simply natural. Only "systematic spirits" set out to "unify" or "integrate" everything.[31]

The idea of representation had, therefore, to function in two rather different ways. Since, Sieyès noted, it presupposes the idea of having something done (*faire faire*), not simply leaving something to be done (*laissez faire*), it presupposes choice, not chance.[32] But choices are made in several different ways, and the difference between them amounted to an important distinction between political and nonpolitical representation. Changing a political society had to involve finding a way to change it peacefully, without interfering with the ordinary nonpolitical choices that individuals also make. This, Sieyès argued, was why it was important to respect the distinction between means that were singular and means that were plural. The former belonged to the unitary nation known as France while the latter belonged to the multiplicity of different individuals making up the nation called France. At first sight, he noted, it might seem that the way to change a political society would be to assert the democratic principle of majority rule and subject every government to

---

[30] An excellent text-based guide to this dimension of Sieyès' thought and a full bibliography of the secondary literature on Sieyès' admirers in the German-speaking world can be found in François Azouvi and Dominique Bourel, *De Königsberg à Paris. La Réception de Kant en France* (1788–1804) (Paris, Vrin, 1991), pp. 77–83, 102–12.

[31] A. N. 284 AP 5, dossier 1[2] (sheet entitled, "Besoin de la société = respect de la liberté individuelle").

[32] A. N. 284 AP 5, dossier 1[2] (sheet entitled "Liberté n'est pas jalouse de faire").

the principle of popular sovereignty. But this, he wrote, would make a political society look like two distinct entities, with a government made up of a head but no body, representing a society made up of a body but no head, or, if it did not, it would imply that there were actually two whole bodies in any one political body. Neither was a particularly viable formula for identifying how the decisions involved in managing change might be made or what any political majority might be a majority of.

Mixing up the idea of representation with a "purely democratic system" would, Sieyès wrote, lead to a "chaos of contradictions."[33] To assume that there was first a nation and then its representatives was "an obscure and false" idea because it presupposed something more than an association based upon individual choice. It presupposed a community to which individuals already belonged and a capacity for collective action within that community that made the notion of representation superfluous, an assumption that lay behind a long tradition in European political thought justifying the right to resist.[34] Sieyès was concerned with finding a way to make resistance compatible with his own idea of representation. If, he claimed, a people or a nation were to act, it could not also be represented by someone acting on its behalf. But if it were to act directly, rather than by way of representation, then the various individual means that the members of the nation also used to meet their several different needs would be subject to the same decision-making processes as those used by the nation itself. This, Sieyès noted, was why it was important to see that there was a fundamental difference between the two kinds of representation, individual and collective, that gave the representative system its systemic nature. The public establishment, he insisted, was the correlate of the whole association, which was singular, not of all its individual members, who were plural.[35] The nation was one, although its members were many. Its government represented the nation's common interests, not its many members' several interests. The common interest might, from time to time, have to change. But changing it had to avoid interfering with the other interests that individuals would also have. This, he argued, was why this kind of change also had to involve representation, not the unitary power of the whole nation. The kind of representation re-

---

[33] A. N. 284 AP 5, dossier 1[2] (sheet entitled "Représentation du tout n'a rien au-dessus").

[34] For a comprehensive overview of early-modern resistance theory, see Quentin Skinner, *The Foundations of Modern Political Thought,* 2 vols. (Cambridge, U.K., Cambridge University Press, 1978), vol. 2.

[35] A. N. 284 AP 5, dossier 1[3] (sheet entitled "Ordre politique, base démocratique, édifice représentation").

quired would act as if it were the nation, functioning, as Sieyès put it, as a *constituting* power in order to redesign the *constituted* power that was the nation's government. "To organize the people," he wrote, using terminology similar to that used by the authors of *The Federalist*, "is to degrade it. It involves creating two bodies to do the same thing, which is contradictory. The people is only the sum of individuals and these spontaneous elements are always able to federate and choose, by federal means, their agents to manage the *common affairs* of the federation."[36]

This idea of association by way of representation (rather than representation based on a preexisting association) was, Sieyès argued, why a political society had to be conceived of as a system based upon the three-sided relationship between a state, its members, and its government, rather than the more simple relationship between rulers and ruled. Representative government had to have a democratic starting point (if it did not, it would represent something partial) but it also had to be able to represent both the whole association and its various single members in somewhat different ways. The two forms of representation, one involving something unique, the other involving switching from one representative to another, gave the system of representative government its nature. But, in terms of Sieyès' theory, both also had to be a matter of choice, not chance. The difficulty was to see how it might be possible to *choose* a single representative of the whole association without collapsing political representation into the ordinary choices of means involved in everyday life. Choosing a sovereign (as Bishop Bossuet, France's most famous advocate of absolute royal sovereignty, pointed out in his attack on late-seventeenth-century French Protestant resistance theory), looks like a radically incoherent idea, because it is hard to see how a sovereign can be sovereign if this involves someone else's choice.[37]

In the eighteenth century the usual way of circumventing this problem was to draw upon two somewhat different notions of representation, one involving the claim that hereditary sovereigns represented their states, the other that elected representatives of one kind or another represented the members of those states. The absence of one or other type of representative was often singled out for comment, especially in periods of political conflict. In republics like the United Provinces of the Netherlands before 1747 or mixed systems of government as in Sweden before 1772, a single hereditary representative was sometimes said to be a

[36] A. N. 284 AP 5, dossier 1^2.

[37] Jacques Bénigne Bossuet, *Cinquième avertissement aux protestants sur les lettres du Ministre Jurieu contre l'Histoire des Variations,* in his *Oeuvres* (31 vols., ed. F. Lachat. Paris, 1862–1868), vol. 15.

solution to political deadlock. In absolute monarchies like France during the reign of Louis XV or the Holy Roman Empire under Joseph II, elected representatives were sometimes said to be a check upon the arbitrary use of sovereign power. But even where the two were combined, as in eighteenth-century Britain, the result was a mixture of choice and chance that, Sieyès argued, meant that the fabled British constitution was largely a set of measures taken to correct the unforeseen effects of combining inheritance and election within a single political system (130–3).

Sieyès' key theoretical move was to conceive of a single system of political representation that was designed to produce both kinds of representative. This innovation lay at the heart of the new conceptual matrix that he began to create. It was one that cut across long-established distinctions between royal, republican, and mixed forms of government. The opposite of a monarchy, Sieyès wrote, was not a republic, but a *polyarchy*, or a government with a multiple, rather than a single, executive head (the term was revived in a more elaborate but still similar sense by the twentieth-century American political scientist Robert Dahl).[38] The word "republic," he noted, did not refer to any particular kind of system of government at all. It was simply a modernized version of the Latin *res publica* (a term that Sieyès usually rendered as *la chose publique*—or public thing—when referring to the state's institutions, including its government). The opposite of a republic was, therefore, either a *ré-privé,* if sovereign power was in the hands of a single person, or a *ré-total,* if sovereignty was exercised directly by the whole community. Both types of system, Sieyès claimed, were incompatible with the long-term joint survival of the two different kinds of means, one plural, the other singular, involved in every durable human association. Representative government was therefore a system of government designed to prevent the occurrence of either of these forms of political pathology. "In representation," Sieyès wrote, "the plenitude of power cannot be exercised anywhere."[39] This, he argued, was why a representative government had to have a constitution that was able to maintain the means (including a head of state, an electoral system, a legal system, a fiscal system, a defense establishment, and a currency) used by the members of a state or a nation to manage their common affairs, as these applied not only to the present generation, but also to all the many generations to come. A nation, Sieyès noted, was not like a physical individual. It was instead more like a biological or

---

[38] Robert A. Dahl, *A Preface to Democratic Theory* (Chicago, University of Chicago Press, 1956), pp. 63–89.

[39] A. N. 284 AP 4, dossier 4 (plan of a work on politics, ch. 8).

zoological species. Its individual members would live and die, but as a "civil species" a nation could live indefinitely.[40] But to do so, it needed a system of government able to respond to change and, by doing so, to maintain its ability to be what it was.

Sieyès and the Revolution of 1789

This was the central theme of *What is the Third Estate?*, the most famous pamphlet that Sieyès wrote. It was published early in 1789, three months before the first meeting of the French Estates-General to have been held since 1614 was due to begin its deliberations at Versailles. Until then, Sieyès was almost entirely unknown. He was born in 1748 in the small southern French town of Fréjus, the son of a minor tax official responsible for collecting the royal stamp duty levied on legal transactions and printed publications. In 1765 he entered the prestigious Parisian seminary of Saint-Sulpice. Although he was not ordained as a priest (he never went beyond his vows as an *abbé*), he took a degree in theology at the Sorbonne and, between 1770 and 1789, followed a career within the ecclesiastical government of the Catholic Church, eventually rising to the position of vicar-general of the diocese of Chartres. He published nothing before 1788. Then, in the space of six months, he produced three pamphlets. All of them appeared anonymously, but by the spring of 1789 he was famous. The first to appear, in November 1788, was the *Essay on Privileges* (*Essai sur les privilèges*). It was followed early in January 1789 by *What is the Third Estate?* The third pamphlet, published four months later, in May 1789, was actually the first of the three that Sieyès wrote. It was written in July or August 1788 and seems to have circulated in manuscript under the title *Views on the means to guarantee the nation against the double despotism of ministers and aristocrats* (*Vues sur les moyens de garantir la nation contre le double despotisme des ministres et des aristocrates*).[41] When it was published, it was entitled *Vues sur les moyens d'exécution dont les représentants de la France pourront disposer en 1789*. The near-contemporary English title of the work, *Views of the executive means, which are at the disposal of the Representatives of France, in 1789*, captures its intent quite well.[42] It was Sieyès' plan for a revolution.

[40] A. N. 284 AP 3, dossier 21.

[41] This is the title under which it appears in A. N., 284 AP 4, dossier 8.

[42] This is the title used in the contemporary English translation of the biography written under Sieyès' own direction in 1794 by his Prussian admirer Konrad Oelsner, *An Account of the Life of Sieyes* (London, 1795), p. 21.

The kind of revolution that Sieyès envisaged had a single radical aim. He insisted repeatedly in everything that he published in the spring of 1789 that it would be politically catastrophic for the Estates-General to take on the huge task of addressing all the many calls for reform contained in the petitions and lists of grievances (*cahiers de doléances*) that the royal government had solicited from all the established institutions of the kingdom. Instead, it had to focus on the single task of imposing a constitution on the government of the kingdom. The strategy laid out in the *Views* was designed to ensure that it could. As Sieyès emphasised when the pamphlet finally appeared in print (see below, p. 4), circumstances in France in the spring of 1789 were very different from those facing the nation in the summer of 1788 when he had written the *Views*. On 5 July 1788, after eighteen months of increasingly intense political conflict over the question of how to fund the deficit in the royal finances, Louis XVI's principal minister, Etienne Charles Loménie de Brienne, had announced that the king would convene an assembly of the French Estates-General and, since it would be the first to have met since 1614, would welcome views on how it should be constituted. On 8 August 1788, Brienne indicated that the Estates-General would meet on 1 May 1789. This was the context in which Sieyès wrote the *Views of the executive means*. He did not know then that in September 1788 the Parlements, the French high courts of appeal, would demand that the Estates-General should be convoked on the same basis as it had met in 1614 or that the princes of the royal blood would echo their demands in December 1788. These events, and, in particular, the posture adopted by the Parlements, led Sieyès to publish the *Essay on Privileges,* explaining why, in the light of what he took a privilege to be, their demands were unacceptable. He followed this up, in January 1789, by publishing *What is the Third Estate?* Its aim was to show why the representatives of the Third Estate had a right to implement the plan that, in the *Views of the executive means,* he had commended to the Estates-General as a whole. That earlier pamphlet was based on the assumption that, although it would be made up of representatives of the three great orders of the kingdom (the Clergy, the Nobility and the Third Estate), the Estates-General would make its decisions in common. When, by January 1789, it had become clear that this would not occur, Sieyès simply transferred the strategy laid out in the *Views* to the representatives of the Third Estate alone. *What is the Third Estate?* was designed to explain why they, and they alone, were entitled to implement the plan laid out in the *Views of the executive means*.

In immediate terms, the plan consisted of a unilateral declaration by the Estates-General abolishing all existing taxes. It was to be followed directly by a further declaration reinstating them on a provisional basis until the Estates-General had completed the work of drafting a new constitution for the government of France. This, Sieyès pointed out, would mean that any attempt by the royal government to prevent the Estates-General from completing its work would produce an immediate cessation of tax-payments. To strengthen its position, he also proposed that the Estates-General should issue a declaration taking responsibility for honoring the nation's debt, so that any attempt by the royal government to bypass the Estates-General either by borrowing additional funds without prior authorization or by defaulting unilaterally on interest payments on the existing debt would also provoke a cessation of tax-payments. He hinted too that the Estates-General could (and should) apply the same principle to the army (see below, pp. 23, 59). As the pamphlet's original title indicates, the aim of the plan was to deny the royal government power over the three key institutions of the state—the fiscal system, the public debt and the army—until the Estates-General had done its work. Although Sieyès never used the word, it amounted to a straightforward assertion of sovereignty. The term he used instead was "constituting power" (*pouvoir constituant*), the power that was the source of a "constituted power" (*pouvoir constitué*). That power belonged solely to the French nation, but (as he explained both in the *Views* and, more emphatically, in *What is the Third Estate?*) it could also be exercised by an extraordinary assembly representing the nation (Sieyès used the term "federal power" or borrowed the English word "convention" to describe such an assembly). When, by late December 1788, it had become clear that the whole Estates-General would never be able to put the plan into effect, Sieyès simply assigned its implementation to the representatives of the Third Estate alone and, in *What is the Third Estate?*, proceeded to set out the reasons why, as he construed them, the representatives of the Third Estate were entitled to act as a constituting power, invested with all the sovereign rights of the French nation, and able, therefore, to draft a constitution for its government.

It is clear, in other words, that the three pamphlets that Sieyès published between November 1788 and May 1789 were informed by a single, consistent strategy centered on replacing the sovereign power of the monarch by the sovereign power of the nation. It was wrong, he argued in *What is the Third Estate?*, to think that the kingdom of France consisted of three great orders or estates, the Clergy, the Nobility, and the Third Estate, and that the representatives of these three orders might meet as three separate bodies to form the Estates-General of the kingdom in order to work out, in conjunction with Louis XVI, a solution to the financial problems affecting the French monarchy. The Third Estate, he wrote, was not just one of the three great orders of the kingdom of France. Nor, despite the fact that it was many times larger and more prosperous than the two other estates, was it simply the largest and most important of the three. It was, instead, as Sieyès put it, "a complete nation." This was why the answer to the question *What is the Third Estate?* had to be "everything." A nation, he wrote, needed both private employment and public service to be a nation. Private employment encompassed agriculture, industry, trade, and the various professions; public service included the army, the legal system, the church, and the administration. All these functions, he claimed, were actually carried out by the Third Estate, even though some parts of the royal government were headed by members of the privileged orders (pp. 95–7). It followed that since the members of the Third Estate were responsible for doing all the things that a nation needed to do in order to be itself, the Third Estate was a self-sufficient, independent nation and, like any "complete nation," it could not be subject to a higher power. It was, in fact, just like a state.

Sieyès' substitution of the word "nation" for the word "state" as the ultimate source of political right and power allowed him to echo the language of many of the pamphlets published by the loosely associated French patriot party between 1787 and 1789 and the many, often contradictory, calls for regenerating or reforming the nation and its government that they contained. But Sieyès' use of the term differed quite radically from contemporary usage. He made this clear in the opening paragraphs of the *Views of the executive means,* with their coruscating attack on the advocates of what, recently, has been called the "French idea of freedom."[43] It did so most obviously by referring to the French nation as a single, unitary entity rather than the sum of all its several members. If France had a population of 25 or 26 million people, they were still all members of one nation. It was this single sovereign entity that was entitled to establish a constitution for its government. This was why Sieyès placed so much emphasis, both in the *Views* and in *What is the Third Estate?* (below, pp. 34, 135–40), on the difference between a constituting and a constituted power. A constituting power was something representing the nation as a singular entity. A constituted power (or powers) was something representing the many different members of the nation. This distinction served to place quite rigid limits on what, as a constituting power, the representatives of the Third Estate were entitled to do. As Sieyès emphasized in the concluding chapter of *What is the Third Estate?* their task was to draft a constitution, not to become a government. Their role, in other words, was to be very similar to that of the American Constitutional Convention. As it transpired, however, the French National Assembly (as, on 17 June 1789,

[43] See Dale Van Kley (ed.), *The French Idea of Freedom* (Stanford, California, Stanford University Press, 1994).

it proclaimed itself to be) became very much more. Practical problems soon got so heavily in the way of principle, that Sieyès' distinction between a constituting and a constituted power very quickly got lost.

Sieyès' use of the word "nation" as a synonym for a state also meant that the relationship between the nation, its members and its government had to follow the same logic as the relationship between a state, its members and its government. A representative government had to represent both the nation and its members. This meant that it could not be based simply upon electing a legislature and an executive from below, but had to be based upon a double system of election in which both the single sovereign nation and its many different members each actually elected their respective representatives. An outline of this dual system of election was already visible in the *Views of the executive means* and in the many references to that pamphlet in *What is the Third Estate?*. But it was set out rather more fully in the public debate that took place between Sieyès and the famous Anglo-American political radical Tom Paine in the summer of 1791. It is worth describing this debate in some detail because its significance as a guide to Sieyès' political thought has often been overlooked.[44] It took place during the period of intense political uncertainty caused by Louis XVI's flight from Paris and arrest at Varennes in June 1791. This unexpected event raised a major question mark against the stability of the new post-revolutionary French constitution and the provisions for a constitutional monarchy that it contained. Paine was one of a number of political figures to call for the establishment of a republic. Sieyès publicly came out against the call. His endorsement of monarchy was seized upon by both his royalist and republican critics as evidence of his theoretical incoherence or political opportunism (or both) and has usually been taken subsequently to have been no more than an expression of prudence in circumstances of acute political instability. Although it was also this, it was still compatible with his broader theory. Paine's position corresponded to the one that he had set out many years earlier in his celebrated *Common Sense* (1776). Sieyès, in his reply, claimed that his own position was also well established. His "researches and results," he noted, "preceded the Revolution" (172). The discussion that took place between them was therefore a concise summary of two quite different conceptions of what a representative government might be.

---

[44] For contemporary assessments of the significance of the debate, see the comments made by Joseph Lakanal in the *Journal des patriotes de 1789* (11 Ventôse IV) and by Pierre Samuel Dupont de Nemours in *L' Historien* (14 and 23 Ventôse IV). For more recent descriptions see Alfred Owen Aldridge, "Condorcet et Paine. Leurs rapports intellectuels," *Revue de littérature comparée,* 32 (1958), pp. 47–65 (p. 55) and his *Man of Reason. The Life of Thomas Paine* (London, 1959), ch. X.

In his open letter to Sieyès, Paine made it clear that by "republicanism" he meant, as he put it, "government by representation." It meant electing a legislature and an executive (as well, perhaps, as an appropriate number of suitably qualified judicial officials). This, he concluded, was why a republic could not have a monarch, because monarchy was necessarily hereditary (an elective monarchy would be a republic). Sieyès, in his reply, argued that Paine's notion of political representation did not go far enough. It was insufficient to ensure that some or all of the members of a nation were represented. The nation too had to have a representative of its own. Government by representation in Paine's sense called for quite a high level of patriotic self-sacrifice for things to go well but, Sieyès warned, relying on this kind of republican patriotism could also lead to very considerable political dangers if things did not. As he put it in the notes that he made in drafting his reply to Paine, an elected executive required a much higher level of virtue and self-abnegation than a ministry appointed by a permanent head of state because any competent minister would be bound to provoke "public ingratitude" and, unless he was prepared to "devote himself to misfortune for the pleasure of serving his fellows," he would be tempted to abuse his power and "acquire an influence contrary to the interest of his country." This, Sieyès argued, was why the nation had to have a single representative of its own as well as an elected legislature representing its members. "The royalists claim this advantage for themselves," he noted, "but to have it, it is not necessary to move away from a good representative system or a monarchical republic."[45]

The result would be a system that relied less heavily on civic virtue. "It would be a grave misjudgment of human nature," Sieyès had written in *What is the Third Estate?* "to entrust the destiny of societies to the endeavors of virtue" (154). This was why constitutional design mattered. "Neither the ideas nor the sentiments which are called Republican," Sieyès informed Paine, "are unknown to me; but in my design of advancing towards the *maximum* of social liberty, I ought to pass the Republic, to leave it far behind, and to arrive at *true Monarchy*" (172). This "true Monarchy" was also representative. It was not "the character of a true representation," Sieyès argued, that it should have to bear "the distinguishing attributes which mark republicans." Representation, he pointed out, was quite distinct from republicanism. Although every "social constitution of which representation is not the essence" was "a false constitution," not all representative constitutions needed to be republican. It all depended, he argued, on how the government was chosen. If it was

---

[45] A. N. 284 AP 5, dossier 1 (sheet headed "Pour mon dispute avec Payne").

chosen from below, then it would have to be republican in Paine's sense. If, however, it was chosen from above, "by an individual of superior rank, in whom is represented the stable unity of Government," then it would not need to display "the distinguishing attributes that mark republicans." The difference between a republic and a "true" or "monarchical" republic turned therefore "upon the manner of *crowning* the government" (169).

Elections can go upwards but they can also go downwards. The difference between Paine and Sieyès' conceptions of representative government was that Paine envisaged a single system of election that would always go upwards, while Sieyès envisaged a double system of election that would go both upwards and downwards at periodic intervals. As Sieyès described it, Paine's system could be depicted as ending in a platform, with an elected executive ministry, chosen either by an elected legislature or by the people themselves. His own system ended in a point, with a single individual electing an executive ministry from a range of eligible candidates so that, as he put it, the government would consist of "a first Monarch, the Elector and irresponsible, in whose name act six Monarchs, named by him and responsible" (169). Although the upward system of election now looks more familiar, the downward system of election, or what is now usually thought of as appointment from a list of candidates, is actually a fairly ordinary feature of many different types of organization. Bishops or cardinals are sometimes selected from a list of eligible candidates, as are the members of university faculties or the coaches of football clubs. Not all of the electors who elect them are elected themselves. But Sieyès' system also made provision for electing an elector. This Monarch Elector, as he named the occupant of "the first public function," was to be chosen by a system that, as he put it, "combines all the advantages attributed to *hereditary,* without any of its inconveniences, and all the advantages of election, without its dangers" (170). The result was something like a monarchy, but without a hereditary monarch. Although it was obviously not a parliamentary regime, it was also not quite like a modern presidential regime, not only because of the Elector's life-tenure of office but also because of the very much more limited constitutional powers of the office itself.

The most concise way of expressing Sieyès' consistent concern with the different kinds of representation involved in the various means used to meet human needs was the idea of the division of labor. "The more a society progresses in the arts of trade and production," he wrote in the *Views of the executive means,* "the more apparent it becomes that work related to public functions (*la chose publique*) should, like private employments, be carried out less expensively and more efficiently by men who make it their exclusive occupation" (48). He took some pride in this idea, noting that he had thought of it after 1770, well before the publication of Adam Smith's *Inquiry into the Nature and Causes of the Wealth of Nations* in 1776, a work he greatly admired, and adding that Smith himself had not seen that the division of labor was also a representative system.[46] Since, Sieyès noted, neither the nation as a body nor every individual citizen went about producing everything serving to meet the nation's needs, it could be said that all the labor of society was representative. The person who made the shoes worn by a rich, delicate lady in the most luxurious of cities was her representative in much the same sense as the person who made her laws.[47] This way of describing the fundamental principle underlying the representative system provided a fairly stable criterion for assessing the content and possible effects of legislation. Anything that was likely to reduce the representative character of economic and political life was equally likely to be incompatible with the nature of the system as a whole. Designing a constitution thus meant applying the principle of representation not only to the task of legislation, but to all the many other functions of government as well. Everything, Sieyès argued, was best carried out by way of representation, not only because of the efficiency gains that representation entailed but also because of the increasing differentiation of office and power that it produced. The greater the provision for specialization provided by the constitution of the government the less danger there would be of the abuse of power.

The representative system was designed therefore to perform two major functions. The first was to work as a bridge between the largely

---

[46] A. N. 284 AP 2, dossier 13 (sheet headed "Travail").

[47] The analogy to shoemaking can be found in A. N. 284 AP 4, dossier 5: "Since it is not the nation as a body, since it is not every citizen who goes about producing everything needed to meet his needs, it can be said quite truthfully that all the work undertaken in society is *representative*. The rich, delicate lady living in the most luxurious of cities whose daily occupations are the furthest removed from those of the humblest artisan should know that her existence is very highly based on representation and that what he does amounts to her most essential capital. She should not therefore despise someone entrusted with her commission since, if the worker who supplies her with slippers stopped working, the result would be that she would have to do it herself, and would do it a great deal less well and at a great deal more cost." ("Puisque ce n'est pas la nation en corps, puisque ce n'est pas tout citoyen qui vaque à la production de tout ce qui sert à remplir ses besoins, on peut dire avec vérité que tous les travaux de la société sont *représentatif*. Il faut que la femme riche et délicate qui dans la ville la plus luxueuse se trouve par ses occupations journalières la plus éloignée du travail du plus grossier artisan sache cependant que son existence est fort représentative et [que] son capital essentiel est ce qu'il fait. Elle ne doit pas mépriser son chargé de procuration, car si l'ouvrier qui la fournit des souliers ne travaillait pas, il suivrait bien qu'elle y travaillerait elle-même et qu'elle ferait beaucoup plus mal et qu'il lui coûterait beaucoup plus cher.")

political functions of the nation and its government and the largely non-political activities of its members, just as the system of representation that Paine envisaged was also designed to do. The second was to function as a buffer separating the political from the nonpolitical so that the power of the state could be kept at arm's length from the lives and goods of its members in a way that Paine's idea of representative government was not designed to do. Paine's system relied quite heavily upon the moral integrity of its members for keeping public and private interests apart. Sieyès' system relied more strongly on constitutional design and the dilution of power produced by dividing it among a multitude of decentralized representative institutions. Although he simply hinted at how the system would work in his exchange with Paine, noting only that a public debate was not the place to describe it in detail, there is no reason to think that he was exaggerating in claiming that his research and its results had preceded the Revolution. In the *Views of the executive means* he had already outlined a modified version of the system of indirect elections used for electing representatives to the Estates-General.[48] This version was based upon a three-tier division of the kingdom into municipalities, arrondissements and provinces. Later, at the time of the elections to the Estates-General in the spring of 1789 and in light of the breach between the two privileged orders and the Third Estate, Sieyès dropped the idea of provincial representation and called for the creation of a new territorial unit, the department, to replace the division of the kingdom into provinces. It proved to be his most obviously durable achievement. Although the new territorial division was presented to the National Assembly by Jacques Guillaume Thouret, another of the members of the Assembly's constitutional committee, Sieyès took a proprietary pride in his creation. When asked, sometime after his return to France in 1830, whether he was one of the principal authors of the division of France into departments, he replied vigorously that he was not its principal author but, in fact, its only one.[49]

The new territorial division was a key component of the representative system. It formed a framework that was designed to house a system of indirect elections in which eligibility for election to office at the national,

[48] On the indirect system of election standardly followed in eighteenth-century France, see Malcolm Crook, *Elections in the French Revolution* (Cambridge, U.K., Cambridge University Press, 1996), ch. 1 and Patrice Gueniffey, *Le Nombre et la raison: La Révolution française et les élections* (Paris, Editions de l'Ecole des Hautes Etudes en Sciences Sociales, 1993), ch. 1.

[49] Charles Mignet, "Notice historique sur la vie et les travaux de M. le Comte Sieyès," *Mémoires de l'Académie royale des sciences morales et politiques de l'Institut de France*, 2nd series, vol. 2 (Paris, 1839), p. xxxix.

departmental or arrondissement levels would depend on having been elected successfully to an office at the level immediately below. The whole system was designed to function as an immense filtering mechanism. Anyone might enter the system at the bottom provided that they could show that they were prepared to be active members of the nation (Sieyès could see no reason why women should not be able to do so too, even though, he noted, prevailing prejudices currently ruled out the possibility). Although Sieyès is sometimes identified with the property-based distinction between active and passive citizens that the French National Assembly adopted in December 1789, his own idea of political eligibility was less like a property-based qualification for participation in political life and more like the voluntary payment of a membership fee to join a political party or (in an analogy that Sieyès often used) the purchase of a share in a public corporation in order to be able to vote for the membership of its board of executive directors. Since progress up the representative system called for substantial political commitment and continued electoral trust, active citizenship in Sieyès' sense amounted to making politics a career, as it has subsequently become. There is every reason to think that an unsuccessful attempt in December 1789 by the comte de Mirabeau (at that time one of Sieyès' closest political allies, although they later moved quite far apart) to establish what its advocates called a system of "graduated public functions" as part of the new constitutional arrangements was based on Sieyès' idea of how the representative system would work.[50] A further, equally unsuccessful, attempt to establish the same "graduated" system was made in the summer of 1795 during the discussions preceding the establishment of the French republican Directory.[51] It was only in 1799, with Sieyès' draft of what became the Constitution of the Year VIII, that all the details of the representative system came clearly into view. It was a very elaborate solution to the problem of how a representative government could represent both a nation and its members.

The draft Constitution of the Year VIII (a draft that was subjected to substantial revision by Napoleon Bonaparte) provided for the existence of five great state institutions and a dual system of indirect election for electing their members.[52] At its apex was a Great Elector and two Consuls. The Great Elector would hold office for life and was responsible for

---

[50] M. J. Mavidal, E. Laurent, and E. Clavel (eds.), *Archives Parlementaires,* vol. 10 (Paris, 1878), pp. 496–7, 577–9.

[51] British Library F 787 (4), *Opinion de Thibaudeau (A. L.) représentant du peuple sur la gradualité des fonctions publiques prononcée le 4 Thermidor an III* (Paris, 1795), pp. 3–4.

[52] It can be found in Antoine-Jacques-Claude-Joseph Boulay de la Meurthe, *Théorie constitutionnelle de Sieyès* (Paris, 1836).

electing the two Consuls. They in turn were responsible for electing fourteen ministers of state, responsible in their turn for managing the affairs of government and, as a Council of Ministers, for proposing legislation to the legislature. The legislature was to consist of two different assemblies. The first was a 400 member Legislative Assembly that would vote, but would not deliberate. The second was a 120-member Tribunate that would receive petitions and propose legislation, but would not vote. The Legislative Assembly would hear arguments and proposals for laws drafted either by the Council of Ministers or the Tribunate and would accept or reject them, but would not debate their content. Alongside them would be a third assembly, a College of Guardians (*Collège des Conservateurs*), whose hundred members were elected for life, with a power to review and, if necessary, to veto legislation approved by the legislature. A quarter of the membership of the two legislative bodies would be replaced annually by the College of Guardians and would not be eligible for re-election for two years. Elections were to be carried out from above from lists of eligible candidates elected from below by electors at three different levels of political representation, making three great lists of eligible candidates: one list for each arrondissement, another list for each department and, finally, a single national list from which the College of Guardians would replace the outgoing members of the Tribunate and the Legislative Assembly every year. Every adult male was entitled to vote. But since all elections were indirect, not direct, the number of eligible candidates for the various assemblies making up the national legislature was surprisingly small.

The nineteenth-century Hungarian political philosopher József Eötvös compared Sieyès' system to a process of distillation by which "the whole French people would be sublimated through several retorts until it finally became a single 'great elector'."[53] It had four main features. The first was the combination of upward and downward election on which the system was based. The second was the regular rotation of office produced by the fixed period of tenure of almost all elected offices (apart from the members of the College of Guardians and the Great Elector, who were elected for life). The third significant feature of the system was that it provided for the existence of a system of political parties. Sieyès did not refer to this possibility in any of the pamphlets he published in 1789, but was quite explicit about it in 1795 in his outline of a new constitution for the

---

[53] József Eötvös, *The Dominant Ideas of the Nineteenth Century and Their Impact on the State* [1851–1854], translated by D. Mervyn Jones, 2 vols. (Social Science Monographs, Boulder, Colorado; Atlantic Research and Publications Inc., Highland Lakes, New Jersey. Distributed by Columbia University Press, 1996 and 1998), vol. 1, pp. 251–2.

French republic in the wake of the Jacobin Terror of 1793–1794. "The existence of two parties, similar or analogous to those known elsewhere as a ministerial party and an opposition party is inseparable from every kind of representative system," he informed the Convention in July 1795.[54] The combination of the dual electoral system and the rotation of office supplied a framework that could readily accommodate the division between a ministerial and an opposition party. As a royalist periodical later noted, the party-system was designed to become the basis of a system of collective ministerial responsibility, leaving the Great Elector with no executive power at all.[55] But it also supplied the fourth significant feature of the representative system. The party-system meant that whenever a Great Elector died, there would be only one candidate eligible for election as his successor. The leader of the largest party would automatically be the only available candidate to be the next Great Elector. This was why Sieyès emphasized that the difference between his own and Paine's idea of representative government turned upon "the manner of *crowning* the government" and why he was able to inform Paine that he had found a way to elect a head of state that "combines all the advantages attributed to *hereditary,* without any of its inconveniences, and all the advantages of election, without its dangers" (170). He had produced something like a constitutional monarchy without having to rely on a system of hereditary succession to the throne. The monarch or Great Elector represented the nation; the electoral system represented its members. Periodically the two systems of representation would intersect. The party-mechanism delivering the next Great Elector out of the electoral system would guarantee the nation from the risks and dangers of unmanageable political conflict arising from disputed elections to the office of head of state. But the same party-mechanism would also provide for a manageable level of ordinary conflict between government and opposition to keep the activities of the nation's elected representatives subject to permanent public scrutiny and the diffuse power of public opinion.

---

[54] The speech is printed in the *Moniteur,* issue 307 (7 Thermidor an III). See p. 1238 for the passage cited and Paul Bastid, *Les discours de Sieyès dans les débats constitutionnels de l'an III (2 et 18 Thermidor)* (Paris, 1939), pp. 27–8.

[55] "L'idée de transférer la puissance exécutive aux ministres a été conçue, dans l'origine, par un des premiers agresseurs du pouvoir royal en France, par l'abbé Sieyès; c'était la base de la Constitution qu'il proposait après le 18 brumaire, et dont Bonaparte ne fut pas la dupe": *Le Drapeau Blanc,* vol. 2 (Paris, 1819), p. 50. ("The idea of transferring executive power to the ministry as a body was originally conceived of by one of the foremost agressors upon royal power in France, the abbé Sieyès. It was the basis of the constitution that he proposed after the 18 Brumaire, but Bonaparte was not caught out.")

The Representative System in Historical Context

The most obvious question raised by this elaborate system of political representation is why Sieyès should have thought of it at all. One answer has usually been that he did so rather gradually and that he added more and more institutional complications to the system first outlined in 1789 in response to the violent sequence of events that led first to the Jacobin Terror of 1793–1794 and then to the slow death of the first French Republic between 1794 and 1799. From this perspective, Sieyès was, as has often been said, the man who both opened and closed the French Revolution, the advocate of liberty in 1789 and the supporter of authority in 1799.[56] But the description does not fit Sieyès' own claim that he had conceived of all the elements of his system before 1789. Nor is it easy to reconcile with his consistent reluctance to have anything to do with the many attempts made after 1789 to bring the Revolution to an end. The political strategy set out in the *Views of the executive means* and *What is the Third Estate?* effectively wrecked the attempt by Louis XVI's most popular minister Jacques Necker to use the Estates-General to transform the French monarchy into something more like the combination of King, Lords, and Commons that was the hallmark of the English system of government. It set a powerful limit on every subsequent attempt to establish a constitutional compromise between the supporters of the monarchy and the leaders of the Revolution. Sieyès made no effort to align himself with any of the various figures who, at one time or another between 1789 and 1795, tried to find a way to end the Revolution. He was never a political ally of Mounier and the Monarchiens in 1789, or of Barnave, Duport and the Feuillants in 1790 or 1791 or of Brissot, Roland and the Girondin leaders after 1792, or of Boissy d'Anglas and the other major supporters of the Directory after 1794. He broke with Mirabeau in 1791 when the latter began to organize a campaign headed by the departmental authorities to revive the authority of the monarchy as the basis of a final compromise between the king and the National Assembly. This consistent unwillingness to abandon his own system of political representation and find a way to compromise with the advocates of a mixed or balanced system of government was matched by a vigorous insistence upon the unprecedented opportunity for freedom and justice provided by the events of 1789 and an emphatic refusal to allow that opportunity to be lost. Privately, Sieyès was even more adamant. "Fate," he wrote in

---

[56] See, most recently, William J. Sewell, Jnr., *A Rhetoric of Bourgeois Revolution: the abbé Sieyès and What is the Third Estate?* (Duke University Press, Durham, North Carolina, 1994), p. 197.

a note to his political ally, the former marquis de Condorcet during the winter of 1790–1791 (at a time when Condorcet was considering leaving the Jacobin club and endorsing Mirabeau's rapprochement with the king and the court), "told a man, 'I will give you immortality in exchange for a guinea (*un écu*)'. He accepted the bargain but then didn't have the means to pay. Those who I see working for that man are those whom I value the most."[57]

From this perspective, the turn to Bonaparte in 1799 looks less like an admission of defeat and more like a last, determined attempt to establish the system that he had failed to establish in 1789. This was what he emphasized in his own handwritten introduction to the draft of the constitution of the Year VIII that he went on to dictate to Antoine Joseph Boulay de la Meurthe.[58] This second (or, if his failure to influence the republican constitution of 1795 is included, third) attempt to establish the system of representative government suggests that Sieyès had quite consistent reasons for advocating the elaborate system of political representation that he had devised and that these were largely the same in 1789 as they were to be in 1799. They were connected to a conception of revolution that has all but disappeared from the historiography of the French Revolution, mainly because the French Revolution did not, in the first instance, follow the course that, before 1789, a modern revolution was widely expected to follow. One of the many reasons why it did not was because Sieyès published his three pamphlets in 1789. The strategy that they contained played a causal part in turning what might have been possible into what, with hindsight, now looks like no more than lurid political speculation, deliberately exaggerated by the opponents of the French royal government to increase support for the Patriot cause. But this was not how things looked in the summer of 1788 at the time when Sieyès began to write what became the *Views of the executive means available to the representatives of France in 1789.*

The Revolution of 1789 was not quite like the revolution that was often predicted in eighteenth-century political speculation. Instead, it was the Jacobin phase of the French Revolution that was the revolution that had long been foretold. The looming menace of something like the Terror, either in France or in Britain, the most powerful European states, was a widely and vividly predicted feature of eighteenth-century assess-

[57] A. N. 284 AP 4, dossier 14: "Le sort avoit dit à un homme, je te donne l'immortalité pour un écu. Il a accepté le marché, mais il n'a pas eu de quoi payer; et c'est toujours pour cet homme que je vois travailler les personnes que j'estime le plus."

[58] Antoine-Jacques-Claude-Joseph Boulay de la Meurthe, *Théorie constitutionnelle de Sieyès* (Paris, 1836), pp. 4–5.

ments of the future of the modern world. "I see," wrote Jean Jacques Rousseau in 1772, "all the states of Europe rushing to their ruin. Monarchies, republics, all those nations with all their magnificent institutions, all those fine and wisely balanced governments, have grown decrepit and threaten soon to die."[59] The outcome of this race towards ruin was not expected to be positive. "The singular revolution with which Europe is threatened," warned the journalist Simon Nicolas Henri Linguet in 1777, would eventuate either in the total collapse of modern civilization or would throw up "some new Spartacus" to establish an "absolute division of the goods of nature" after destroying the "murderous and deceitful" system of laws and government underlying the property-based regimes of the modern world. "One or other of these two calamities," Linguet concluded, "is inevitable."[60] Although his prognosis was lurid, it was far from unusual. From the marquis de Mirabeau's warning that the "necessary consequence" of the modern "social revolution" would be "absolute decadence, corruption and, eventually, the dispersal of existing political societies," to the Scottish philosopher Adam Ferguson's observation that the "boasted refinements of the polished age" would serve simply to "prepare for mankind the government of force," to the abbé Gabriel Bonnot de Mably's prediction that the modern world was "nearer than one might think to the revolution that Asia underwent," so that "the time may not be too far away when Europe will languish under the splendor and misery of despotism and slavery," claims about decline and fall, leading to crisis, revolution and a despotic, highly militarized republican regime were one of the staples of Enlightenment thought, particularly in the four decades between the end of the War of the Austrian Succession in 1748 and the beginning of the French Revolution.[61] From this perspective, the modern world was hurtling towards a cycle of conflict and

---

[59] Jean Jacques Rousseau, *Considérations sur le gouvernement de Pologne* [1772], ed. Barbara de Negroni (Paris, Nizet, 1990), p. 164. I have slightly modified the translation given in Jean Jacques Rousseau, *The Social Contract and Other Later Political Writings*, ed. Victor Gourevitch (Cambridge, U.K., Cambridge University Press, 1997), p. 178. The best starting point for the study of eighteenth-century conceptions of revolution can now be found in Reinhart Koselleck, *The Practice of Conceptual History: Timing History, Spacing Concepts* (Palo Alta, Stanford University Press, 2002), chs. 5, 8-10.

[60] Simon Nicolas Henri Linguet, "De la société en général. Révolution singulière dont l' Europe est menacée," *Annales politiques, civiles et littéraires du dix-huitième siècle* , 1 (1777), pp. 83–103 (pp. 83 and 103).

[61] Victor Riquetti, marquis de Mirabeau, *Entretiens d'un jeune prince avec son gouverneur,* 4 vols. (Lausanne, 1785), vol. 3, pp. 234, 318; Adam Ferguson, *An Essay on the History of Civil Society* [1767], ed. Duncan Forbes (Edinburgh, Edinburgh University Press, 1966), Part V, section iv, pp. 231–2; Gabriel Bonnot de Mably, *Notre gloire ou nos rêves* [1779] in his *Oeuvres*, 13 vols. (Paris, 1795), vol. 13, p. 396.

revolution similar to the one that had destroyed the ancient world, a revolution from which there might be no way back.

A particularly vivid example of this kind of speculation was laid out in a pamphlet entitled *La Voix du citoyen* (*The citizen's voice*) published shortly before the Estates-General assembled at Versailles in May 1789. Its author, Charles François Lebrun, had been a political advisor of the French chancellor René-Nicolas de Maupeou, drafting some of Maupeou's legislation during the last great demonstration of royal authority in 1771 and, as the duc de Plaisance, was to become a prominent political figure during the first Empire. In *La Voix du citoyen* Lebrun issued a stark warning of what might happen if the Estates-General failed to deal with the monarchy's financial problems. Disagreement between the three estates over how to apportion the tax-burden needed to fund the deficit would, he warned, precipitate a bankruptcy whose economic and social effects would be catastrophic. It would destroy the authority of the state and shatter every social bond, leaving the French nation exposed to the depredations of all the other European powers. If France managed to survive at all, it would be reduced to the least of all the powers.[62] But, Lebrun continued, in this final extremity, patriotism would find its appointed place. It would recognize necessity as the supreme law and, adopting the ancient republican maxim that the public safety had to be the supreme law (*salus populi suprema lex esto*), the French nation would dispense with legality and justice in order to preserve itself. It would sacrifice both the nobility and the clergy to the "tumultuous equality" of democracy. And if democracy was in turn to fail, France would still find a way to ensure that she was not effaced from among the European powers. A "determined *leveller*" would emerge from within the Third Estate to found a new constitution upon the ruins of the old.[63] Not content with the destruction of the nobility and the clergy, this "audacious leveller" would summon the citizenry to even greater liberty and prosperity. But he "would lack the authority needed for his beneficent views."[64] At every step, perpetual meetings would distract the people from industry, agriculture, and commerce. At once, Lebrun predicted, a general desire (*le voeu général*) would lead him to be entrusted with all public power as a legal despot, thus bringing the long cycle of political conflict to an end. Not surprisingly, Lebrun republished his pamphlet in 1810. It was a very graphic prediction of the sequence of events running from 1789 to the Jacobin Terror and the first Empire.

---

[62] Lebrun, *Voix*, p. 83.

[63] Lebrun, *Voix*, p. 84.

[64] Lebrun, *Voix*, p. 85.

The Jacobin phase of the French Revolution may well have come after the revolution of 1789, but in imaginative terms the Terror came first. This has an important bearing both on Sieyès' political thought and on the wider question of the origins and nature of the French Revolution itself. Once Sieyès' system is set in the context of eighteenth-century predictions of revolution, it looks less inexplicably radical in its premises and effects than the best modern historians have sometimes taken it to be.[65] If, to use the terminology of the modern historiography of the French Revolution, the revolution of 1789 was a "political revolution with social consequences," this was because something like "the social interpretation of the French Revolution" was already in existence as a nightmarish vision of modernity's future.[66] From this perspective, Sieyès' system might best be described as one of the last of an elaborate sequence of theoretical attempts (not only in France and not just before 1789) to conceive of a system of government compatible with those of the properties of the modern world that were taken to be likely to maintain its potential for peace and prosperity while, at the same time, forestalling those taken to be likely to condemn it to repeat the cycle of decline and fall that had destroyed its ancient counterpart. The context from which Sieyès' idea of representative government emerged was shaped by this kind of concern with modernity's potential for catastrophe and the accompanying search for a better understanding of the mechanisms underlying modernity's capacity for civilization. The elaborate system of political representation that he tried unsuccessfully to persuade his contemporaries to adopt, first

---

[65] "The sovereignty of the king was transferred to the people; aristocratic society was replaced by the world of free and equal individuals, a dual upheaval, carried out so radically—and this is still the mystery of 1789—that it gave the question of the reconstitution of society the character of a philosophical question analogous to those treated by the philosophers of natural jurisprudence. . . . So much so, that of the two great classical problems that the French Révolution has posed for historians—that of the causes of 1789 and that of the lurch from 1789 to 1793—the latter is perhaps less of an enigma than the former." ("La souveraineté du roi est passée au peuple, la société aristocratique a été remplacée par le monde des individus libres et égaux: double basculement opéré si radicalement—c'est encore le mystère de 1789—qu'il donne à la reconstitution du corps politique le caractère d'une question philosophique analogue à celles qu'ont traitées les philosophies *jus* naturalistes. . . . Si bien que des deux grands problèmes classiques que la Révolution française pose à l'historien: celui des causes de 1789, et celui de la dérive de 1789 à 1793, le second est peut-être moins énigmatique que le premier"): François Furet and Ran Halévi, *Orateurs de la Révolution française* (Paris, Gallimard, 1989), pp. xciv–xcv.

[66] The phrases were coined by George V. Taylor, "Non-capitalist Wealth and the Origins of the French Revolution," *American Historical Review,* 79 (1967), pp. 469–96 and Alfred Cobban, *The Social Interpretation of the French Revolution* (Cambridge, Cambridge University Press, 1964).

in 1789, then in 1795 and again, in 1799 was designed to prevent, not promote, the long-predicted "social revolution" of eighteenth-century speculation about the future and the despotic outcome that it was expected to entail.

As many eighteenth-century political theorists had claimed, the most immediate source of the threat was the deficit. "The revolutions that the system of public loans will produce all over Europe have no precedent in the history of the ancients," noted one French commentator at the beginning of the reign of Louis XVI.[67] The potential effects of using public credit to fund the costs of war had been described most vividly by the Scottish philosopher David Hume in 1752. Either, he wrote, "the nation must destroy public credit, or public credit will destroy the nation."[68] Hume's warning was widely noticed. In his *Inquiry into the Principles of Political Oeconomy* of 1767, the exiled Scottish Jacobite Sir James Steuart drew out the wider geo-political implications of allowing the modern system of war finance to run unchecked. Suppose, he wrote, that a Prince was to contract debts up to the value of the whole property of the nation, as Hume had surmised, taking the land-tax up to twenty shillings in the pound "and then let him become bankrupt to the creditors," such a ruler would at once have emancipated himself from the public debt and have at his disposal "the income of all the lands...for the use of the state." "I ask," Steuart commented, "what confederacy among the modern European Princes, would carry on a successful war against such a people?...And what country could defend itself against such an enemy?"[69] This had been why Hume had issued his warning with its brutal recommendation that it might be better to destroy the debt by a voluntary state bankruptcy than allow the debt to destroy the nation. When, in 1787, the English political commentator Arthur Young made an assessment of the likely outcome of the developing conflict in France over the royal government's financial deficit, his prognosis followed Hume's logic. "Dined today," he

---

[67] Pierre Jean Grosley, *Londres,* 3 vols. (Neuchâtel, 1774), vol. 3, p. 331.

[68] David Hume, "Of Public Credit" [1752], in David Hume, *Essays, Moral, Political and Literary* ed. E. F. Miller (Indianapolis, Indiana, Liberty Press, 1985), pp. 360–1. More generally, see Istvan Hont, "The Rhapsody of Public Debt: David Hume and Voluntary State Bankruptcy," in Nicholas Phillipson and Quentin Skinner (eds.), *Political Discourse in Early Modern Britain* (Cambridge, U.K., Cambridge University Press, 1993); Michael Sonenscher, "The Nation's Debt and the Birth of the Modern Republic," *History of Political Thought,* 18 (1997), pp. 64–103, 267–325.

[69] Sir James Steuart, *An Inquiry into the Principles of Political Oeconomy* [1767] (ed. Andrew Skinner, Edinburgh and Chicago, University of Chicago Press, 1966), Bk. II, ch. xiv, pp. 226–7.

noted in Paris on 17 October 1787, "with a party, whose conversation was entirely political." "It is very remarkable," he continued,

> that such conversation never occurs, but a bankruptcy is a topic; the curious question on which is, *would a bankruptcy occasion a civil war, and a total overthrow of the government?* The answers that I have received to this question appear to be just; such a measure, conducted by a man of abilities, vigour and firmness, would certainly not occasion either one or the other. But the same measure, attempted by a man of a different character, might possibly do both.[70]

Sieyès himself drafted a model of the long-term effects of public debt that followed the same logic as the one that Hume and Steuart had outlined.[71] But France was an absolute not a constitutional monarchy. The implications of a failure to take responsibility for dealing with the deficit out of the hands of the royal government were set out most fully in the *Views of the executive means.* A considerable part of the pamphlet (see below, pp. 24–32, 60–7) was devoted to a discussion of the possibility that, faced with a choice between preserving itself and preserving public faith (its obligations to its creditors), the royal government would opt for the first. There were, Sieyès wrote, two moments at which a bankruptcy was possible. The first, which would have averted summoning the Estates-General altogether, had passed. But the second remained a real possibility because it might be carried through with the support of the Estates-General itself. Instead of a bankruptcy engineered by ministerial fiat, the representatives of the nation might be persuaded that "at bottom" what was at issue was no more than "a combat between landowners and capitalists" (as investors in the public funds were known in eighteenth-century France) and, rather than meet the costs of funding the debt, would prefer to sacrifice the capitalists to the interests of landed property. Bankruptcy, Sieyès pointed out, had its partisans. Some claimed that the nation could not be responsible for the debt because it had not given its consent to the original loans. Some argued that the loans themselves were usurious and therefore illegal. Others preferred to balance the advantages of a bankruptcy against the disadvantages and were prepared "coldly" to opt for the advantages. The majority, frightened of any further addition to the tax-burden, might be prepared to contemplate any alternative to a new tax.

If, Sieyès warned, the Estates-General was to opt to default on the debt, the results would be catastrophic. By "subscribing to a bankruptcy" it would have lost the most favorable and least costly means of acquiring

---

[70] Arthur Young, *Travels in France*, ed. Constance Maxwell (Cambridge, U.K., Cambridge University Press, 1929), pp. 84–5.

[71] A. N. 284 AP 2, dossier 12 (note headed "finances").

a constitution ever offered to a people. What might appear to free the nation of its debt would, at the very moment of liberation, restore the independence of the royal government to spend its revenue as it liked. Once the royal government was again able to exercise its "omnipotence," any departure from servile obedience by the Estates-General towards ministerial despotism would lead to it being broken like a reed. In the worst case, a bankruptcy might lead to a war with nations such as England whose citizens were among the creditors of the French state. Having disowned its debt, the French state would then have to borrow funds at exorbitant rates of interest and would find itself saddled with an even greater debt-burden once the war had ended. Even in the best case, with no war, the court and the ministry would maintain public expenditure at its present level, but revenue from existing taxes would collapse, either because of the sharp fall in consumption and production caused by the bankruptcy itself or because of widespread tax evasion. The result would be a drift towards despotism as the rising costs of tax collection led to further demands for revenue and an increased reliance upon force to fund public expenditure. The strategy that Sieyès laid out in the *Views of the executive means* and then transferred to the representatives of the Third Estate in *What is the Third Estate?* was designed to ensure that this scenario would not happen. The increasingly lengthy notes that he added to the three editions of the latter pamphlet contained a sequence of warnings about what could be expected if it did. (His coruscating note—below, p. 98—on a pamphlet by the Protestant minister Rabaut Saint-Etienne, himself no friend of the established order, is a particularly vivid example of his impatience with those who were unable or unwilling to see that it might).

In a broader sense, the system of representative government was designed to ensure that, even in the longer term, it would not. In part, this would be an effect of the decentralized system of decision making that the representative system entailed. Since as many as possible of the steps involved in both law-making and law-enforcing were to be entrusted to separate representative bodies, no single body would have the power to affect the decision making capacity of any of the others. This meant that the representative system was much less capable of the absolute exercise of sovereign power than either a monarchy or a democracy. The structure of decision-making embodied in the constitution also supplied a stable point of reference for assessing the compatibility between projected legislation and the nature of the system itself. This built-in reflective capability made it easier too to build a set of checking mechanisms into the decision-making process itself. Although Sieyès famously rejected the idea of giving the king a veto (because it would endow the monarchy with a legislative, rather than a purely representative function), he was careful to equip the system with constitutional checks. They had, however, to be part of the legislative process itself, working like a regulator in a watch or a governor in an engine. The first person to have introduced a regulator into the design of a machine, Sieyès commented sarcastically in September 1789 during the debate on the royal veto, would have been careful not to have placed the regulator outside the machine itself if he wanted to prevent it from going too fast.[72] He was consistent in advocating a three or, occasionally, a two-chamber legislature (one to be called the blue chamber, the other the red chamber, he remarked in a private note) respectively responsible for deliberating, deciding, and reviewing.[73] He also left room for a veto. But it would be a veto exercised by one or other of the branches of the ministerial executive (which, unlike the Great Elector, would be accountable and subject to the confidence of the legislature) or, in 1795, by the Constitutional Jury or, in 1799, College of Guardians. If deadlock could not be prevented, the issue would be referred to an extraordinary Convention for resolution. Later, in his draft of the Constitution of the Year VIII, Sieyès proposed a further check by stipulating that the College of Guardians would have a power to co-opt any political or military leader it deemed might be a threat to political stability. Anyone selected for this sort of political ostracism would not be entitled to refuse. Unsurprisingly, Napoleon Bonaparte rejected this provision from the final version of the Constitution, as well as the office of the Great Elector itself. Apart from its other functions, that office was intended to be a final insurance against political crisis. In grave emergency, there would be a single decision-maker, not a Committee of Public Safety, to decide what to do to maintain the nation's sovereignty. Since, under the provisions of the constitution, the Elector would not have any share of legislative or executive power, any decision of this kind could not be conflated with a decision by the government itself. It would be an extraordinary decision made in exceptional circumstances. This was one reason why Sieyès had little confidence in Necker's alternative to absolute government (below, pp. 7, 14, 93, 159). If it was faced with a difficult decision over the future of the debt, a mixed system would find it hard to avoid either deadlock, or revolution, or (as Hume had predicted) a drift towards a constitutionally sanctioned despotic regime.

---

[72] "Le premier qui, en mécanique, fit usage du *régulateur*, se garda bien de le placer hors de la machine dont il voulait modérer le mouvement trop précipité": Emmanuel Joseph Sieyès, *Sur l'organisation du pouvoir législatif et la sanction royale* (Paris, 1789).

[73] Fauré, Guilhaumou, and Valier (eds.), *Des Manuscrits de Sieyès 1773–1799*, p. 349.

In part, however, Sieyès envisaged a set of mechanisms binding everyone to the representative system by way of a considerable number of precommitments. The most important of these would be generated by the debt itself. The key to political stability under modern conditions of private property, Sieyès recognized, was a fiscal-state (or taxation-state) and the basis of a taxation-state was a permanent public debt. This, he wrote in his draft Declaration of the Rights of Man in August 1789, was why the modern theory of landed property could not accommodate the prepolitical principles of occupancy or labor that might once have been applicable to a world without states. He copied out a comment by the Anglo-Welsh Presbyterian minister and political reformer Richard Price that if there had been a public debt in seventeenth-century England, both Charles I and James II would have remained on their thrones.[74] "The true doctrine of taxation," he noted, "true social theory, does not require either repaying the debt, since it was going to set all production under the hands of the state, or freeing the landowners from their fiscal obligations to the state."[75] He made this note in the autumn of 1789, when the French National Assembly was debating the question of whether to reduce the debt by confiscating the property of the church (a course of action that it decided to pursue that November). It is well known that Sieyès was opposed to this way of trying to solve the problem of the deficit. His opposition was not, however, motivated by his own position as a member of the church but rather by the massive increase in governmental responsibility that nationalizing church property was likely to produce.

He was not at all averse to a very radical reform of the Catholic Church.[76] Unless it was assumed to be the best of all possible known or imagined religions, he noted in a draft of a speech to the National Assembly's constitutional committee, the Catholic Church was simply the church that happened, *de facto,* to exist in France and did not need to have the ecclesiastical government it presently had (it could also, he later noted, exist alongside any other church). Like everything else, the new system that Sieyès envisaged was based on the principle of representation. Priests, like the magistrates responsible for police and local justice, would

---

[74] A. N. 284 AP 2, dossier 14 (note headed "Angleterre. Fonds circulans en 1783").

[75] "Ce plan est dans la supposition des théories politiques reçus jusqu' à ce jour. La véritable doctrine de l'impôt, la véritable théorie sociale ne demande ni le remboursement de la dette puisqu' elle alloit à mettre toutes les productions entre les mains de l'état, ni l'affranchissement des propriétaires terriens envers l'état." A. N. 284 AP 4, dossier 9, "Destination des biens ecclésiastiques."

[76] A. N. 284 AP 4, dossier 9, "Croquis de mon discours au comité [de constitution]."

be appointed by the primary assemblies of the municipalities. They would, of course, have had to be ordained (just as magistrates, doctors or lawyers needed some proof of professional capability), but ordination as well as confirmation, would be carried out by other priests (as, Sieyès noted, had been the case with the primitive church). There would, therefore, be no need for many bishops. There would in fact be only six. They would be ambulatory (so that there would be no dioceses) and responsible for overseeing church government under the aegis of the ecclesiastical committee of the legislature. The church would, therefore, become a simple professional body that, like any other, would be subordinate to the state. It would, however, still have its own source of funds. This was one reason why Sieyès was opposed to both the abolition of the clerical tithe without compensation and the unilateral confiscation of ecclesiastical property (the other was that doing so amounted to an immense windfall for the rich). Instead of simply nationalizing the church, he suggested that it would be better to buy its unused property and pay for it by floating a loan of 1,500 million *livres* secured against the income from its subsequent sale. The capital that the church would then own could then be invested in the public funds to produce an income to pay the clergy and cover the costs of the education and welfare that they provided. A further 2,500 million *livres* could be raised against the revenue from the clerical tithe by turning it into a straightforward tax on landed property.[77] The capital could then be used to convert short-term debt into longer term annuities, locking the landowners into a system of taxation predicated upon the continued existence of the nation's debt. The details varied from draft to draft. But the general aims were quite consistent. The first of these was to prevent the church from becoming the responsibility of the state (Sieyès was privately appalled by the civil constitution of the clergy introduced by the National Assembly in the summer of 1790, proposing—anonymously—in the 18 November 1791 issue of the *Chronique de Paris,* a law stipulating that as from 1 January 1792 no religion would have the backing of the legislature).[78] The second was to use public credit to turn church revenue into state revenue without confiscating ecclesiastical property, so that the landowners rather than the church would carry the cost of the national debt.

---

[77] See also the interesting description of the same debt-reduction scheme by the very royalist comte de Montlosier in his *Mémoires,* 2 vols. (Paris, 1830), vol. 1, pp. 254–5. According to Montlosier, Sieyès, Necker, and the Bishop of Chartres (whose vicar-general Sieyès had been) had already prepared plans to use the capital in the way that Sieyès suggested but these were overtaken by the Assembly's abolition of the tithe.

[78] A. N. 284 AP 4, dossier 9.

The permanence of the debt meant that Sieyès was also committed to the existence of a permanent fiscal system. Taxes would have to be raised to pay interest on the nation's debt. This, in turn, meant that both electors and elected would have a permanent, if conflicting, interest in the workings of the fiscal system and in ensuring that public revenue was properly used. The pyramidal structure of representation that Sieyès envisaged was intended to be matched by a decentralized system of public finance. Each of the various levels of representation running from the municipalities at the bottom to the national government at the top was to be equipped with a tax-collecting and revenue-spending capability. The result would be a permanent bridge between the political and the economic life of the nation. The natural tension between ministerial and opposition parties was designed to ensure that the use of public funds would be subject to permanent public scrutiny, while the irredeemable character of the national debt was designed to ensure that agriculture, industry, and trade would all be subject to a permanent pressure to reduce costs, increase output, or raise productivity by innovating on products or production processes to reduce the burden of taxation that they had to pay. This, in turn, would have the effect of increasing the number of specialized tasks performed within society and, by doing so, of raising the threshold of risk associated with economic and political instability. In a system in which everyone in some sense represented everyone else, the risks associated with collapse might, over time, come to be seen to be very high indeed.

The Intellectual Origins of Sieyès' System

Early in December 1791, the future Minister of the Interior of the first French Republic, Dominique Joseph Garat, published a valedictory report on the period he had spent reporting on the debates in the National Assembly for the *Journal de Paris* between 1789 and 1791. In it, he offered an assessment of what the Assembly had achieved and what the new Legislative Assembly would still have to do. Its chances of success, he wrote, would depend on its ability to achieve a level of debate commensurate with the political theory that Sieyès had begun to develop. That theory, Garat claimed, had its origins in the work of the seventeenth-century English political philosopher Thomas Hobbes. It was also connected to the eighteenth-century conceptual innovations made by Charles Louis de Secondat, baron de Montesquieu, in his *The Spirit of Laws* of 1748 and by the Genevan Republican Jean Jacques Rousseau in his *Social Contract* of 1763. Despotism, Garat wrote, "had ranged among its defenders the only one, among all the political writers, who best understood the true foundations of societies, the rights of man, and the principles of peace among nations, Thomas Hobbes."[79] But none of its more recent defenders in the French National Assembly had come at all close to the level of sophistication that Hobbes had achieved. If, Garat wrote, there had been a combat in the National Assembly between "a man like Hobbes on one side and a man like the abbé Sieyès on the other" the entitlements of the human race "after having been found again and proclaimed anew" would not "have experienced the outrage to which they had been subjected even by those who had proclaimed them."[80] The need now was for a common intellectual enterprise, modeled on the great French *Encyclopédie* of the third quarter of the eighteenth century, to build on what Garat, borrowing the term that Sieyès had coined, described as "the primary givens of *science sociale*." The first of these was the idea of the separation of powers contained in Montesquieu's *The Spirit of Laws*. The second was the conception of sovereignty as the general will set out by Rousseau in his *Social Contract*. These, according to Garat, had to be the starting point for any further developments in social science.

The line of intellectual descent running from Hobbes to Montesquieu and Rousseau and then to Sieyès and his idea of *science sociale* that Garat laid out was not entirely direct. Both Montesquieu and Rousseau were openly critical of the idea of representation that was the cornerstone of Hobbes' political theory. Hobbes had described the idea most famously in Chapter 16 of his *Leviathan* (1651). "A multitude of men," he wrote, "are made *One* Person, when they are by one man, or one Person, Represented; so that it be done with the consent of every one of that Multitude in particular. For it is the *Unity* of the Representer, not the *Unity* of the Represented, that maketh the Person *One*."[81] Montesquieu was not impressed by this theory of attributed action. "Hobbes' principle" he noted, "is very false: namely, that the people having authorized the prince, the actions of the prince are the actions of the people, so that the people cannot complain about the prince nor demand that he give any account for his actions because the people cannot complain about the people."[82] Rousseau was even more emphatic, rejecting the idea of a personified

---

[79] Dominique Joseph Garat, *Dominique Joseph Garat, membre de l'assemblée constituante, à M. Condorcet, membre de l'assemblée nationale, seconde législature* (Paris, 1791), pp. 25–6.

[80] Garat, *A M. Condorcet*, p. 26.

[81] Thomas Hobbes, *Leviathan* [1651], ed. C. B. Macpherson (Harmondsworth, Penguin Books, 1968), Part 1, ch. 16, p. 220.

[82] Charles Louis de Secondat, baron de Montesquieu, *Pensées*, ed. Louis Desgraves (Paris, Robert Laffont, 1985), No. 224, p. 253.

representative sovereign altogether. The general will, he wrote in his *Social Contract,* could be represented only by itself. Quite a lot, in other words, had to be added to turn Hobbes' idea of representation into Sieyès' system of representative government.

Hobbes' theory of representative sovereignty turned largely upon the *de facto* power of overwhelming force and an argument about how submission to that kind of power was still compatible with human choice. Crudely summarized, that kind of power might impede your ability to act, but it did not impede your ability to will, and if this was the case, it could be authorized to act as a purely artificial person (a state), acting as the representative of the many different members of a civil association in a single collective act.[83] From this perspective, a state, not a natural person, was the locus of legitimate sovereign power. But since states are not human, they need to be represented by real people in order to be able to act. These representatives might be one or many, but they would still be mortal and have to be replaced. The difficult part of Hobbes' legacy was to find a way to build a rather more obvious amount of human choice into the idea of the state as a representative of its members without falling back upon the idea of electing a sovereign, thus reviving the problems of partiality, division, and conflict that Hobbes' theory of sovereignty was designed to overcome.

A starting point could be found in an idea of representation that was closely related to Hobbes' idea of states as artificial persons. According to this idea of representation, buildings and other physical things could also be represented, either by their owners or by those responsible for their upkeep (Hobbes used the examples of bridges and hospitals to illustrate the point). Sieyès' conception of the representative system owed a great deal to this notion of representation and the use to which it was put, first by Montesquieu in *The Spirit of Laws,* and then by Rousseau in his discussion of government as the executive representative of the general will in the third book of his *Social Contract.* It opened up a way of thinking about representation that could encompass both the kind of representation involved in ordinary life and the sort of representation involved in political society but still did not reduce the one to the other. This idea of representation was not connected (at least in the first instance) to anything to do with political or legal representation but referred instead to a particular way of thinking about the inheritance of property that in early modern Europe was held to be a feature of ancient Roman property law.

---

[83] Quentin Skinner, "Hobbes on the proper signification of liberty" now in his *Visions of Politics* (Cambridge, U.K., Cambridge University Press, 2002), vol. 3, *Hobbes and Civil Science,* ch. 7.

In this account of Roman law, property passed from one generation to the next by right of representation. An individual's surviving lineal or collateral descendants could inherit the goods that he (and in some circumstances, she) had owned because they were held to be the representatives of the individual who had died and were entitled, by right of representation, to a share of the property that he (or in some circumstances, she) had owned. Although there was some discussion of how literal a representative someone had to be (whether, for example, a daughter could represent her father), it was always accepted that a representative was someone standing in for someone else and, as that representative, was held to possess the goods that he or she had owned under the same entitlements and conditions.

The most important institution to which this idea of representation was held to apply was the French monarchy. As the seventeenth-century Dutch natural jurist Hugo Grotius described it in his *The Rights of War and Peace* (1625), the French crown was successoral, lineal, and agnatic (meaning that it passed successively only from one generation to the next, never laterally to uncles or cousins, and only through the male line), making the royal succession, as he put it, "representative."[84] The system was often associated with what were called the Salic laws, a much-interpreted body of customary law that, it was said, was followed originally by the Frankish invaders of the Roman province of Gaul and according to some interpreters contained the original principles of the French monarchy. The rules of representative succession meant that the heir to the throne could not be chosen by the incumbent king nor could he be the incumbent's closest blood relative but had instead simply to occupy the appropriate position in the line of succession, coming to the throne either as the first direct male descendant of the previous king or as the representative of that heir in the line of lineal, agnatic descent, so that in legal terms he was held to be exactly the same person as the previous king.[85] This meant, as it was put in the early eighteenth century, that "in facts of succession, it is not he who is nearest to the throne who succeeds, but he who represents it."[86] The effect of this conception of the rules governing

---

[84] Hugo Grotius, *De jure belli ac pacis* [1625], translated by Jean Barbeyrac as *Le Droit de la guerre et de la paix* (Amsterdam, 1724), Bk. II, ch. vii, § 12–37.

[85] Grotius, trans. Barbeyrac, II, vii, 30, note 7.

[86] This characterization of the rules governing the royal succession can be found in several pamphlets bound in British Library. FR 1, particularly [Anon.], *Maximes de droit et d'état pour servir de réfutation au mémoire qui paroit sous le nom de Monsieur le duc du Maine, au sujet de la contestation qui est entre lui & Monsieur le Duc, pour le rang de prince du sang* (n. p. 1716), pp. 10–12 and [Anon.], *Raisons courtes et fondamentales pour les princes du sang & pour la nation contre les princes légitimez* (n. p. n. d.), p. 3.

the royal succession was to drastically reduce the possibility of conflict between rival candidates to a vacant throne. The idea of representation by lineal, agnatic descent meant that even if an incumbent king was to die childless, it was always possible to identify a single legitimate heir by going back up the line of descent to reach a point in the linear and agnatic sequence that could then be traced back down to identify a single living individual. This had the practical effect of making the distinction between elective and hereditary succession nugatory, because the rules of representation meant that in the event of a vacant throne there would always be only one eligible candidate.

But this feature of the rules governing the royal succession created a political and analytical conundrum when Louis XIV died in 1715. At his death, the French throne passed to his five-year-old great-grandson, Louis XV. If (as seemed quite possible) Louis XV was to die without an heir, the throne would go to Philip V of Spain (1683–1746), the second son and only surviving representative of Louis de France (1661–1711), Louis XIV's defunct oldest son and heir, reopening the prime cause of the War of the Spanish Succession. The possibility that this might occur affected French domestic politics and European international relations for nearly two decades until the birth of Louis XV's own son (Louis XVI's father) made the question of the royal succession a practical irrelevance in both domestic politics and European diplomacy. Until then, the question generated considerable interest. Applying the rules governing the succession to the French throne amounted to opting for the possibility of a unified Franco-Spanish crown and the near certainty of a major European war. Dropping them meant reopening all the problems about disputed claims to vacant thrones that the system of representative succession was designed to avoid.

The title of Montesquieu's great work, *The Spirit of Laws,* was in a sense an indication of a solution to the dilemma. If the law itself could not offer an acceptable course of action, then its spirit had to be taken into consideration. The problem of the royal succession had to be soluble without either war or civil war, because it was fairly obvious that the rules of representative succession were designed to prevent them both. This meant that if the rules of representative succession threatened to produce a perverse result, there had to be an alternative to a potentially divisive electoral contest. It was not hard to see that there was a significant difference between the idea of representative succession as it applied to the French throne and the notion of representation that was held to have been a feature of ancient Roman property law. In Roman law, the goods that could be transferred from one generation to the next could be divided between several representatives. The French throne, however, was indivisible, and the notion of representation that applied to inheriting the French crown was considerably narrower than anything in Roman law (most obviously because women could not inherit the throne). For Montesquieu the interesting question seems to have been the question of how the Roman idea of representative succession had become the basis of the French system of indivisible, hereditary monarchy. By identifying the reasons for this change, it might then be possible to identify the reasons for making a less than literal interpretation of the laws governing the succession to the French throne.

Montesquieu's answer was based upon three passages in the Roman historian Tacitus' *Germania,* the classical source of information about the Germanic invaders of Roman Gaul. These passages described three features of the system of government of the Franks, the Germanic people whose king, Clovis, was usually held to be the first king of France. The first passage stated that "the power of their kings is neither unlimited nor arbitrary" (*Nec regibus infinita aut libera potestas*). The second stated that "minor affairs were submitted for discussion to the chiefs; major affairs were discussed by all" (*De minoribus rebus principes consultant, de maioribus omnes*). The third passage—"kings were chosen in terms of their nobility, generals in terms of their valour" (*Reges ex nobilitate, duces ex virtute sumunt*)—was particularly significant. As Montesquieu interpreted it, it meant that the civil and the military powers were exercised by two different representatives. This, he noted, was "the key to the beginnings of the French monarchy."[87] The reason why it was "the key to the beginnings of the French monarchy" was because when it was combined with the two other features of Germanic society that Tacitus had described, and was applied not to the original Frankish peoples who did not cultivate the land but to the conquering Frankish people who had all the land of Roman Gaul at their disposal, it became the basis of a type of monarchy that had no counterpart in the ancient world. By showing how the Roman idea of representative succession had come to be grafted on to the feudal system of fiefs, Montesquieu was able to describe the outcome as a kind of monarchy in which, as he put it, "intermediate, subordinate, and dependent powers constitute the nature of monarchical government, that is, of the government in which he alone governs by fundamental laws." The "most natural" of these "intermediate, subordinate, and dependent powers," he added immediately, was a nobility.[88] Monarchy, as Montesquieu

[87] Charles Louis de Secondat, baron de Montesquieu, *Pensées,* ed. Louis Desgraves, No. 1906, p. 584.

[88] Charles Louis de Secondat, baron de Montesquieu, *De l'esprit des lois* [Geneva, 1748], Bk. 2 Ch. 4.

defined it, was a dual system. In it, the sovereign (the king) could be distinguished from the government (the subordinate, dependent, and intermediate powers), or to use his language, the prince could be distinguished from the state.

Montesquieu had, in short, made a distinction between a state and its government by showing how their respective powers might be separated without using the historically implausible idea of a social contract and without equating the separation of powers with either a mixed system of government or solely with the peculiar system of government that had grown up in post-Reformation England, the system that he described with such skill in two famous books of *The Spirit of Laws*. By making this distinction, he also showed how it might be possible to identify a connection between representatives and represented that made it easier to see how a government representing a sovereign state could also actually represent the interests of the members of that state rather than, as with Hobbes, simply make decisions in their name. The connection between representative and represented was formed by indivisible hereditary property. By showing how the old Roman idea of representative succession had, during the first three dynasties of Frankish rule, been transformed into a combination of hereditary monarchy and hereditary fiefs (a process culminating in the election of Hugues Capet to the throne when "the owner of the greatest fief" became the reigning king), Montesquieu was able to claim that the modern French monarchy was based not, as might intuitively be thought, upon some original set of founding political laws, but instead upon a congeries of civil laws (notably the Roman law of succession and the Frankish Salic laws), which, over the course of time, had acquired a political and institutional character. (Montesquieu was extremely proud of this demonstration of the paradoxical way that a civil law could be seen to have been the cause of a form of government that did not yet exist, when logic suggests that the relationship between cause and effect ought to be the reverse.) One implication of this claim was that if the rules governing the royal succession seemed likely to produce a potentially perverse outcome (as with the case of Philip V's right to inherit the French throne if Louis XV had died without an heir), it was then possible to refer not to the law but to the spirit of the law and apply the original civil law principle affecting the inheritance of fiefs to the inheritance of the throne, so that once again the owner of the greatest fief (which, necessarily, would be situated within the kingdom) would be the only eligible candidate to fill a vacant succession.

A second and equally important implication of this claim was its bearing upon the relationship between a state and its members. Unlike the old Roman system of representative succession, the feudal version, as it applied to the inheritance of the throne and the inheritance of fiefs, stipulated a single representative heir to either a throne or a fief. The language in which this notion of representation was couched was indisputably feudal, not Roman. It used the terminology of entails and substitutions to explain how it was possible for either a fief or a throne to pass from a single individual in one generation to a single individual in the next as one indivisible entity. Montesquieu went to considerable lengths to show how this feature of the feudal version of representative succession could not be found in the ancient Roman system (devoting Book 27 of *The Spirit of Laws* to showing how the Roman law of inheritance, unless sanctioned by a political decision, never provided for a single exclusive heir). It was instead an outcome of the way that feudal fiefs had come to be passed from one generation to the next by means of testamentary wills and the provisions for substitutions and entails that they contained. The result was that the transmission of property by way of a last will and testament had come to occupy a much more prominent place in the modern world than it had ever had in ancient Rome or Greece. This in turn had a significant bearing on the relationship between states and their members, because it meant that decisions affecting the distribution of property could not be the direct concern of the state. It was this, Montesquieu claimed, that served to make monarchies different from both republics and despotic governments. In both republics and despotic forms of government, decisions affecting the distribution of property were matters for the sovereign. Peculiarly, in a monarchy, decisions affecting the distribution of property were not matters for the sovereign, because they were decisions that had been made by the dead (Montesquieu, almost uniquely, was prepared to defend the application of the same principle to the ownership of the thousands of venal offices attached to the French system of royal government). The living were simply responsible for upholding what the dead had decided in their last wills and testaments. Since the dead were the authors of some of the actions of the living, this had the effect of ensuring that the state had no direct concern with the mechanisms determining the social distribution of wealth and the property arrangements underpinning the hierarchy of ranks. From this perspective, inequality was not a regrettable, potentially reversible, development in most modern European societies (which considered action by a reforming government might aim to reduce), but was instead what made monarchy, uniquely, the type of government it was, giving it, as Montesquieu put it, its *nature*. This, according to Montesquieu, was why it was a different kind of system of government from either a republic or a despotism and why, accordingly, its peculiar principle of honor and the system of ranks on which it was based had no counterpart in any other type of political society.

Although Rousseau's political thought is usually taken to be the polar opposite of Montesquieu's, the distance between their respective theories of the relationship between states and their governments was not as considerable as it has sometimes been made to seem. In a pamphlet entitled *Jean Jacques Rousseau à l'assemblée nationale* published late in 1789, a minor political writer named the abbé François Jean Philibert Aubert de Vitry commented quite acutely that Rousseau's political thought had been "spoiled by reading *The Spirit of Laws*" with the result that "it could not but fail to be infected, in certain places, by the venom of aristocratism."[89] The comment was directed at the fourth book of the *Social Contract* and the description of the ancient Roman system of political representation that it contained. Rousseau was notoriously suspicious of the idea of political representation. "The idea of representatives," he noted, was "modern; it came to us from feudal government."[90] But however distasteful its origins may have been, it was nonetheless the way of preserving the liberty of the moderns (as Rousseau pointed out, it was the price paid by the moderns for the abolition of the slavery that had served to preserve the liberty of the ancients).[91] The key problem was to find a form of representation that was compatible with both the absence of slavery and the fact that everyone was equally entitled to membership of a modern state. Taking the ownership of property as the basis of a system of political representation was, Rousseau showed in his *Discourse on the Origins of Inequality,* bound to lead to despotism. It would do so, he argued, because the representative would have to act and, to do so, would need resources of its own. This, he insisted, was why the state-person should never be represented by any actual person. The state-person had to be a general will which had to be kept entirely distinct from the flesh and blood members of its government. To maintain this distinction, Rousseau dropped the Germans and went back to the Romans. Doing so allowed him to follow Montesquieu's logic without having to adopt Montesquieu's property-based approach to the distinction between a state and its government.

Liberty, Rousseau wrote at the beginning of Chapter 8 of the third book of the *Social Contract* was not the fruit of every climate and not

---

[89] [François Jean Philibert Aubert de Vitry], *Jean Jacques Rousseau à l'assemblée nationale* (Paris, 1789). p. 220.

[90] Jean Jacques Rousseau, *Du contrat social,* Bk. III, ch. 15, in Rousseau, *Oeuvres,* vol. 3, p. 430, and in Jean Jacques Rousseau, *The Social Contract and Other Later Political Writings,* ed. Victor Gourevitch (Cambridge, Cambridge University Press, 1997), p.114.

[91] Rousseau, *Du contrat social,* Bk. III, ch. 15. *Oeuvres*, vol. 3, p. 431, and Rousseau, *The Social Contract,* ed. Gourevitch, p. 115.

within the capacity of every people. "The more one reflects on this doctrine of Montesquieu," he added, "the more one is conscious of its truth."[92] In order to be able to govern, every government in the world, he continued, had to rely on the surplus produced by the members of the states that they ruled. It followed that political society, or "the civil state," could subsist "only if men's work yields more than what is required for meeting their needs."[93] In some settings the surplus could be produced quite easily; in others, however, producing a surplus called for substantial effort. The same absolute surplus would have a different relationship to the size of the population and the needs of the government. If the population was small or its needs were few, the government would have a larger relative surplus at its disposal. If the population was large or if its needs could be met only with substantial amounts of effort, the relative size of the surplus would be smaller. The first state of affairs, Rousseau argued, favored despotic governments. The second favored free states. Under this kind of government—in which a large number of citizens produced a small per capita surplus without relying on any external resources—population and prosperity would go hand in hand. This, Rousseau argued, was the only reliable measure of good government.

Government, Rousseau emphasized, was "an intermediary body established between the subjects and the sovereign." The phrase was evocative of Montesquieu. But Rousseau's idea of an intermediary power was inside the political system, not outside it, as a nobility generated by the inheritance of property was in Montesquieu's theory of monarchy (Sieyès made the same distinction between a "true" and "false" hierarchy in a note in his *Essay on Privileges,* below p. 82). The model that Rousseau adopted to illustrate his theory of government was taken from republican Rome. The Roman system of government, as Rousseau described it, was a system of representation based on persons, not property.[94] It was also indirect, not direct. Every Roman citizen was a member of a tribe, a *curia,* a class, and a hundred. These, rather than each individual Roman, elected the membership of the government of the Roman Republic. Since membership of some tribes and hundreds was massively more exclusive than others, the electoral system was designed to filter out the majority of potentially eligible citizens. Rousseau's description of the Roman

---

[92] Rousseau, *Du contrat social,* Bk. III, ch. 8. *Oeuvres*, vol. 3, p. 414, and Rousseau, *The Social Contract,* ed. Gourevitch, p. 100.

[93] Rousseau, *Du contrat social,* Bk. III, ch. 8, *Oeuvres,* vol. 3, p. 414, and Rousseau, *The Social Contract,* ed. Gourevitch, p. 100.

[94] Rousseau, *Du contrat social,* Book IV, ch. 4. *Oeuvres,* vol. 3, pp. 444–53, and Rousseau, *The Social Contract,* ed. Gourevitch, pp. 127-36.

system of government was something like a republican parallel to Montesquieu's version of monarchy, with an elected aristocracy replacing the property-based system of ranks that made monarchy the kind of system of government it was. Since it was a republican system and since, as Rousseau emphasized (and as Montesquieu himself had also pointed out), only a relatively small republic was able to serve as a setting for the intense emotional compound that made patriotism the basis of anyone's ability to internalize the general will, it was able to dispense with a personified sovereign. It was a system of government suitable for Geneva, not modern France. Any more extended political society, Rousseau argued, would have to be a federation or, if it were not, it would be ruled despotically. Later in his *Considerations on the Government of Poland,* written between October 1770 and April 1771 but published only in 1782, he went on to outline a system of government for a large territorial state that would still be compatible with these principles.

Since Poland was a large territorial state, it could not have "the severe administration of small republics." But "the constitution of a large kingdom" could, Rousseau argued, still have "the solidity and vigor of a small republic."[95] One essential move was to make the system of government a federal system based upon the thirty-three palatinates into which the kingdom was divided. The second was what Rousseau called a system of "graduated promotions." This, he wrote, was "the strongest, most powerful" means to maintain liberty and, "if well implemented" would be "infallibly successful" in "carrying patriotism to the highest pitch in all Polish hearts."[96] All the "active members of the republic" would be divided into three classes. Eligibility for election to the Polish Diet would depend initially on some earlier form of public service in local administration. Eligibility for the second grade would require election to the Diet on three occasions. Membership of the Polish Senate would be drawn from this class of citizens. Finally, those who had been elected to the Senate on three separate occasions would be eligible to become guardians of the law, from whom the heads of the palatinates and other high offices would be drawn. Thus, "after fifteen or twenty years of being continually tested under the eyes of the public" the "foremost positions of the state" would be filled by a suitably qualified combination of talent, experience, and virtue.[97] These would include the monarchy itself. "A hereditary crown prevents trouble," Rousseau observed, "but brings on

---

[95] Rousseau, *Considerations,* in Rousseau, *The Social Contract*, ed. Gourevitch, p. 193.

[96] Rousseau, *Considerations,* ed. Gourevitch, p. 238.

[97] Rousseau, *Considerations,* ed. Gourevitch, pp. 239–42.

slavery; election preserves freedom, but shakes the state with each new reign."[98] To avoid either possibility, he proposed that the Polish kings should be chosen by lot from among the thirty-three heads of the palatinates. The names of three candidates would be selected in this way, and one of them would then be elected by the Polish Diet to become king. With this form, Rousseau wrote—using a phrase that was rather similar to the one that Sieyès used later in his debate with Paine—"we combine all the advantages of election with those of hereditary succession."[99]

In purely formal terms Sieyès' system of representative government was quite similar to Rousseau's system of graduated promotion. But it was designed to serve a different purpose from the one that Rousseau associated with his own system. The system of indirect election that Rousseau envisaged was designed to maintain and promote patriotism by subjecting everyone involved in public life to the permanent scrutiny of public opinion. Sieyes' system of indirect election was designed to maintain and promote all the means that individuals used to meet their needs. Sieyès' starting point was human need; Rousseau's starting point was rather different. Rousseau was intensely suspicious of any needs-based theory of human association because, he argued, humans have no natural capacity to prevent themselves from turning luxuries into needs and no natural ability to prevent their increasing dependence on others from spilling over into political life. Something other than need had to be the fundamental principle on which a political society was based. But it could not be something that could be identified by rational inquiry because, Rousseau argued, humans are far too quick to use their reason to justify their own interests rather than identify the common interest. It had, therefore, to be feeling and the intense compound of patriotic emotions that could be awakened in everyone's hearts by music, public festivals, and all the pageantry of public life. The *Considerations on the Government of Poland* was a detailed description of how this could be done.

Sieyès was consistently hostile to this kind of patriotism. Although he admired Rousseau as a writer (some passages in his *Essay on Privileges* are very like parts of Rousseau's *Discourse on the Origins of Inequality*), he rejected the weight that Rousseau attached to human emotions as the basis

---

[98] Rousseau, *Considerations,* ed. Gourevitch, p. 248.

[99] Rousseau, *Considerations,* ed. Gourevitch, p. 251. Sieyès later placed the words he used in his debate with Paine in quotation marks in a long manuscript entitled "Bases de l'ordre social," which he wrote at the time of the constitutional discussions of 1795. It is not clear whether this was a gesture towards his own earlier words or to the passage in Rousseau. The text is printed in Pasquale Pasquino, *Sieyès et l'invention de la constitution en France*, pp. 181–91 (see p. 191 for the passage in question).

of human association. Emotions, he noted, are by nature indefinite and can be associated with a wide variety of different objects. Reason, on the other hand, limits itself because it deals with one object at a time.[100] If Sieyès' system of representative government had some similarity to the model that Rousseau proposed for Poland, its purpose was somewhat different. The combination of means and ends on which it was based meant, as Sieyès put it in *What is the Third Estate?*, that it was a rather like a machine and as he consistently emphasized, the best machines were not usually the ones that came first. In this sense, the system of representative government that Sieyès devised was rather like a purely artificial analogue to the dual system based on inheritance found in Montesquieu's description of monarchy. It followed the same logic as the mechanism generating a representative of the state, which Montesquieu had identified in the feudal system, but for the system of fiefs, it substituted a complex electoral system as the mechanism producing the state's representative. Sieyès added a further modification to the hereditary principle underlying the system of government described by "the aristocrat Montesquieu," as he often referred to him. Instead of a system of political power that originated in the hereditary transmission of a particular kind of property, he envisaged a particular kind of property system based on the elective transmission of political power. In his draft of the Constitution of the Year VIII, he was insistent that both the Great Elector and the members of the Council of Guardians should not only hold office for life but should also have very large and imposing landed estates. They would be very highly paid and would enjoy a landed income of at least 100,000 francs a year for as long as they lived. But when they died, the land that they owned would revert to the nation before becoming the property of the next incumbent. There would therefore be a system of ranks, but it would not depend on hereditary property. The connection between property and office would run in the opposite direction from the one that Montesquieu had described, from public office to private property rather than from private property to public office. The result would be a nobility based on public service, divested of any ability to transmit its property from one generation to the next. The rotation of property would be driven by the great electoral cycles generated by the representative system and would follow the rotation of office from one lifetime to the next. Property would follow power, not the other way around.

Dropping the connection between representation and property made it easier to revive the old Roman law principle of representation and apply it to property that was individually owned. Doing so was also the key to elim-

---

[100] A. N. 284 AP 5, dossier 1.

inating the economic and social effects of the feudal system. If Montesquieu's version of monarchy made inequality inseparable from its nature, Sieyès' monarchical republic could find more room for equality because its stabilizing principle was industry not honor. "The peoples of modern Europe," he stated in his speech to the National Assembly on 7 September 1789 explaining the difference between "representative government" and "true democracy," "barely resemble the peoples of antiquity."

> All that matters for us are trade, agriculture, manufacture, etc. The desire for wealth seems to have turned all the states of Europe into vast workshops where more thought is given to consumption and production than to happiness. Political systems today are thus based exclusively on labor. Man's productive faculties are everything. It is hardly at all possible to derive much benefit from his moral faculties, even though they could become the most fertile source of the most genuine enjoyment.[101]

This disabused assessment of modern political systems and their bias against the improvement of the moral faculties of their members (one that Sieyès shared with Jacques Necker) was one reason for reviving the old Roman principle of representative succession and for reinforcing it by giving anyone unable to work a legal right to welfare provision. Sieyès had no illusions about the dignity of modern industrial work and wrote quite extensively about its demoralizing effects on anyone living in a giant city (in one note he toyed with the rather hair-raising idea of breeding a race of humanoids to do this kind of work).[102] This was one reason why he preferred the term *onéologie* to political economy. He was unimpressed by the claim first made by John Locke that modern industry made the poorest member of a commercial society richer than an African king. But the rotation of property that industry entailed could, he argued, be combined with a more extensive system of inheritance to reduce the more socially divisive effects of inequality. He emphasized in his draft Declaration of the Rights of Man in 1789 that the modern theory of property, and landed property in particular, had rather less to do with identifying legitimate reasons for individual ownership and more to do with social stability and the needs of the state.[103] This was one reason why

---

[101] M. J. Mavidal, E. Laurent, and E. Clavel (eds.), *Archives Parlementaires*, vol. 8 (Paris, 1875), p. 594.

[102] See the note reproduced in Emmanuel Joseph Sieyès, *Ecrits politiques,* ed. Roberto Zapperi (Montreux, Editions des archives contemporaines, 1985), p. 75.

[103] "*Landed* property (*propriétés territoriales*) makes up the most important part of *real* property. In its present state, it has less of a connection to individual need than to social need. Its theory is different; this is not the place to discuss it here." Emmanuel Joseph Sieyès, *Reconnaissance et exposition raisonnée des droits de l'homme et du citoyen* (Paris, 1789), p. 27. See also his comment on the effects of a permanent public debt, cited above, p. xliii.

he preferred taxing the landowners to confiscating church property in 1789 and why, like many of his contemporaries, he was anxious to reform the inheritance system to extend the notion of representation to a wider number of collateral kin so that property would be divided up among a larger number of legitimate heirs when it passed from one generation to the next. Sieyès seems to have been particularly concerned to see this Roman law principle reinstated as fully as possible, going to some lengths after the coup of Brumaire to try to ensure that the legal experts involved in drafting the new French civil code were specialists in Roman law.[104] Reinstating the old Roman idea—representative succession under the aegis of a fiscal state with a permanent public debt—fitted the broader aim of the representative system as a whole, because of both its long-term redistributive effects and the stimulus to individual industry that it was likely to entail.

Conclusion

The proximate origins of Sieyès' system were apparent to both its supporters and opponents when it was discussed in the National Assembly during the constitutional debates of the winter of 1789–1790. When Mirabeau commended it to the National Assembly in two speeches, on 10 and 15 December 1789, he highlighted the praise that the system of "graduated promotion" had been given by Rousseau, "the man," as he put it, "who had reflected the most on human affairs."[105] In a speech opposing it, the future Jacobin leader Bertrand Barère reminded the Assembly that since it had already "wisely proscribed" an earlier proposal to establish a three-tier electoral system and had also rejected the idea of a "civic tribute" (alluding to Sieyès' way of distinguishing between active and passive citizens), it could not now reverse its position by limiting eligibility for administrative office to those who had been elected already to a lower office. The proposal, he argued, would limit eligibility to those with the means to spend ten years or more working their way up the electoral hierarchy and "would soon come to resemble those derisory grades that the laws once prescribed to encourage the study of law and letters as con-

---

[104] A. N. 284 AP 16, dossier 5 (Durenaudet to Sieyès, 15 Germinal VIII). See also the proposal to reform the inheritance laws presented by Sieyès' *protégé* Jean Pierre Chazal, *Motion d'ordre et proposition d'un voeu à émettre pour des améliorations aux lois sur les successions et la faculté de tester* (Paris, 16 Floréal An VIII).

[105] M. J. Mavidal, E. Laurent, and E. Clavel (eds.), *Archives Parlementaires,* vol. 10 (Paris, 1878), pp. 496, 579.

ferring an aptitude for the possession of benefices or judicial offices, so that administrative functions will be no more than the vain titles of ambition and vanity."[106] The same awareness was apparent in the summer of 1795 during the constitutional discussions in the French Convention preceding the establishment of the Directory. As one of its critics, A. L. Thibaudeau, noted, the system was modeled on the Roman republic's indirect system of representation. But this, he argued, made it entirely unsuited to the complexity of modern government. If implemented, he warned, it would be "the greatest attack on the sovereignty of the people that there can be."[107] Hindsight and modern historiography make hostility from a Barère or a Thibaudeau (both influential members of the Jacobin club) seem predictable enough (for Robespierre it was simply "the bizarre system of absolute representative government").[108] But it is important to emphasize that the bulk of the early opposition to Sieyès' idea of representation came from the mainstream of the National Assembly and most particularly from the group of deputies associated with Joseph Barnave, Adrien Duport, the Lameth brothers and the marquis de Lafayette that, eighteen months later, came to be known as the Feuillants. "If, to annihilate the constitution with a single blow, it was enough to wrap oneself in contrary principles, some moral ideas and marks of erudition," Barnave began his speech attacking Mirabeau's motion of 10 December 1789, "then the previous opinant might be able to flatter himself that he was able to produce that effect on you."[109] Duport's language was less strident, but his hostility was no less strong. The proposal, he commented, was simply "a copy of that harmful system" consisting of three degrees of election that the Assembly had already rejected "with a generous unanimity."[110]

It is also important to remember that this hostility was shared by Jacques Necker and, a decade later, by Necker's most gifted protégé, Benjamin Constant. Sieyès himself was intellectually quite close to Necker. He read and annotated Necker's *De l'administration des finances* with care. He shared Necker's interest in public credit as the basis of a permanent

---

[106] Bertrand Barère, *Opinion . . . sur la motion de M. de Mirabeau, concernant les grades administratifs, du 10 décembre 1789* (Paris, 1789).

[107] British Library F 787 (4), *Opinion de Thibaudeau (A. L.) représentant du peuple sur la gradualité des fonctions publiques prononcée le 4 Thermidor an III* (Paris, 1795), pp. 3–4.

[108] Maximilien Robespierre, *Oeuvres,* vol. 5, ed. Gustave Laurent (Paris, 1961) p. 19.

[109] M. J. Mavidal, E. Laurent, and E. Clavel (eds.), *Archives Parlementaires,* vol. 10 (Paris, 1878), p. 497.

[110] M. J. Mavidal, E. Laurent, and E. Clavel (eds.), *Archives Parlementaires,* vol. 10 (Paris, 1878), pp. 577–9.

fiscal system and as a permanent stimulus to human industry. He also shared Necker's objections to the ambitious program of political and economic reform produced by the advocates of Physiocracy (or government based on a particular construction of natural law) and accepted his argument that a combination of industry, taxation, and welfare was the only one capable of countering the divisive effects of an established system of private property. But he was skeptical of Necker's ability as a political theorist. He had no confidence in the constitutional settlement that Necker tried to reach in 1789, because the mixture of popular and royal representation that it contained (with sovereignty divided between the king, a second chamber, and the commons) made it difficult to see how it would be able to decide what to do in a crisis. The difference between the roles of the philosopher and the administrator that Sieyès set out in the epigraph of *What is the Third Estate?* (p. 92) signaled a demand for a more radical constitutional reform than anything that Necker envisaged. In Sieyès' system, the representative of the whole nation had to have no constitutional power at all. Only then, if something like a choice between preserving public credit and preserving sovereignty became unavoidable, would it be safe to leave the decision to that person. Giving the king (or the Great Elector) any kind of constitutional power beyond that of simply acting as a sign or symbol of the nation itself would leave more room for the possible transformation of the government into despotism. From Sieyès' point of view, Necker's system was not a strong enough guarantee against this possibility.

Necker was equally circumspect towards Sieyès. From his point of view, Sieyès' system was not a strong enough guarantee against apathy and would lead to despotism from another direction. His most extensive criticism of Sieyès (although it never referred to him by name) was contained in his *Dernières vues de politique et de finance,* his last work on politics, published in 1802. It was an attack on the Constitution of the Year VIII, the short-lived constitution that Napoleon (as Necker predicted) destroyed. "The spirit of a republican constitution," Necker observed, "is undoubtedly to attribute to the people . . . all the political rights that it can exercise with order." But the Constitution of the Year VIII, despite its republican patina, ruled this out. "Good faith should require it to be agreed," Necker commented, "that one should cease to give the name republic to a form of government in which the people would be nothing, nothing other than by fiction."[111] The system of indirect representation that was its most prominent feature gave the people a right that, accord-

---

[111] Jacques Necker, *Dernières vues de politique et de finance* [1802], in Jacques Necker, *Oeuvres,* 12 vols. (Paris, 1821), vol. 11, pp. 15–16.

ing to Necker, it would find "a matter of perfect indifference."[112] However much praise might be lavished on the new system for eliminating hereditary distinctions of every kind, it was doomed to die of apathy because it had no real connection with the people it purported to represent.

> The prime utility of participation by the people in the nomination of its magistrates and its legislators is to form a continuous, more-or-less tight link between the leaders of a state and the whole mass of its citizens.
>
> Destroy that relationship, whether by divesting the people of the only political right that it can exercise or by changing that right into a simulacrum, a simple fiction, and there will no longer be a republic or it will exist only in name.[113]

There was no substitute, Necker argued, for "the free, direct elections that form the essence of a republic."[114] In this, he was echoed by Constant (who, like Necker's daughter, Germaine de Stael, always maintained a fairly distant relationship with Sieyès).[115] In this respect the liberalism now associated with Benjamin Constant was somewhat different from Sieyès' conception of representative government, not only because of its reinstatement of direct elections but also because of the much stronger emphasis on citizens' involvement in public life that this implied.

The twin dangers that Sieyès and Necker each highlighted have not gone away. Making governments more democratic, as Necker proposed, may make government more difficult, as Sieyès feared. Making governments more representative, as Sieyès proposed, may entail apathy, as Necker feared. If representative government is not quite the oxymoron that its most hostile early nineteenth-century critics sometimes took it to be, it still has to manage the combination of the one and the many that Sieyès' system was designed to maintain.[116] The dilemma (as well as some sense of the system's intellectual provenance) was captured quite well in

---

[112] Necker, *Dernières vues de politique et de finance,* p. 16.

[113] Necker, *Dernières vues de politique et de finance,* p. 21.

[114] Necker, *Dernières vues de politique et de finance,* p. 94.

[115] "L'élection directe constitue seule le vrai système représentatif," Constant wrote in the *Mercure de France* in January 1817, referring to Necker's "courageous, eloquent and profound" *Dernières vues de politique et de finance.* See Ephraïm Harpaz (ed.), Benjamin Constant, *Receuil d' articles. Le Mercure, La Minerve et La Renommée,* 2 vols. (Geneva, Droz, 1972), vol. 2, pp. 38 and 39 (n. 3) and, on Constant's views on Sieyès, Norman King, and Etienne Hofmann, "Les lettres de Benjamin Constant à Sieyès avec une lettre de Constant à Pictet-Diodati," *Annales Benjamin Constant,* 3 (1988), pp. 89–110.

[116] "Is it not self-evident (allowing for the triviality of the terms) that what is called *representative government* is an example of defining black by white or white by black": [Saint-Roman], *Réfutation de la doctrine de Montesquieu sur la balance des pouvoirs et aperçus divers sur plusieurs questions de droit public* (Paris, 1816), pp. 70–1.

the early nineteenth century by a French constitutional theorist named Jean Pierre Pagès, who was later to edit Benjamin Constant's *Cours de droit politique*. "Thus," Pagès wrote,

> that system of representation that has come to us from feudal government would be impracticable in a nation that has the energy of youth, a consciousness of its manners, its strength, its love of country and that would seek to enjoy the freedom to which it is entitled. But it is wonderful for peoples who have fallen into softness, corruption, avidity, and egoism because it denies them the possibility of completing the process of their depravation and of succumbing to anarchy through licentiousness. In states like these, representatives are harmful only to kings. With respect to the people, they are like viziers in whom its idleness can find repose from all political care.[117]

The history of representative government has taken place under the sign of the twin dangers that Sieyès and Necker highlighted. At one time or another, economics has not been quite enough to enable people to "find repose from all political care," and politics has had to take the strain. Sieyès tried very hard to devise a system of government designed to enable politics to do so and still leave room for economics to survive. But practical problems repeatedly engulfed his theoretical principles. The Estates-General did not become a constitutional convention in 1789. Nor did the Republican Convention in 1795. Nor, finally, did Napoleon Bonaparte become a Great Elector after 1799. In the longer term, however, his efforts to identify a system of government suitable for what, in the late eighteenth century, was already the modern world, have been broadly confirmed. Representation has become the basis of modern economic and political life. Sieyès' great insight was to see that the two kinds of representation that this involves amounts to something that is both more complicated than it might first seem, but is still sufficiently simple to be accommodated within a single political society. The combination of political authority and economic liberty that is the hallmark of modern systems of representative government follows from this. Sieyès' system was designed to reconcile the one with the other and make them both, ultimately, a matter of human choice. Reading his works is a very good way to find out what this involves and what it might mean for thinking about the nature and future of the system of government that we now call democracy. Words may not matter all that much. But there may still be a price to pay by forgetting the questions about the relationship between one state and many people that Sieyès addressed and why, in the setting

---

[117] Jean Pierre Pagès, *Principes généraux du droit politique dans leur rapport avec l'esprit de l'Europe et avec la Monarchie constitutionnelle* (Paris, 1817), pp.483–4.

in which he addressed them, the answers that he gave were based on the logic of representation, not democracy. "The real benefit of earlier centuries to the present age should not be confined to aristocratic families," Sieyès wrote in one of his notes. "If that benefit is to be confined to anyone it should, on the contrary, be limited to those who, in the arts and reason, have best been able to profit from the efforts of our predecessors. The old age of the world belongs to everyone but is there to be used advantageously only between birth and death. No one ought to have any door closed to him on the pretext that he did not start trying to get in before he was born."[118]

---

[118] A. N. 284 AP 4, dossier 8 (sheet entitled "noblesse"): "L'avantage réel des siècles antérieurs pour l'époque présent n'est pas particulier à des familles aristocrates, au contraire s'il était particulier à quelqu'un, ce serait à ceux qui dans les arts et la raison ont le mieux sçu profiter des efforts de nos devanciers. La vieillesse du monde appartient à tous, l'on n'en peut tirer parti qu'entre la naissance et la mort. Il ne faut donc fermer à personne quelque porte que ce soit sous prétexte que ses efforts pour entrer ne datent pas d'avant sa naissance."

VIEWS OF THE EXECUTIVE MEANS AVAILABLE TO THE REPRESENTATIVES OF FRANCE IN 1789

As was pointed out in the Introduction, the Views of the executive means *was the first of the three pamphlets that Sieyès wrote between 1788 and 1789, although it was the last of the three to be published. This is a translation of the first of the two editions of the pamphlet published in 1789. Notes in the text indicated by Roman numerals are Sieyès' own and have been placed at the foot of the page. Notes indicated by a bracketed asterix (*) have been added to the text to enable the reader to identify the individuals or institutions referred to by Sieyès and can be found, under the relevant page number, in the* Notes on French Terms *at the end of this volume.*

Views of the Executive Means Available to the Representatives of France in 1789

"Projects should be tailored to the available means"

Table of Contents of the Principal Objects Discussed in this Work

Preliminary Notice

This work was written in the last days of a ministry (*) that had excited an unprecedented measure of public hatred and scorn. It should not be surprising, therefore, if truths that at any other time would be set down calmly are here mixed with a little bile. In reassuming responsibility for the financial administration, M. Necker (**) has succeeded, not in changing the meaning which the word *ministry* always ought to have but at least in dispelling those ideas that the word *minister* used to call to mind. I confess with regret that I have used the word here with a humor and a bitterness that are no longer in season. Apart from this, however, and since the subject which forms the substance of this work is still entirely new, even though it dates from last summer, I have decided not to suppress it. It contains nothing related to the unhappy discussions that have since arisen between the three orders of the kingdom. (***) That question now stands poised between the nation on the one hand and unlimited power on the other.

I wish to repeat that the minister in question in this memorandum is not, and could not have been, M. Necker. I have no personal acquaintance with so justly famous a man. I can therefore pay homage to his virtues and talents, which is all the more pure since, free from all party spirit, I am equally free from all enthusiasm. I honor, respect, and even admire him as an administrator without, however, going so far as to idolize him. If I have an infinite esteem for his sentiments in morality, I do not like *all* his political principles. Doubtless I can think of no one I would want to put in his place. But to put it in a word, it has to be recognized, painful though it may be, that he does not have the power to give us a constitution. Let us hope that the Estates-General will be able to make good for what he cannot do.

Views of the Executive Means Available to the Representatives of France in 1789

There are plenty of other authors who appear to believe that we ought to ask earlier barbarous centuries for laws that are suitable for civilized nations. We, however, do not propose to lose ourselves in an uncertain quest for ancient institutions and ancient errors. Reason is made for man's use and, especially when it speaks to him of those interests that he holds to be most dear, reason should be listened to with confidence and respect.

Would we, disdaining the modern products of an improved art, turn to Otahiti or the ancient Germans for models in providing for the needs of life? Order a clock from a clockmaker, and see if he is inclined to consult the history of clock making, whether it be true or false, to extract the different ways of measuring the time that infant industry once decided to adopt. Rightly, he will be more disposed to view the long-drawn-out hesitations of the human mind over centuries of ignorance as less fit to guide him in his art than the fixed laws of that part of mechanics that have at last been revealed by the genius of the modern age.

The study of social mechanics has been no less enriched in our own age by the nocturnal meditations of legislative genius. Why then should we refuse to consult social mechanics to find the true means to provide for the great needs of political societies?

Considering how much ardor we display in seeking to enjoy the most trifling improvements to be seen in the arts of trade and luxury, why should we withdraw into dull indifference as soon as it comes to the progress of the first of all the arts—the social art, whose skilful combinations serve to keep the well-being of the human race under their firm safeguard?

But there is no reason to despair. Force of circumstance, richer in wisdom than mere humane interest, has put us in a position that cannot but seem striking to the mind or fail to awaken our energy. There cannot be any doubt that a movement towards freedom will also become a movement towards reason and that we will at last come to consult mankind's one true benefactor, the source of all the knowledge and all the useful institutions that gradually have served to improve the lot of the human race.

Part of the public has begun, not without some shame, to grasp the essential character of what it is that makes it possible to distinguish a nation organized as a political body from an immense flock of people scattered over a surface of twenty-five thousand square leagues.

Already in various parts of the kingdom there have been forceful claims that it is high time to put an end to being the cowardly victims of inveterate disorder. There have been appeals to the fundamental principles of the social order, and it has come now to be perceived that for any people the first and most important of all the laws of the social order is to have a good constitution. This is because only a good constitution can give and guarantee citizens the enjoyment of their natural and social rights, can confer stability on everything that may be done for the good, and can progressively extinguish all that has been done for the bad.

Already patriotic and enlightened citizens who for so long have looked with sadness and indignation upon those millions of men now piled together without any plan or order, have begun to allow themselves some feeling of hope. Now they can believe in the force of circumstance and can see at last that the moment is at hand when we can become a *nation.*

The Estates-General has been summoned.(*) It will undoubtedly be held because the Estates-General has come to be necessary even to those who think they have the most to fear from it. And, not to let our gratitude be misplaced, it ought to be said—and publicized most widely—that the convocation of the Estates-General will not be the fruit of any sort of good intention on the part of the ministry. We owe it to an excess of evil alone. Excess of evil did it all.

The record of what has just occurred is in this respect something that we owe to posterity. Posterity will learn how the great political machine established to provide protection, but which unaccountable administrators continually diverted from that goal, came to ruin the fortunes and crush the persons of its citizens; how the workings of this cruel machinery came to be part of the ordinary course of events; and how we were prepared to put up with it! . . . And how it would have lasted for a long time more unless in a moment of madness the royal ministers had not themselves bent or broken its springs.

Posterity will then learn that, horrified by their handiwork and trembling at its consequences, they tried, albeit uselessly, to forestall its effects and that it became essential to make their embarrassment and their failings known. But (and who would believe it?) true to the superb pride of their place and with all the insolence acquired from long impunity, these royal ministers now dared to beg for help in that confident and generous tone used in announcing a benefaction.

But the deplorable condition of the public establishment was clear for all to see. Ordinary resources seemed to be insufficient. Both the notables and the parlements could not prevent themselves from reminding the government of council that had become almost criminal, namely, to have recourse to the one true engine of every administration.(**)

Thus the words "Estates-General" were finally heard to pass the lips of the French vizier, even if his hatred of the thing itself could not be effaced from his heart. He hoped much, in the depths of his soul, both of his hypocrisy and of the passage of time. But the veil of hypocrisy was pierced, and the passage of time did no more than bring him yet more imperiously towards the much-redoubted Estates-General. He could see it before him and, forgetting imperious necessity and attending all the while only to his own danger, he exhausted every measure and maneuver to have the Estates-General deferred. He committed illegalities as others use expedients. Finally, and the fact is certain, these royal ministers pushed criminal audacity to the point of coldly contemplating and calculating the consequences of the horrible project of a bankruptcy and the even more infernal project of a civil war.(***) And if, in the end, these execrable means were rejected, be careful not to attribute the honor of the decision to remorse. Instead, after careful examination, those very means were simply deemed to be insufficient.

And so after following such different paths, both the friends and the enemies of the nation will finally come to meet at the same point. The path bearing the national interest is one that has been followed by all good citizens. The path involving abuses and excess has been the one followed by the government. A national assembly could never have been its open and honest aim; it has simply become the final and inevitable end point of its depredations. How is it possible not to have a deep feeling of indignation in thinking that the Estates-General might still belong to the realm of fantasy if the crimes of the king's ministers had been pursued with more energy and effective power than were the just, necessary, but impotent, desires of twenty-five million men?

It will therefore be impossible to avoid holding that national assembly that so many voices have called for, that so many hopes will accompany, and whose fruits will be all the more precious insofar as conduct that is at once enlightened, courageous, and measured will be added to the force of circumstance.

Many good patriots will hasten to draw its attention to vices that should be reformed, or tell it of the good that should be done, or offer it legislative systems replete with useful views. In our case, persuaded as we are that the majority of deputies will add knowledge of true solutions and a real desire for effecting real remedies to an experience of existing evils, we would like to assume that they will not only want to do what is right but will also know in what it consists.

But however fine or full may be the plan of action that they aim to follow to secure the people's interest, it will still be no more than the work of the philosopher. It will still be no more than a project. The viewpoint of the administrator is concerned with executive means. His concern is with the possibility of realizing the philosopher's good intentions. These two points of view imply two distinct kinds of meditation. Will the Estates-General have executive means? Will those means be sufficiently solid? This is the subsidiary question to which this work is confined. It follows that this work should be seen as no more than an addition to the large number of works to which present circumstances will give rise.

Its aim is to show that the Estates-General cannot be broadly and solidly useful unless, in addition to the knowledge and will that it can be supposed to have, it also has legal executive *power.* Will it?

Three conditions constitute power of this kind. The first is the *right* to do things. The second is complete *freedom* to do so. The third is *permanence* for what has been done.

This division is clear. To develop it, the aim of the following three sections is to show:

1. that the Estates-General has the right to legislate;
2. that it is up to the Estates-General alone to exercise that legislative power freely;
3. that the Estates-General can establish and make the results of its deliberations permanent and independent.

Section I. The Estates-General Has the Power to Legislate

It is certain that the Estates-General will not be able to do much good unless it has a great deal of power. To find out how much power it should be entitled to have, there is no point either in consulting that swarm of mandated officials whose opinions and beliefs will be those of their place and whose places are part of the established routine of getting things done, or in consulting those self-important inhabitants of the anterooms of power whose all-too-honorable lives have been devoted to begging, hating, and intriguing against that very same people which then has to pay for their haughty mendicancy. To listen to them, one might just as well think "the Estates-General exists simply to supply money.(★) Should it also need to be consoled by having an opportunity to draw up a list of grievances, this is purely a matter of form.(★★) In fact, it will be no more than a list of last wishes."

A nation with a right to offer both money and grievances must assuredly be a worthy one! Can it really be credited that the Estates-General alone has a right to complain? Or is it to be assumed that the complaints of a dispersed people do not deserve to be heard? Or does this mean that an assembled nation can do no more than any private individual?

To get to the heart of things we need, first, to establish an idea of the end and purposes of all legislation and of the two parts that make legislation essentially what it is.

The liberty of the citizen consists in an assurance of not being hindered or interfered with in the exercise of his *personal* property or in the use of his *real* property.

The liberty of the citizen is the sole *end* of every law. Every law should be related to that end, either *directly* (and this amounts to civil legislation) or *indirectly* (and this amounts to those laws that concern the government). Our aim is to show that the Estates-General has the right to make laws falling under both these different points of view.

It is generally agreed that *the right of granting a tax belongs to the nation alone*. What, at bottom, does granting a tax mean? It means that each citizen is obliged to cede a part of his property to maintain the public establishment. What makes a law lawful is that it creates in those it affects a moral *obligation* to be subject to its provisions. Tax officers can certainly pursue the taxpayer who is subject to the law. Public force can certainly assure its execution. But the law is not the work of either the tax officers or public force. It is instead the manifest will of whoever has a right to establish a duty. If therefore it is a recognized principle that only a nation can oblige a taxpayer, it follows as an immediate principle—and one that ought to be recognized too—that this part of the legislative power belongs to the Estates-General.

But if it is assumed that the nation could never have transferred the privilege of disposing of even the tiniest portion of its real property to some master, how can it be imagined that it could ever voluntarily have branded itself with the most pronounced and shameful mark of servility by renouncing its personal property, the first and most basic of all rights and goods, without which all others are merely illusory? It is inconceivable that anyone who had reserved the right to dispose of his real goods could then have renounced his ownership of his person. To do so would be an act of madness.

These two arguments are already enough to prove that the power of the Estates-General must encompass all the laws concerning the two kinds of property belonging to every citizen. But there is more to follow.

We all know that in the most barbarous age of the monarchy laws of every kind were decreed *by* or *with* the people's consent. Nonetheless, since administrators at that time were less ignorant than the people, it is easy to see why the larger influence that they then might have had could often have been compatible with the general interest. Today, the nation is not just worth more than it once was but is also more enlightened than the government. Should this be a reason to assume that it should be reduced to infinitely more narrow bounds in the exercise of its rights?

We take it to be a maxim that there are no slaves in France. The twenty-five million individuals who inhabit the kingdom are free. How then can it be conceivable that the nation is not? If slavery cannot be imposed upon any particular head, how then can it possibly apply to them all? In general, any citizen deprived of the right to consult his own interests, to deliberate, and to impose laws upon himself is rightly taken to be a serf. It follows that the right to consult its own interests, to deliberate, and to impose laws upon itself must necessarily belong to the nation.

To pursue this important question further, examine the nature of legislative power in itself and consider in what it has consisted among any more or less populous people.

As has just been said, every man has an inherent right to deliberate and will for himself, to impose obligations upon himself, to engage himself towards others, and therefore to impose laws upon himself. Consider this man—first of all outside any association—at the moment when he wants to form an association with other individuals. Here relations internal to the family can be set aside. In a subject like this it is necessary to simplify as much as possible. Even if the basic elements of the association were not simple individuals but the heads of families, this, for the time being, is perfectly admissible. This is not the place to discuss this question now. Here what matters are those members of the union who can be taken to be its integral parts—namely, those admissible as contracting parties—and what has to be said here is that there cannot be any other relationship between them than one based upon a free act of each individual's will.

Either one wills freely or one is forced to will; there cannot be any middle position. In the first case there is a real engagement emanating from its true source because, as has just been said, every man is taken to be able to will for himself. Will and intelligence are two faculties attached by nature to men's constitution to enable them to follow the path that she has laid out before them. Each of these two faculties is as inalienable as the other. Every individual has to make himself the subject of his own engagements and obligations towards others. Only his own will can give his engagement the character of a moral obligation. Outside of it there cannot be anything other than the empire of the strong over the weak and its odious consequences. But that empire can never have any moral force. It is, if the image is allowable, no more than a kind of mechanical compression, which produces an *effect* but not an *obligation* or, if there is an obligation that this violent principle is capable, if not of producing, at least of awakening and exciting in the breasts of the weak, it is the natural and sacred duty to resist oppression without remission and to use every possible means to escape its thrall.

Thus when a number of individuals come to be united by a social engagement, the only principle underlying that engagement is a free act of the will. A man can offer and *exchange* one thing for another or one engagement for another. Anything among men can be a matter of exchange, and in any act of exchange there is necessarily, both on one side and the other, a free act of the will. No man has a right to *dominate* another's will. The opposite maxim would open a door to every crime, every horror and to the annihilation of every right.

This is sufficient insistence upon this truth. But it is one that is so essential and so fundamental that it has to be insisted upon. It means that the only basic element from which the laws can be composed is the individual will and that a legitimate association can have no other basis than the will of its associates.

Once we suppose that an association exists, it has to have the freedom to will and to engage itself either with other associations, with its own members, or with individuals belonging to other countries. There has to be a *common* will to meet common needs. That will must naturally be the general product of all the individual wills and the very first common will of a number of men who might be supposed to have united to form a political society would without doubt have been exactly the sum of all the individual wills. But to require for the future that the common will should always be the exact sum of every individual will would amount to giving up the possibility of being able to will in common and would mean the dissolution of the social union. It was therefore absolutely necessary to recognize all the characteristics of the common will in an agreed majority. But do not believe that with this kind of convention society is at bottom governed merely by a will that is incomplete. Every citizen, by his act of adherence to the union, makes a continuous engagement to see himself as bound by the majority view even when his own will forms part of the minority. He submits himself in advance, it should be emphasized, by a free act of his own will, reserving only the right to leave the association and to emigrate if the laws that it makes do not suit him. In this way, continuous residence amounts to a voluntary acceptance of the majority will or a tacit, but positive, confirmation of that initial engagement by which he subjected himself in advance to the duty of seeing the common will as his own. But however it may be formed, the common will cannot consist of anything other than the citizens' individual wills. It is this and this alone that entitles it to establish a genuinely binding obligation for all—and to make law for the whole community.

But we need to press further and see how an increase in the number of associates has to give rise to new modifications in the legislative power.

As the number of citizens increases it becomes difficult or impossible for them to assemble to hear each individual will and then reconcile their differences to form a general will. This makes it necessary to divide the community into a number of districts. Each division then has to entrust some members of the association with a vote to be carried to a common *meeting place*. But it soon becomes clear that delegating a number of simple vote carriers is essentially vicious, because those selected as deputies, obliged to adhere scrupulously to the commission of those who mandated them, often find themselves unable to agree, making it impossible to extract a common will from the totality of votes. But there has to be a *common will* and any means that fails to produce one has to be radically flawed. If it is necessary to refer things back to the various districts, to inform them of what has happened, to wait for new instructions and then begin the whole process all over again for as long as no common accord between different views can be found, it comes to be obvious that matters will never end, that the public interest will suffer, and that by trying to keep the use of its will under its direct control, the general mass of associates has actually deprived itself of the ability to use its will at all.

There are further disadvantages to this method. These cannot all be set out here. Suffice it now to point out one that is capable of nullifying every deliberation. In this, what seems to be an apparent majority makes it impossible to establish a genuine majority. This makes it impossible to make law based on a genuine common will. This vice is connected to the practice of counting votes by sections and not by the number of individuals party to the deliberation as a whole. We will elaborate on this truth in the second part of this work, where it is more appropriate.

All this leads the community to give its mandatories more confidence. It gives them a proxy enabling them to meet, to deliberate, to reconcile their views, and to come to a common will, so that it now has genuine representatives instead of simple vote carriers. Note however (since these truths should always be kept in mind) that the mission given to these representatives never involves a formal surrender of the community's original power. It is one that is essentially at the liberty of the delegating power, is constantly revocable, and is limited, at the will of those making the delegation, both in time and in subject matter.

From the moment that the community comes to be divided into districts, the part played by each individual will in the legislative power is less direct. But that power cannot have any other origin or any other constituent element. This is not the place to describe all the nuances involved in this new state of affairs. But one simple observation is still necessary. If each district is to nominate its own representatives separately and has no involvement in selecting those of the other divisions, it would seem, on the basis of the principles outlined here, that it ought to recognize only the work of the majority of its own representatives and not the work of the whole body of representatives as the basis of law. It would then seem to follow that every division would have a *liberum veto* on every other, and it does not need to be said that a right of this nature would make it impossible for a legislative body to carry out its functions. Nothing is more true. A right like this would be genuinely antipolitical and cannot be recognized. Instead, what has to be kept as a maxim is the principle that each deputy represents the whole association. No one would be inclined to dispute this truth if the whole community were able to meet to nominate the whole body of its representatives. But the same applies here. Since the totality of citizens either cannot, or will not, assemble together in a single place, the totality has to be divided into districts and each district has, by agreement, to nominate a proportional number of deputies. To perform this decentralized election, all the districts have, reciprocally, to authorize and entrust their affairs to one another and, by doing so, make the election the work of the whole community. There is therefore no difficulty. The legislative power is always the product of the generality of individual wills.

A large and populous people is even less able to exercise its common will, or legislature, itself. It has therefore to nominate representatives entrusted to will on its behalf, and it cannot be said that the common will of these representatives does not make genuine law or law which applies to everyone.

It can be seen therefore that any nation which is able to form a common will by means of representatives invested with authenticated powers is able to exercise the full extent of the legislative power.

There is no point in invoking a so-called contract between a people and its master by which the former surrendered the right to will by the very first act of their will. A collection of men is no more able to give up the faculty of deliberating and willing in its own interest than an ordinary private individual. What could be the price or purpose of such an undertaking? If it is said to be for protection, how can a single man protect a whole nation? It alone contains that salutary power. Nothing else does. When a nation gives one of its members responsibility for using that salutary power, all of whose elements, combinations, and direction it supplies, it does not contract. It delegates. There is no engagement but a delegation at will.

But it is a mistake to reply in advance to arguments like these. It is now an established fact that no man can be another man's slave. A moral act that would destroy all morality cannot be binding. Even if some unhappy creatures could still be found who were willing to devote their whole lives to this final degree of baseness, their example would still have no effect on their descendants. What cannot be willed for oneself cannot be willed for others. It is always necessary to return to the essence of what makes a free will to identity the sole source from which, directly or indirectly, all the laws imposing a genuine obligation upon a man derive. Thus since the national will is the product of every individual will, the legislative power belongs to the nation, necessarily and in all its fullness. The only thing that can be set above it is natural law that, far from contradicting it, serves rather to enlighten and guide it towards the great end of the social union.

Our opponents will not like the force of the evidence that follows so readily from a simple consideration of the nature of things. They would prefer to remind us of the thousand and one facts and the thousand and one hypothetical occurrences in which the social will has been silent. There must, they would say, have been some other way to make up for its silence.

But what does it matter to us how it might have been possible to cater for the silence of the people's will if they were unable to make it known by way of representatives of their choice? All that is needed is for the nation to be in a position to speak and for no one to be able to deny that it is indeed the nation speaking by way of its representatives. This fact alone serves to make it a contradiction in terms to claim that deliberations made by these representatives will not be genuine, obligatory laws for all those who they represent.

In keeping with its custom, the generation now passing may exclaim that all these new systems will simply overturn everything. Our own reply, in the name of the generations to come and, above all, in the name of all those who between infancy and senility really do have to bear the burden of the present is (1) that we have a little more of an interest than they have in everything to do with the laws and affairs of this world; and (2) that there is nothing more venerable or more respectable than ideas that restore truth. It is not truth but error, which is a novelty under the eternal order of things, and it is high time that men should turn at last towards it to find true social principles.

Things, it is said, should be taken as they are. It is not a question of what might be or what should be done, but what is. . . . True enough. So let us deal with what is. The Estates-General will undoubtedly be held. Now the choice is yours. Either it does or it does not represent the nation. In this latter case, it cannot produce any kind of obligation, not even the duty to pay any kind of tax or anything else. Or it will express itself in the name of the nation, and then it will be capable of everything.

We believe that we have shown with some rigor that a general assembly of representatives is the legitimate organ of the national will, and that in that quality it has a right to make laws on everything pertaining to the nation, and that there is nothing on which it cannot legislate.

Why then, since these principles are drawn from what is self-evidently the case, should there yet remain a certain premonition of regret at not having seen them adopted? Why should what is self-evidently the case still seem to be too little to be a measure and a guarantee of the favorable impression which it ought to make on every man's mind? In the long run, the deplorable course of events has ruined our ability to recognize the importance of anything that relies solely upon the inherent power of truth. Mere truth is simply taken to be an empty ideal and the light that it throws is held to be foreign to peoples' real affairs. Decisions, it is assumed, depend on facts alone. This is because despotism everywhere began as a de facto system, and it has relied upon facts as the basis of the false model that it has at its disposal to present, instead of relying on truth that is separate from that model and stands in judgement against it.

Every day it is customary to see a crude pedantry denigrate the philosopher who aims to go back to the first principles of the social art. To the dull scholastic, useful and fertile meditation looks like no more than idle labor, and when, as much out of disgust as discernment, the philosopher abandons the sorry spectacle of our ancestors' errors, earnest mediocrity takes hold of the material task of assiduously noting down every page of history, seeing the highest degree of intellectual merit as well as the answer to every question in the simple talent of being able to read and to transcribe.

Unhappily, philosophers themselves, who during the course of this century have given such signal services to the physical sciences, appear to have set the stamp of their authority upon this absurd belief and seem to have lent the force of their genius to blind declamation. Rightly disgusted by the systematizing mania of their predecessors, they devoted themselves to the study of facts and proscribed every other method. In the area in question, this deserves nothing but praise. But in moving beyond the physical order and in recommending the use of this method in the moral order, they are mistaken. Before prescribing a single procedure for all the sciences, it should have been necessary to examine the differences between their various objects and geniuses.

Nothing can be more correct for the physical scientist than to observe, collect, and examine the relationship between facts. His aim is to understand nature, and since he is not required to assist the plan of the universe with his advice or practical skills (since the physical universe exists and is able to preserve itself independently of his corrective meditation), it is perfectly right for him to limit himself to the examination of facts. Physics can only be the knowledge of *what is*. Art, which is bolder in its horizons, aims to modify and adapt facts to meet the purposes of our needs and enjoyments. It asks *what should be* for the utility of human beings. Art has us as its object. Its speculations, combinations, and operations are for our own use. The first of all the arts must therefore be one that is concerned with arranging the disposition of human affairs by way of a plan that favors them all. But is it right here to examine the facts in the way that the physicist does? What should be the true science here, a science of facts or a science of principles? Because the physicist is sure to be able to form his science by studying what happens in nature, should the legislator similarly seek to find a model of the social order in the spectacle of historical events? If, for the physicist, the route of experience is a long one, it is at least a useful one, and he is certain, in advancing step-by-step, to add continually to the treasury of his knowledge. But how different is the position of the legislator! How heavy a burden must events lay on his heart and how heartily will he wish to escape from the horrible experience of ages that have passed!

Some readers might find these thoughts out of place. Those who have never considered the objection will never feel the need for a reply. What matter is there for us, they might say, in the difference between sciences based on simple observation and sciences based on combination? Here what matters is the Estates-General. Yes! Indeed! The Estates-General— which will serve only to reinforce your misfortunes and make for yet more, if it were to allow itself to be guided by a sequence of facts but which, by attending to reason, will be able to lead you towards freedom and all the rights that make freedom what it is. Beware of the influence on your representatives' minds of the idea, disseminated all-too-widely by modern scholars, that morality, like physics, can be given a foundation based on experience. Men in this century have been restored to reason by way of the natural sciences. This has been a real service. But we must still beware of allowing a false sense of gratitude to confine us within a narrow circle of imitation and instead must make an unimpeded inquiry into the new instauration that awaits us at the journey's end. It is of course the case that genuine policy and genuine politics involve combinations of facts, not combinations of chimeras, but they still involve combinations. Like an architect who, in his imagination, designs and, in some measure, prepares his plan before carrying it out, the legislator conceives of and, in his mind, realizes both the details and the whole of the social order which is fit for a people. When he presents us with the fruit of his meditations, we should assess its utility, not ask for factual proofs of its existence. Nothing would exist if it had to be brought into existence along with the facts, so to speak, attesting to its existence. Never has it been more urgent to restore reason to all its force and to rid the facts of a power that they have usurped to the misfortune of the human race.

This particular thought brings me—indeed encourages me—to give free rein to my indignation and outrage towards that mass of writers obsessed with asking the past what we should become in the future, who scour miserable traditions full of lies and follies for laws capable of restoring public order, who obstinately persist in delving into every archive to collect and compile countless memoranda, searching for and revering the least scrap, however apocryphal, obscure, or unintelligible it may be, and all in the hope of discovering what? No more than an old title, as if, in their gothic frenzy, they hoped to put the nation in possession of what genealogists call *proofs*.

I wish that it might be suddenly possible to bring among us a being endowed with luminous reason and exquisite good sense but entirely inured to the eccentricities of our opinions, and after explaining the great interest we have in present circumstances, he were left to assess the means we have adopted to draw the greatest benefit from them. What would he have to say about the general rush to scour ancient compilations in which some mention of our old public law has been made, about the importance we seem to attach to interrogating this kind of oracle, and about the extreme willingness with which everyone on all sides seems to be disposed to accept its apparently binding verdicts? He would have to believe that the past must surely contain both an inexhaustible source of enlightenment and a body of rulings that was able to resolve all doubts and dispel every kind of difficulty. Perhaps he would also come to be persuaded that apparently somewhere on earth beyond the range of tyranny and immune to the ravages of time there must be some sacred repository where the authentic archives of every people have been preserved religiously as a resource available to every nation and, whenever it is necessary, that it is possible to go there to consult the original contracts determining the form and rights of every human association. Or even if he wanted fully to explain our absolute trust, how could he be prevented from thinking that it must be possible to withdraw laws from this salutary source of human liberty, laws endowed all by themselves with a power to compel sovereigns to make prompt restitution of rights that were usurped and to force them, as much out of their indolence as through their own strength, to assist in the universal regeneration of political societies? He would be mistaken. All this activity is for us no more than the unhappy effect of that vertiginous spirit that, in driving poor, weak humanity along erroneous paths, has served to ruin the best chances they have had to recover their rights. The archives of peoples have not been destroyed. But they are to be found only in one sure and faithful repository. This is the repository of reason. When injustice holds sway over events and turns societies into a confused mixture of oppressors and oppressed, reason remains to watch over them all, and reason never ceases to display a faithful picture of their rights and their duties for a more fortunate age.

It is time therefore to abandon our so-called origins to the impenetrable darkness in which they have happily been buried forever. We have no need for inhuman nostalgia. Even if these origins were revealed suddenly before our very eyes, what hope would they give us? There can be no doubt that they would be foreign to our present needs, just as the games and quarrels of childhood are useless to the needs of a riper age. I would go even further. Even if our national origins were to contain a full, authentic, guaranteed, and positive list of all our rights (it is impossible to ask for more), it is still quite certain that armed force would be as contemptuous of our positive entitlements, as it has habitually insulted our natural rights.

Yet such futile and false research still continues to win applause! The public seems to have authorized them and to have pinned its fate upon its findings. But stop! Your rights are already there, within yourselves. There they are imprescribable, engraved in immortal characters by an almighty hand. Yet you insist on compromising them, on losing them, by making them hostage to the hazards of a chance discovery or a mark of scholarly prowess! You seem to be willing to allow them to exist or have any value only insofar as they can be found in a few battered parchments written in a servile hand that the tyranny of ages has allowed to be released.

And even if you were able to extricate all your entitlements in all their purity from that scholarly swamp, shining with the truth as if they had been given to you by reason itself, would they (it cannot be asked too often) become any more imposing in the eyes of arbitrary power; would they be any more respected and any more protected from illegal assault?

It is pointless to turn over the ruins of an ancient political edifice; doing so cannot produce a good idea of how it was originally built. The peoples of Europe in particular have continuously changed their constitutions, or rather the forms of their political societies, to the point at which they no longer resemble themselves for two successive ages. All that erudite research will do is to increase the difficulties. The evidence of one century is the opposite of another. A writer making the most positive affirmation is contradicted by someone preceding him and another following him. Witnesses like these are suitable only for giving weapons to every party and every pretension at one and the same time. And during these interminable quarrels, time passes and the moment is lost.

We do not believe that men who are always looking backwards are suitable to be led forwards. We should not, at the end of the eighteenth century, be reduced to having to turn to the legislators of the Sicambrians and the Welches for enlightenment.* What could anyone have ever been able to do if everyone always had to consult their ancestors? And when all is said and done, can it really be hoped that the textual ineptitudes of the Middle Ages will yield up the revelation of a social code?

It has to be repeated, however long these groanings may already seem to certain readers, that most of us are fascinated and degraded by the most cowardly superstition. In vain, a kind of national modesty has made us ashamed of our long political nakedness. In vain we have formed a desire to cover that nakedness from the affronts of despotism. But like awkward children, if the spur of our needs impels us towards the beneficent hand that offers us clothes, an inexplicable timidity makes us withdraw at the same instant; or rather some kind of confused feeling of faith seems to govern our souls, imbuing us with a feeling of horror towards the profane councils of reason and good sense in legislative affairs and drawing us back endlessly to the adoration of the most stupid of prejudices and the most base of customs, because these were those of our fathers! Such sublime devotion, such great and useful instruction, condemning as it does a people to languish forever in infant babble, is capable only of making them delight in the disgusting spectacle of feudal absurdity or in graphic accounts of the ferocious institutions of ancient barbarity!

Better by far to abjure servile superstition and cease to arm ourselves against that enlightenment which presses upon us from every side. In the great light of day that now awaits us, let us show ourselves instructed of our rights. Let us not allow our representatives, responsible for fixing the destinies of twenty-six million men, to fall into vain quarrels and present an attentive universe with the ridiculous and shameful spectacle of a theological conclave, arguing over texts, tearing reason asunder, and ending all this noise and bluster in the most abject impotence.

Section II. It Is up to the Estates-General Alone to Exercise Its Legislative Power Freely

It should not be forgotten that the sheer need to regenerate the royal finances was responsible for the resurrection of the Estates-General. We might already suspect that a cause that was powerful enough to have restored its existence might well be powerful enough to secure its liberty too. But before making this assumption it is worth establishing a notion of the principal objects of which the Estates-General will need to be independent in the exercise of its power. For if it is simply going to be a matter of following ministerial ideas, it can well be imagined how much room for the exercise of liberty and power there will be. Submission and obedience do not need all that much.

According to the ministry, the Estates-General has been convoked to agree to a new tax, because it has not been possible to find any other way to raise one. The circumstances of the state are like those of a great seigneurial magnate who, having ruined his affairs and exhausted his credit, finds himself having to make the extreme and tedious choice of assembling his farmers and agents. His steward hastens to receive them and to address them in the following terms: "Milord needs money and *deigns to approach you* to ask you for some. You will have the honor of seeing him. Be worthy of his goodness by making haste to pay his debts and put him in a position to make his expenditure surpass that of all his predecessors, and be sure that we on our side will make every arrangement that we deem will be suitable for you." Note too that a royal minister can be more secure in making his so-called engagements than the steward of a great lord, who can at least be pursued in the courts.

The nation's deputies might see the circumstances of the public finances in a rather different way. They will be perfectly well aware that private property does not belong to the fiscal system and that citizens are not supposed to be this so-called master's farmers or administrators. There cannot be an honorable man who in accepting so important a trust from the people will not tell himself, "Now that I have become responsible for the nation, I intend to carry out its duties. These duties are not restricted to playing the miserable part of a taxpayer instructed simply to rush to the assistance of a rapacious tax system." The nation's representatives will not degrade themselves so far as to turn themselves into a set of clerks in a public counting house, obediently following the orders of its plundering administrators. The members of the Estates-General will have a more exalted and honorable task, one that they hold in trust from the people and that encompasses all the component parts of the general interest of their constituents.

No one is ignorant of the fact that every political society has common needs and that to meet them several different classes of individuals have to be given a mandate and separated out from the mass of the citizenry. These individuals and the tasks for which they are responsible form what is called the *public establishment.* The costs of this establishment fall upon everyone who benefits from its advantages. This is why there are taxes.

There would not be any taxation if there were no public establishment to support. But the public establishment itself would be no more than a ridiculous show unless it had a more exalted purpose. It was created and exists solely to meet common needs, and its size is proportional to the requirements of the nation's common needs.

Thus in terms of both the order of ideas and real dignity, *national concerns* are the only *goal.* The *public establishment* is the *direct* means used to reach that goal, and the *fiscal system* is no more than the secondary, or indirect, means and should therefore amount to no more than what public necessity requires. Here it is hard not to recall that trivial but fundamental maxim that serves as a rule in all of life's affairs, namely, *one should never sacrifice the end to the means but instead adapt the means to the end.*

It is easy to see that the Estates-General would never be able to deal with public concerns in ways that are useful and in keeping with its electorate's wishes if it were possible to overturn these simple and obvious notions. No one is more willing than I am to put his trust in its wisdom over the choices that circumstances might require or permit it to make.

Whatever the course of its conduct, we are entirely prepared to believe that an inner feeling of its duty and a careful consideration of things as they are will serve to guide its steps. But it must not lose sight of or invert the natural and essential order of the basic social truths. To repeat, that order requires (1) a knowledge of all society's common needs; (2) the elimination of everything extraneous and of no use in meeting these needs; and (3) an examination of the existing means used to meet them and careful regulation of their economic and practical effectiveness in proportion to the reasons that existed for creating them. It is a fundamental principle of liberty that the public establishment should be all-powerful in being able to meet the goal for which it was designed and absolutely impotent to diverge from it, whether to do harm or even to do something good that it was not designed to do. Finally (4) consideration will be given to setting up a national treasury on a scale that is justly proportional to meeting these great objects; (5) this treasury will be placed irrevocably under the control of those who have an interest in public income and will never be at the disposal of those with an interest in public expenditure. It is easy to see the need for this new principle as the basis of all the others. Even if the Estates-General were to have no more than this particular task to deal with, it is more than enough of an indication of the need to ensure that in performing its functions, it cannot remain exposed defenselessly to the enterprises of a ministry displeased by the turn that its deliberations might take.

To turn to the means required to ensure that the National Assembly will be free from fear in this respect. Firstly, I take it for granted that it will display the highest goodwill, and I also believe that it will not hesitate to take possession of a power that both reason and popular commission will have devolved upon it. Precautions will not have to be taken against the National Assembly but against coups of authority or other ministerial enterprises.

Already a thousand and one voices seem prepared to assume that it will have more than enough of a guarantee of not being impeded or troubled in its proceedings provided that it simply takes the precaution of *not granting any subsidy until its grievances have been redressed*. It would seem that we have been reduced to adopting this oblique approach when speaking of the rights of the nation and that no one dares to do so without using terms stamped with the character of servility.

We willingly agree that delaying taxation is the best of measures. But in our view, even supposing that a new tax will have to be agreed to, it is still a measure that has been presented without a proper defense or a proper explanation and under a false rubric.

1. Why, to begin with, make the grant of a subsidy dependent upon the redress of grievances? Will it not leave the nation and all the advan-

tages that present circumstances have given it at the mercy of a promise? And even if you were at once to succeed in obtaining all the formalities of a law dictated and promulgated on your own terms, who is to give you a guarantee that sufficient attention will be paid to ensure its execution once you have dispersed? Is not the uniform experience of centuries past sufficient testimony?

2. What does the expression *grant* a tax mean? To whom? The nation has to set public income on its knowledge of public needs. It should not have to react to a *demand,* and who in any event has a right to make this demand? Whom should it expect it to come from? Does it need notice from anyone other than itself to know that it has to carry out common expenditure and that this can be done only by way of a subsidy that is fixed in size and duration? What does "to grant" mean? It means to bestow. Do we say of a man who covers his expenditure that he grants, or bestows, his annual income to the various people whose goods and services he pays for? What is at issue here is not a gift, or a grant, or, still less, a debt of honor. It is no more than rightful payment.

The people who pay their share of taxation are simply honoring an engagement made by themselves or by those acting on their behalf. A nation that pays for its expenditure is performing an act of justice. A nation that taxes itself is performing an act of necessity and cannot refer to anyone else about how much it needs to raise. Thus the word "grant" and all its cognates should be banished forever from political science. Do not accuse me of laboring a point over a mere word. It is a word that is capable of having real influence, and it is often important to attack the abuse of a term to make it easier to overcome the abuse itself.

3. Finally we have no more liking for the sound of a call for the *redress of grievances*, a call which presupposes that the Estates-General is not itself qualified to do justice to any of the grievances that may cause the people to complain. To adopt so imprudent a procedure would betoken a weakness or a degree of ignorance that is not nowadays to be countenanced by the nation. No, the Estates-General will not commit the great error of failing to recognize its rights even when it may not yet be within its power to guarantee them all. It will not betray so important a beginning by this sort of pernicious negligence. Instead, by taking care to avoid losing any of the advantages capable of promoting the restoration of a rightful order, it will show itself to be armed with all the strength that is already at its disposal without forgetting that perhaps the greatest strength of all is one based on right principles and an unwavering logic.

With this viewpoint in mind it might make an initial declaration couched in something like the following terms:

> "Given that the nation alone has the right to fix and regulate taxes and that there are presently none whose origin or extent is not illegal, the Estates-General proclaims them all to be legally abolished. But because of the time that the Assembly will need to create a new order in this branch of national affairs and also because of the need to avoid the inconveniences that might arise for the collection of any future tax from a total suppression of any relationship between the taxpayer and the fiscal administration, the Estates-General provisionally stipulates that all existing taxes will continue to be paid and temporarily authorized, but solely for the duration of the present session and not thereafter, further stipulating that henceforth there will be no other fiscal contributions than those to be established by the present Assembly before its initial separation."

This would be a clear, full, properly principled declaration, which would not go beyond the powers of the Estates-General even in the eyes of the more reasonable members of the opposite party. It cannot be disputed that by taking this step, the Estates-General would be putting itself under the protection of a power superior to any conceivable enterprise and would be able from that very moment to exist, deliberate, and legislate in a manner fitting the national interest for as long as might be necessary without having to fear anything, even from the most daring of ministers. Any such minister would, in effect, have to be remarkably blinded by ill humor to attempt to carry out a show of force against the whole body of representatives or even a single one of its members (and public opinion would make no distinction between the two), if it was impossible for him to conceal the fact that by doing so he was running the risk of overturning everything. The least act of violence, the most minor enterprise threatening the freedom of the Assembly, would give rise to a movement of revulsion whose effects could be stopped only by ordering its dispersal. If any minister were to go to such an extreme, he would necessarily cause an immediate and legal cessation of all tax payments everywhere. He would be responsible for provoking a mass of disorders, and he would not fail to be their first victim.

This should suffice to prove that the Estates-General, under the aegis of the most imperious necessity, will be fully the master of delaying the establishment of any tax until it has finished and consolidated everything that it thinks should be done for the sake of a national constitution. No kind of dependence can be allowed to be felt. It will be master of the decision to separate only at the moment and for the time it deems to be suitable. It will, in a word, be free because no one can will either to consign it to inaction or to dismiss it. It will be free, because for the ministry its freedom will be less of a danger and less to be feared than its dissolution.

It might perhaps be imagined that it should not be necessary for the Estates-General to seize hold of all the tax revenue with so firm a grasp and that its freedom would be protected sufficiently from any danger by the simple need to cover an immense *deficit*.

But it should be noted that this view, whether well-founded or not, cannot be seen as an objection, because the imperious nature of the necessity that will serve as a safeguard for the Assembly can only be reinforced by following the procedure suggested here, and in addition it is also a sure step towards practicing the right principles.

But there is a further point of view that calls for rather deeper reflection. Up to now we have considered the Estates-General on the basis of a single assumption, namely, the present state of affairs. But suppose that current circumstances were to change. Suppose that it was decided to reduce or even eliminate the deficit! There is nothing impossible in this. It might already have been done by adopting the just and honorable means used in financial distress by any private individual with honor and good sense. If in the absence of morality or energy the ministry were to adopt the frightful expedient of a bankruptcy to escape in an instant from its present position; if it were to see from the prevailing mood that the Estates-General would prefer honorable means to the crushing expedient of surcharging a people who already have too much to pay; and if, seeing that it would have nothing to lose, it were to abruptly dismiss and dissolve the National Deputation, what would become of our national aspirations? How might it be possible to avoid all the horrors of a bankruptcy? In present circumstances, this is a subject that is too important and too closely connected to the plan of this work for it not to be treated with all the length that it deserves.

On the Subject of a Bankruptcy

If, to ensure that any human action was genuinely impossible, all that was needed was simply to show that it would amount to something containing or capable of causing every crime at once, it would be quite easy to reassure the nation against the project of a public bankruptcy.

But if there are weak men who like to commit petty misdemeanors or stronger men who feed on great injustice, then the strongest of all, the vizier who holds the power of a whole people in his corrupt hands, can also create an interest for himself that is the enemy of all morality. That private interest then becomes a public pestilence, a general calamity.

There is no individual or corporate body that is not capable of separating its own interest from the general interest and, as a result, of turning itself into something unjust and criminal. The nation alone is incapable of this because its own interest is the general interest itself. The nation cannot under any circumstance be guilty of a bankruptcy.

But the ministry! It has coveted it; it has projected it; it has just begun to carry it out under the guise of a forced loan. What if with greater foresight and more audacity it was to wipe out the whole deficit?

The subject needs to be envisaged in terms of two different moments. Before the meeting of the Estates-General, the aim of a bankruptcy would be to remove the need for one forever. In this case it would be true to say that all our meditations about the advantages that the nation would be able to draw from that assembly would be superfluous, unless what would still be a legitimate National Assembly were to emerge from the disorder and the boundless opposition that would rise up from every side, because it is the peoples' mandate, not the decision to convoke it, that makes it legitimate.

If, on the other hand, present circumstances were to lead to a meeting of the Estates-General without any crisis or upheaval, by virtue of the promise to convene it, it would then be extremely important that, as has been indicated, it does not lose a moment in binding its future to the totality of the public revenue. As has been said, it is quite possible that a ministry that has been baulked, exhausted, and irritated by a mass of objections that it had not foreseen, might dare to revive and execute the project of a bankruptcy in order to recover its independence by committing the very act that would destroy your liberty unless you had taken the precaution of giving it a more solid foundation than the need to cover a *deficit* which would no longer exist.

On the basis of this conjecture, the Estates-General would be unassailable. It would survive a bankruptcy. It would already have voiced enough opposition to it, or rather the impossibility of dissolving it would be a solid guarantee in advance that a bankruptcy could not be carried out, because no minister would dare to attempt one in the certain knowledge that the Estates-General would find an independent protector in an outraged people.

I do not understand the confused anxiety that has taken hold of a good number of minds. It needs to be proved that the king has neither the right nor the power to order a bankruptcy and, in the second place, that the Estates-General would fall into the most deadly trap either by allowing or by failing to oppose one.

The King Cannot Carry Out a Bankruptcy

It is not the king who owes the money or who supplies the funds needed to pay the debt. It is the nation. The annual wealth used to pay for labor and credit is produced by its citizens, and as a natural consequence, it is they who also have at their disposal all the money used annually to service the nation's transactions. Only the nation has the means to pay, and if it has no intention of suspending its payments and frustrating its creditors, it is obvious that no one has a right to suppose it has a contrary will.

It is not hard to see how intermediaries responsible for receiving and transferring the interest on the debt to its destination might be guilty of infidelity. Either the debtor or the creditor would be robbed. The crime would be a real one, but it would not have any of the hallmarks of a genuine bankruptcy. Would there not still be a debtor with both an intention and a capacity to honor his engagement and a creditor prepared to receive what is his due? For as long as these two terms maintain their relationship, a national bankruptcy is not only legally but also really impossible. It is not in my power to fail to meet someone else's obligations, just as it is not in the king's power to breach national faith. It would be very odd if he were held to have a right to declare a bankruptcy when he is said not to have a right to borrow or to tax!

You might perhaps say that it would still be true that public funds had been lost in transit, in which case, make them take another route. If you are robbed by your cashier, have him punished. In the case of the public funds, it is not too hard to see that since it is not really possible for anyone holding them on deposit to take the whole treasury and disappear, a properly conducted investigation will always be able to put any misappropriated tax revenue back in its rightful place and guarantee exemplary punishment of the guilty parties.

The Estates-General Will Be Lost, and the Nation along with Them, Either By Countenancing a Bankruptcy or By Not Opposing One

It is almost a crime, I acknowledge, to imagine for a moment that the nation's representatives might be capable of lending themselves to a project whose elements could have been combined only by a perverse and vicious soul. But in the final analysis, is there any pestilence beyond the reach of the skilful combinations of despotism? If this is a danger to be feared, it is most to be feared at the very beginning when the true character of genuine representation is not yet well-enough known, when the people are not yet fully appraised of their interest in not allowing themselves to be guided in the choice of their representatives and when hired proxies sent into the provinces may yet be able to exercise a preponderant influence over the elections. Deputies chosen under such conditions might well be less able to resist the seductions of the many different means used to tempt them. Would there be no grounds for anxiety on this score if one were to see a general assembly made up of the shameful products of ministerial omnipotence rather than the natural and free outcome of the people's confidence?

This possibility necessarily suggests another, namely, that the Estates-General might be doomed to a feebleness that would affect its conduct as a whole. It would not find it easy, as a basic principle, to use the imperious necessity to raise taxes to arm itself with the power needed to be of solid utility to its constituents. Instead, every effort to escape former dependence, every honorable initiative, every useful design would, under this unhappy supposition, become an act of courage that cannot be expected.

In this light, what would the ministry aim to do, and how might it conduct its maneuvers with regard to a bankruptcy? Examine its interest. There is no need for much reflection to see that the ministry would simply seek to persuade every class of citizens who had been ruined or had been more or less directly affected by the rotation of so many fortunes, that it was a truly abominable idea to have convoked the Estates-General, that such large assemblies have never done anything but harm, and that sooner or later the representatives of a nation become a pestilence upon it. As can be imagined, all this amounts to an excellent doctrine for despots!

By defaulting on the debt, the ministry would be back in control of its expenditure. It would be restored to the exercise of its omnipotent power and if it were to allow those docile deputies to remain assembled for a period of time, its aim would be to take the most advantage of their presence and use a consent that it could count on in advance to do whatever it wants. What then would it lack to support or reward treason? Its hand would be free to use the great mechanisms of fear and money and it would again be able to spread them about with profusion.

If it is obvious that the ministry has everything to wish for from the project of annihilating public credit, it is indisputable that the Estates-General and the nation have everything to fear. Shame, misfortune, the ruin of all hope, acts of the most absolute despotism—all these evils will befall it. The need now is to examine these various prospects without following a very rigid order.

Before imagining a body of representatives capable of betraying a people by lending support to the sinister project of a bankruptcy, it is worth asking what the reward for such treachery might be. To be capable of becoming the instrument of the avidity and designs of one's enemy, to be able voluntarily to make something detestable of the one means left to nations to regain possession of their rights, to bury, in a certain sense, the last remaining hope with its own hands—all this must require a particular point of view, which is quite the opposite of the interest of all. What might this view be?

Corporate bodies, it is said, always tend to increase their power. But by consigning twenty-five million men to oppression, would the Estates-General be able to do so to its own advantage? Putting oneself at the mercy of one's enemy is a rather strange way of increasing one's strength and power! It is clear that if for a moment deputies of this stamp were to cease to be the servile agents of ministerial despotism, they would be exposed to being broken like a reed. What reward for their ambition, than to return to the bosom of their hearths burdened with the nation's hatred and the bitter despair of having gained no more from such baseness than well-deserved nullity and an opprobrium that will be forever attached both to their persons and their names! Now, consider something more.

It is only too certain that by subscribing to a bankruptcy the Estates-General will have made us lose forever the most favorable and least costly opportunity that has ever been presented to a people to acquire a free constitution. For true citizens this point of view, which affects the political future of the whole nation, is the most grievous of all. This would be the most unhappy of all the countless and harmful effects of a bankruptcy. Were it to occur, we would have to abandon patriotic aspirations forever. You, who have so lively an interest in civil liberty, in the condition of the people, and in a national constitution and who imagines so fondly that progress will soon be made towards a rightful order in every possible sense, do not believe any longer in the patriotic rebirth of our country. For there will no longer be a country or any liberty. The great maw of despotism will have swallowed them all.

But it is not enough to show that the nation would lose all hope of anything better and would be forced to put up with the fate to which she had been accustomed. Its fall would be far greater. New misfortunes and a new ignominy would lie in store.

A bankrupting nation! Such would be the title with which the entire universe would be entitled to besmirch a people who once proclaimed themselves to be frank and generous and who dared once to pretend to liberty. Such would be the fruit of the first use that it was allowed to make of liberty. Like a body of vile and vicious slaves released by chance from their irons—uncertain and rapacious, unworthy of the liberty offered to them by fortune—they would know no more than how to mark their first steps with theft, violence, and disorder before bowing their heads beneath the whips of commanders who would soon return them to their accustomed chains.

Peoples who are our creditors would not be satisfied with despising us. England seeks to give us enemies wherever she can. She will inflame and combine resentment from every corner, and we will not have long to wait to find ourselves embroiled in the horrors of a war that will have to be funded without any credit (meaning with funds acquired at grossly usurious rates). After heavy loss of life, to nobody's great concern, and after the ruin of part of the fortunes that the bankruptcy seemed to have spared, France, forced to sue for a shameful peace, would find herself in a new state of disorder with a new debt that usury would have raised to double the level of the enforced military expenditure.

A new debt would give rise to new taxes. This is not quite what those who were disposed to acquiesce in a bankruptcy would have proposed to themselves. All they wanted was to avoid any new tax. It should therefore be useful to consider what the probable effects of a bankruptcy might be in relation to taxation. It is not even necessary to imagine a war to come to a conclusion that is not very different from the one we believe we have reached.

What sort of disposition can be conceived of a court that would decide to cancel or effect the cancellation of the state's debt? Would it do so with a view towards frugality or with the design of increasing its power and profligacy? If the ministry were not inclined to opt for genuine reform when, during a period of difficulty, it had powerful motives for doing so, is it in good faith conceivable to think that it would be prepared to regulate its conduct voluntarily when, after recovering the fullest extent of the most absolute authority, it no longer had to fear any obstacle capable of obstructing its proclivity for indulging its passion for the most extravagant expenditure? Would it be more disposed to close all those hidden porticos from which the public revenue has leaked out of the royal treasury?

Follow the natural effects of a bankruptcy upon the two sources of tax revenue. It is clear that there would immediately be a prodigious fall in consumption of every kind. This reduction in demand, coupled with the suppression of a mass of the capital which previously supplied funds to manufacturing industry, would for some time give rise to an enormous reduction in production of every kind. The result would be an incalculable fall in every part of the public revenue.

In this new state of affairs, would it be possible to guarantee that nonpayment of taxes would be confined to those unable to pay because of their poverty? Would it not be more likely that the general discontent and the ease with which it would be possible to hide behind a misfortune whose limits could not readily be fixed would cause the greater part of ordinary tax revenue to dry up? What then would the ministry try to do? It would have recourse to force. It would spend even more considerable sums in raising the size of the military establishment.

Thus by way of the inevitable reduction in receipts and the forced increase in expenditure as well as of that long habit of dissipation that has to be regarded as incurable for as long as the public treasury does not belong to the nation, new needs will come to be established, calling for new financial assistance. I wonder whether it is too much to foresee that with an impotent nation and an all-powerful ministry, it would not be long for new taxes to be established.

But along with those who are incapable of considering the most probable consequences of any event when it begins to look a little too far-removed from those they are accustomed to see going on all around them, I am still prepared to envisage the outcome of a bankruptcy in the most favorable possible light. The least harm it might do would still be greater than the disadvantages of a new tax. Not that this should be taken to mean that I think that to avert a bankruptcy a new tax is unavoidable. I will have more to say on this very soon but will say here that if the nation were to have to choose between the disadvantages of a new tax and those of a bankruptcy, it should not hesitate to opt for the tax. This is not only in the interest of the state's creditors and all those with a relationship to them, but also in the interest of the universality of citizens. The aftershocks of so violent a measure, the paralysis of trade and the manufacturing arts for fifty years, and three hundred thousand men forced to take to the highways should be enough to make everyone decide which of the two evils it is better to avoid.

We have not examined a state bankruptcy in terms of its connection to the rights of citizens who are creditors of the state. It should not be necessary to point out to anyone that an act like this has all the hallmarks of the most grave injustice. Anyone who is unable to rebuff with indignation someone who needs it proved that it is not permissible to dishonor one's engagements or who starts coldly to discuss the question of whether the public faith is subject to the same moral code as the good faith of a private individual, deserves to be despised.

A more vivid image of the troubles, misfortune, despair, calamities, and crimes of every kind to which rage and misery might lead might also serve to throw a further shade of horror over the very thought of a project capable of producing so many evils. But the purpose of this work has been rather to consider the political influence of a bankruptcy upon the fate of the nation taken as a whole.

This means that it is necessary now to reply to objections, because it cannot be disguised that there have been objections. A bankruptcy has its partisans. Some claim that the debt is not the nation's because the nation was not convoked to give its consent to loans that were raised, etc. Others view the debt as usury and argue that it is possible to revoke an engagement in which, they claim, there was a manifest lesion. Others still make a studied effort to consider the advantages and disadvantages of a bankruptcy and opt, in cold blood, for its advantages. Finally, the majority, terrified at the prospect of a surcharge hanging over the people, refuse to contemplate anything else than wanting at any price to remove the need for new taxation. It should be apparent that the considerations we have given up to now will not seem to be sufficient in the eyes of all those moved by one or other of these latter concerns. It is therefore essential to reply, and in order to reply to everything it ought to be sufficient to clarify the state of the question and then show its true relationship to both rightful principle and the present situation of the state. But developing these arguments here makes me fearful of slowing down the steps leading towards the main object of this work. Better, therefore, to consign them to its end, where the reader will find them addressed under four questions.

We will therefore bring these reflections dealing with a bankruptcy to an end here by noting that everything that has the character of property is equally sacred before the law. My annuity is mine; its interest is my income just as my land and its annual rental income are mine. There can be no difference on this score. No one can have a right to despoil me of either the one or the other. Even the nation, although it may well be the highest legislative power, cannot take away my ownership of either my house or my annuity. By going back to rightful principle, one meets with the guarantee of the ownership of property as the aim of all legislation. How then can it be imagined that the legislator might take it from me? Legislative power exists only to protect it. When in comparing the power to effect a bankruptcy to the power to consent to a tax, we would have offended against justice and denied the true end of society if we were to conclude that the Estates-General has a right to nullify the entitlement to co-ownership of the universality of the kingdom's goods that belongs to the state's creditors. Moreover a legislative body is also the representative of the nation's common will and acts by way of general laws, never by particular acts of authority. It cannot therefore despoil some to the benefit of others, and its mandate, however extensive it may be, cannot authorize it to crush one class of citizens to lift the tax burden from the others.

This is the moment to take leave of so painful a conjecture. No, the Estates-General will not suffer anything with the least connection or similarity to the indignity of perjuring the public faith. It will instead feel that this is the issue on which it will set the final seal on its own freedom and power and by doing so will acquire that overwhelming moral authority in public opinion that ought to be its goal. With this view in mind, it is to be desired that it should enact a declaration couched in something like the following terms:

> It is constant that
>
> Every public loan presupposes two engagements on the nation's part: (1) to pay annual interest and (2) to effect a gradual and successive reimbursement of the debt.
>
> Since these two operations can be put into effect only by one of the following three ways: either (1) by establishing a new tax, or (2) by changing the destination of part of an existing tax, or finally (3) by a fiscal surplus arising from a tax yield which is naturally susceptible of increase;
>
> Since, for these reasons, it is indisputable that the power to borrow in the nation's name can belong only to the nation;
>
> Since the Estates-General also notes that every part of what presently amounts to the public debt and in particular every loan raised up to this day in the king's name having been endowed with the full panoply of all existing legal forms, it was impossible for those lending funds to identify any radical vice in that form. And since the Estates-General also considers that any necessary and projected national restoration cannot be compatible with the rotation of fortunes and the innumerable disorders that would be the result of the suppression of the public debt; guided by two such powerful motives the Estates-General declares that it has adopted the debt in the name of the nation. It stipulates that the debt will be consolidated and that provision will be made under its orders both for the payment of annual interest and for the gradual reimbursement of the capital which should always accompany any loan.

This is how to calm the people's fears, how to show that one is worthy of representing them, how to reinforce right principle, how to enable citizens to know their rights and the power of their union, and how to march towards one's rightful destination by following the path of equity and honor. In our eyes such a declaration would in every respect make a national assembly worthy of the title of public savior. Interest, zeal, love, and that devotion which seeks only to feel patriotic sentiment would then follow their natural course towards the Estates-General, which would thus become the rallying point of every opinion and sentiment and, soon, of everything that will come together to produce true power.

This is the moment to bring this long digression to an end, if digression is the right word to use for a subject linked so intrinsically to the plan of this work and in particular to the question of the freedom of the Estates-General.

The question of the freedom of the Estates-General involves, in addition to its external independence, finding that form of full and easy internal organization needed by any collective body in order to be able to fulfil its functions. Without wanting to deal with the subject in any depth, its main details will have to be outlined here. We will end this section by offering a word or two about the current prejudice towards the putative disadvantages of large deliberative assemblies, because we would, if possible, prefer to defend the Assembly's freedom even from an unjust public view.

It might seem superfluous to prove the need for an official code of conduct for an assembly of a thousand or twelve hundred individuals, particularly if it is accepted that it is essential for the members of any legislative body to be exempted from legal actions initiated from the outside, a prerogative that could not survive if there was not some sort of tribunal responsible for enforcing justice within the Assembly itself. As can be seen, we have tried to deal with the subject by adopting the form of a model vote or a set of statutes, even though whenever it has seemed to be necessary to make our own views clearer and more precise within the confines of this framework, this has not been the easiest of tasks for its author.

Statutes of Personal Conduct

1. No deputy can be held to be externally responsible for anything that is said or done within the Assembly.
2. The Assembly will nominate from among its members three *disciplinary* officials and a *judicial* committee made up of twelve individuals.
3. The three disciplinary officials will be responsible for (1) calling to order those who speak or act out of order, (2) *provisionally* withdrawing the right to speak from those refusing to return to order, (3) summoning and bringing before the judicial committee anyone who refuses or fails to obey their provisional order suspending the right to speak of any member responsible for committing an offence or grave injury in the Assembly.
4. Seven of the twelve members making up the judicial committee will suffice to give a majority verdict.
5. The functions of the judicial committee will consist (1) of *summarily* punishing any refusal to obey a provisional suspension order made by a disciplinary official (punishment will consist of a longer period of withdrawal of the right to speak or even in suspension from the Assembly for a greater or lesser period); (2) of pronouncing a *final* verdict on all other infractions that do not entail *absolute exclusion* from the Assembly; (3) of trying, with a right of appeal, any member charged with an offence deserving absolute exclusion or deserving trial by the ordinary processes of the law as these would apply to any other citizen.
6. Appeals will be heard by the whole Assembly, which will pronounce a *final* verdict of absolute exclusion and, if appropriate, refer the case to the ordinary judicial process.

7. Since any member who has been excluded will no longer be held to belong to the Assembly, notice will be given to his constituents, along with the minute of the judgment against him, to proceed to the election of another deputy, for which position the excluded member will no longer be eligible.

As this implies, it was necessary both to outline a sphere that is confined to the internal system of justice particular to members of the Assembly and to indicate clearly the point at which it joins the external system of justice common to all citizens.

Many people will think (and I strongly share their view) that at the outset—until a good constitution has been established to provide protection from any violence by the administration, it would be just to extend the deputies' privileged immunity to all those of their *external* pronouncements and actions that have a bearing on public affairs.

Details of the Procedural Formalities to Be Adopted by the Assembly

It will be no less important for the Assembly to use its initial sittings to give itself the organization and procedural formalities appropriate to the functions that it will be called upon to exercise. This ought not to be taken to mean that at bottom any ordinary legislature can be responsible for giving itself its own constitution. There must not be any confusion between a constituting power and a constituted power. But, since the nation has made no provision for carrying out the great task of constitution-making by way of a special deputation, it has to be supposed that the forthcoming Estates-General will combine the two powers. It would moreover take us too far afield to deal with this interesting subject, which deserves a separate memorandum. Here it is enough to point out that since the general assembly necessarily has to be in the most perfect independence of the executive power, it would render itself guilty towards the nation as well as towards reason if it were to allow its procedure to be modified by any extraneous authority. The only rules to which it will be obliged to give credence will be those it has made for itself, and it will observe them notwithstanding any contrary usage, decision, or ruling by the Royal Council.

A representative body cannot admit anyone who is not a deputy, freely elected by the people, to take part in its deliberations. Officers of the crown, dukes, peers, or princes cannot sit in it under any of these latter qualities. All influence that is alien to the quality of a deputy should be regarded as contravening the laws of a genuine representative body.

Propositions emanating from the king should not be carried to the Assembly other than by properly accredited commissioners. If any member of that assembly were to appear unafraid of adopting the quality of King's Commissioner, it would be visible from that very fact that he had abandoned his mission as a representative. He was expected to form his views as part of the legislature. By making himself the mouthpiece of the executive power he will have changed his role and should therefore be excluded from any deliberation. It probably ought to go without saying any more particularly that the Assembly should not undertake any deliberation in the presence of the king or his commissioners.

Just as no province has a right to dominate any other, it would be absurd for any one of them to pretend to the privilege of supplying the Estates-General with its presiding officer. In France there are some unusual prejudices about the importance of the presiding officers of assemblies. They are held to be in charge of the task at hand and fit to guide the assembly in question. So dangerous a misapprehension has its origin in the ministry's interest in having every assembly in the kingdom deliberate only under its authority. The ministry has the king proclaim that he will hold, or arrange to hold, *his* Estates of Brittany, *his* Estates of Artois, *his* Assembly of the Clergy, *his* Estates-General, as if they are all no more than emanations of his power or of his council or simple administrative offices belonging to one or other of the departments of the secretaries of state.(*)

It is understandable that with ideas like this, the government must have come to regard the officers presiding over these various bodies as mandatories designed to account to it for everything that occurred. Soon all the presiding officers of every assembly came to fall, directly or indirectly, under its nomination. They became its natural accomplices. Their influence and authority increased in a thousand and one different ways. Their hand was everywhere. They proposed, guided, and governed. Public affairs were their private concern, concerted in advance with a ministry with whom they made it a matter of honor to be on intimate terms.

It ought to go without saying that the Estates-General will not adopt a system like this. The presiding officer, or officers, whom it will elect freely along with every other of its own officials solely from among the Assembly's members, will not deviate any more than any other official from the functions attributed to him. Those of the presiding officer will consist of collecting votes according to the prescribed forms and of speaking in the name of the Assembly on ordinary occasions and on those occasions such as, for example, a deputation or an important affair where no ad hoc orator has been nominated. Finally the president will have responsibility for explaining the state of the question to those who do not seem to have understood it. Were you to allow your president or any other member to act more or less openly as the voice of an extraneous power; or to cause you to understand that he is, in certain respects, aware of things of which the Assembly is ignorant; or to become a bearer of promises on behalf of the ministry; were you, in any possible way, to permit any attempt to *influence the debate,* as the English put it, you will open the way to abuse of the most dangerous consequence.

Nor should you allow the presiding officer to set up committees at will or nominate the members of committees to which the Assembly might refer the preparatory discussion of important or difficult matters. Although he will generally be given a casting vote when the number of votes is divided equally, it ought to be recognized that this is an enormous privilege that should not be turned into a prerogative of the office. Any decision made in this way will depend too obviously on a particular will. A casting vote should be put off as far as possible until there is some indication of the general will, which if it cannot be pronounced directly, can at least be ascertained indirectly. It is therefore consistent with rightful principle for the Assembly to elect the person who has the right to collate votes, and consonant with sound politics for this public function to be performed by a number of different individuals. I propose therefore that every week or every fortnight the Assembly should nominate a member of each order who has a reputation for virtue, and whenever opinions are equally divided its members should draw lots to determine which of them will exercise a casting vote. To this effect there should be a weekly or fortnightly ballot to elect officials empowered to make a casting vote in advance. But I begin to see that I am exceeding my brief.

It is probable that after restricting the president to his proper functions it will be easier to move towards the principle of equality and prudence specifying that any officer presiding over the Estates-General should have no more than a weekly term and that the same principle should apply to every individual elected by each of its sections, bureaus, and committees. Moreover since no province or section can have any pre-eminence within the Assembly, this proposal will give the Estates-General the advantage of being able to choose its presidents from each province or section in alternation. Let it not be said, finally, that the first two orders will never allow themselves to be presided over by a member of the Third Estate. The way to get the best and most honorable presiding officer is to choose someone oneself. Any positive exclusion would amount to a gratuitous insult to a particular individual and would be an absurdity in public affairs.

In the eyes of the philosopher and the man of good sense, disputes over rank and precedence may seem despicable. But it is easy to foresee that a large assembly made up of people who, up to now, have been entirely unacquainted with the great principle of equality and who have not yet agreed upon or adopted habits appropriate to their weakness will be exposed to the loss of a large amount of time in vain disputes. The way to circumvent this initial obstacle to proceedings will be to nominate, perhaps by acclamation, a special committee responsible for hearing and elucidating all claims of this kind and for it then to refer them back to the general assembly to be adjudged as a whole.

Concurrently it will be necessary in an initial general session to nominate the membership of a much more important committee responsible for drafting a plan of the internal organization and procedure to be adopted by the Assembly. Until that plan has been adopted, its sittings can only be preliminary. This is not to say that it has no power to adopt provisional regulations. Whatever the way by which votes may be cast, it will be enough to collect them and identify the majority to establish the common will, which must always be what makes law.

Since the general view[1] can be known only by way of a majority, every statute or law whatsoever must be the work of a majority. That majority may be larger or smaller according to the nature of the affair, but it will always be a majority, and it would be remarkably odd if anything were to be decided on the basis of a minority vote. What then is to be thought of the means that have been used up to now to collect and collate votes! They are of a nature as to make for only the appearance of a majority, effectively allowing a minority to make law. This is the disadvantage of the method of voting by sections. I have heard it said that M. de Calonne in convoking the Assembly of Notables relied heavily on the vicious character of this particular form to give himself an apparent majority.(*) He divided 144 or 147 voters into seven different bureaus, each made up of twenty-one members. A majority of the total membership would have amounted to seventy-four votes, but by taking the views of each bureau, four out of seven amounted to a majority, and since in each of these four bureaus eleven votes were enough to carry the day, no more than forty-four out of a total of 147 voters were enough to produce the appearance of a majority. This vice would be the greatest of all. No argument in favor of efficiency, ease, or saving time can override the danger of making a law based on a minority view. The old way of voting by provincial governorships and, within governorships, by bailiwicks (*bailliages*) was detestable.(**) It is absolutely essential to correct it because it has the drawback—the highest of all—of being able to nullify the outcome of any deliberation at its very root.

---

[1] I have assumed that each deputy, without any distinction between orders, will represent the whole nation. Without this there cannot be a general view.

On the other hand, it would be impossible to call a thousand or twelve hundred individuals to give voice to their views, and sections have great advantages that ought not to be lost. There has to be some way of reconciling the two forms. I can imagine that every important affair will be discussed, analyzed, and cast into its most fundamental terms within a general assembly and that votes will then be taken and collated by section. Everyone will be able to take advantage of the light thrown on matters by everyone else, and those unable to make their voices heard in an assembly of a thousand or twelve hundred people will readily be able to do so before an audience of thirty discussants. No good idea will be lost, and the views of the assembly will not be exposed to the charge of having been captured by a sudden shift of mood or an artful intrigue. The best means has to be one that leaves deputies with as much of their enlightenment and wisdom as possible.

But sections will not be formed to combine individual views or to bring back one single view to the whole assembly. Having collected the votes, the president of section A will say, for example, that there were eighteen voters for the motion and twelve against. The other sections will do the same so that in this way there will be a true majority just as if no one had left the assembly hall and as if the universality of votes had all been collected and collated by the same individual.

To ensure that this procedure is followed as usefully as possible, it is important to find a way to prevent votes from getting lost among as many opinions as there are sections. This is why we have specified that questions of any importance should be presented, discussed, and analyzed in the presence of all the deputies, almost up to the point of whittling them down to a yes or a no. That will be the time to divide into sections. Then if any new interest or new point of view were to lead a bureau to want to examine the state of a question in a different way, it could proceed accordingly to communicate with the other bureaus by way of a deputation. In this case either a certain number of sections will join together to demand a fresh discussion of the matter in the general assembly, or the wishes of the section making the deputation to the others will be rebuffed, or it might be decided to adopt a third point of view, namely, not to change the terms of the matter under consideration but to agree that this was not the time to discuss it.

When dealing with ordinary questions there will be no need to leave the place where the general assembly meets. It will be enough to gather together into separate groups in the hall itself. In most deliberations, it is perfectly usual for there to be no need for a vote at all.

In a subject like this, it is not enough to arm the assembly against ministerial enterprise as well as against mistakes in its own internal governance. The public, too, can be unjust and the following reflections are addressed to it.

A Reply to Several Opinions Hostile towards Large Assemblies and Freedom of Speech

First, there is some disapproval of the complication and slowness that matters seem to take on in large deliberative assemblies. In France this may have something to do with being accustomed to arbitrary decisions made in silence in the recesses of ministerial cabinets. A question that is handled in public by a large number of participants, all able to exercise their right to discuss it with more or less prolixity and all prepared to express their ideas with a vigor, and often with a heat, foreign to the tone found in polite society, affords a spectacle that will naturally horrify our good citizens, just as a noisy concert of loud instruments is bound to offend the feeble ears of the patients in a hospital. It seems hard to imagine how any reasonable view could emerge from so free and lively a debate, and it is tempting to wish that it might be possible to call upon someone with an obvious degree of superiority over the whole crowd to impose some sort of order upon people who otherwise look like they will waste all their time in quarrelling.

But in dealing with public affairs, is it right to prefer methods that make the least noise and can be concealed more easily to those that are visible to all and that best combine all the characteristics required of a decision in the general interest? Has enough thought been given to how much of a mistake it generally is to arrange public administration for the convenience of the rulers rather than the utility of the ruled? What would one say about a skilled artisan who did not hesitate to sacrifice the essential purposes of a machine to the idea of simplifying how it works?

You might say that a great deal of time will be wasted in all these discussions. But what does time matter, if the public is well served and enlightened by good laws? What kind of waste of time can there be if that time is set against the greatest chance ever given to a man to find what he is seeking and when what he is seeking is of essential interest to a nation?

In every deliberation there is a kind of problem to be solved. This is to know, in any given case, what the general interest would prescribe. When the discussion begins, it is not possible to identify the direction it will take to reach that discovery with certainty. Doubtless, the general interest would be nothing if it were not someone's interest. It has to be the one interest among the various individual interests that is common to the largest number of voters; hence the need for a clash and coincidence of opinions. What you take to be a mixture and confusion that serves to obscure everything is an indispensable preliminary towards enlightenment. All these individual interests have to be allowed to jostle and press against one another, to take hold of the question from one point of view, then, another, each trying to push it according to its strength towards some projected goal. In this trial, views that are useful and those that are harmful will be separated from one another. Some will fall while others will maintain their momentum and will balance one another until, modified and purified by their reciprocal interaction, they will end up by becoming reconciled with one another and will be combined together in a single view, just as in the physical universe a single, more powerful movement can be seen to be made up of a multitude of opposing forces.

At this point I agree it will now be possible to single out from the broader mass those opinions that should never have been heard. But beforehand, would it have been right to have expelled any single one of them from the place in which each of them had a right to be heard, when everyone asserted how compatible with the general interest all of them were and announced that the final outcome would be just the same as the genuinely unknown decision lying at the conclusion of the debate? By arbitrarily eliminating any one, would you not have risked a more or less substantial degree of divergence from that final course of direction that would have taken the Assembly towards its true goal?

I would like to impose silence on that mass of critics who seem to be preoccupied with French frivolity and inconsequentiality. Certainly if large assemblies are held to be incapable of all order and any regulation, the disadvantages will be innumerable. But it must surely be misguided to suppose that the Estates-General is incapable of drawing up a set of rules to make its sittings orderly.

There is moreover no need to reply to every censorious critic. Some reproaches and some expressions of hatred deserve to be worn as badges of honor. Is it surprising that an assembly in which every deputy will have both a right and a duty to reveal the failings of the administration with complete freedom will arouse fear in anticipation among that multitude of agents interested in former abuse and all those, in particular, who were often able to bury the most heinous of mistakes simply by finding ways to seduce a departmental head who was susceptible to petty interest? Their hypocritical anxiety about the conduct of the forthcoming Estates-General is simply bad faith. Their aim is no more than to sow despondency wherever they can. There is no reason to waste time discussing anything with this sort of person since they are not to be persuaded. The best reply is to leave them to taste the lash of events. Good patriots will notice with joy that a feeling for the public interest is now widespread among every order of citizens and that it has already come to form an imposing body of opinion. Yes, we can now be quite open in showing our hatred of the internal enemies of the nation. That patriotic feeling is spreading rapidly and is becoming something like a first, initial act of public justice.

As for those cowards (and who has not met one?) who adopt the title of the sage and play the man of moderation, do not bother to seek to arouse any feeling or idea of honor among them. Better to leave them with their willingness to suffer every outrage rather than resist a single one. Let them keep that moral inertia that they prize as a condition for maintaining the tranquillity of the state. Better to be resigned to the fact that, their spirits being paralyzed beyond repair, they will flinch from any liberal movement. Leave them to the effrontery of daring to say that the mere sight of the energy and honor of others is a cause of fatigue. What matter are such degenerate nullities? They are no more than corpses, best fitted for the grave.

If every tongue could be silenced, patriots would not have to answer all that many objections. But no such assumption or power can ever be availed upon to rid us of the anxious censure of the old. Nature, by allowing them to survive into the present age, has still condemned them to be yesterday's men. They cannot forget either the feelings or the mistakes of yesteryear. The words "liberty" and "patriotism" have no part in their lexicon. It is futile to try to explain these things to them; every explanation cannot but fall on deaf ears. The prejudices of our contemporaries can be dissipated, and their reason, enlightened. But nothing can repair the reason of a sixty-year-old. Were I to dare, I would say, (like the character of *M. le Bailly* [the high sheriff] in the play), that men enfeebled by age know only how to preach *moderation*, when what matters is to be active and able. With their endless concern for persons and proprieties and their eternal deference towards anyone with a place or a rank, they would end up by suffocating every useful initiative and by destroying every hope of anything better.

It does not surprise me that men who have grown old in long servility might want, and yet not want at one and the same time—would like, but would not dare—to attack abuse and, trembling, would commend no more than the use of an outworn tool with a blunted edge, revering the authors of their misfortune from force of habit and never allowing themselves to express even the smallest grievance to them except with the most base of compliments and the most servile prostration! Yes, offer to free these slaves and, if they agree, it will be on condition that they do not have to surrender the livery that disgraced them for so long and that they can still die faithful to the yoke that they have borne. But should we, who at least in thought and will are free and able to preserve our original vitality, still borrow the language and attitude of slaves!

It has to be hoped that these shameful feelings, these futile considerations, these miserable complaints will no longer defile public opinion. The people's representatives will be well to be rid of such dangerous traps. There will be a time—and I say so for the honor of the nation—there will be a time when its assembly offers the spectacle of one of those outbursts of virtuous indignation that, in bringing great abuse to book, fearlessly overcomes those limits that weakness, much more than so-called wisdom, dared to impose upon courage.

These marks of honor and public spirit will become common, despite the disapproval of perfidious spirits, despite the opposition of depraved souls, and despite the treachery of those cowardly informers whose ears are open to the words of the virtuous only so that they can denounce them and who are ever ready and always quick to manufacture in secret some new entitlement to an honor and a place from some shameful service.

But to revert to the subject of the public and public opinion, which, sometimes confounding good sense and adding its blindness to the injustice of its censors, has gone so far as to condemn the authors of opinions that it has deemed to be too bold and seemed willing—shameful to relate—to accept that the punishments inflicted by despotism were as merited as the risks that they ran.

Consider the matter without any heat. However impetuous or indiscrete an individual opinion might appear to be, some attention should also be given to the fact that these things happen in any deliberative body just as any ordinary individual will be subject to a host of half-formed, fleeting thoughts before coming to a decision in an important matter. What would become, if not of a dullard, but of even the wisest of men if he were to be held to account for all the extravagances, all the hurtful thoughts or, to put it more truthfully, all the satisfying malice that sometimes enters his head before he comes to a decision worthy of a sound mind and an honest heart?

Now think. That host of barely perceptible and multiple movements spinning in every direction within the tissue of a single individual's brain is like an image of every individual view in a deliberative assembly. Both are the materials of deliberation, the elements of which it is made up, the first, preliminary parts of a judgement. They supply the motives that are combined together to form that final combination of mind and will that amounts to what is called a *resolution*. An assembly would never be able to form a common will without hearing the individual views that precede and go into its making. But once a resolution has been made, everything that is useless or dangerous in these preliminary views has, like those views themselves, to be discarded. An assembly can only answer to, and be held to account for, its own work, and its own work cannot be anything other than a common decision. If all the thoughts that served to bring about a decision by an individual remain at his disposal in the impenetrable secrecy of the brain, the views that excited and served to bring about a decision in a collective body are necessarily open to public scrutiny. But they must still be regarded as incapable of compromising their authors. Every opinion should have something like a sacred and inviolable right of asylum attached to the place in which it once had a necessary moment of existence.

In addition, that much-maligned publicity is rarely the cause of a little harm and almost always the source of a great deal of good. This is a truth that could easily be shown if it was possible to say everything that comes to mind. But even if some inconvenience has to be attached to the boldness of some views, the public should still not deal with them with such severity. If it understood its interests properly, it would instead protect and encourage freedom of speech, especially when there seem to be so many reasons for arguing that it should not be exercised courageously. But if this were so, it would then be the public itself that would suffer and its enemies alone who would benefit. Punishing a voting member of a legislature for his views, whatever they may be, is barbarous. In law it would amount to an absurd self-contradiction; for a government with armed force at its disposal, it is an act of horrible tyranny. The most complete freedom of expression is an inherent, unassailable right, sacred to every member who speaks in a legislative body. License or excess begin only when the internal order of the assembly is affected, and in matters of this kind, we have seen already that it can and should rely upon its own disciplinary regulations.

This is the moment to conclude, in keeping with the heading of this second section, that the Estates-General, after beginning by setting all taxation under its safeguard, can then, if it so wills, deliberate on and legislate in the most entire freedom for whatever it judges to be useful to the nation. Since we have not yet embarked upon an examination of what those laws that would be so fitting for the nation might in present circumstances be, it is necessary to proceed further. In the next section we will examine whether a people is to be condemned to draw no more than a fleeting benefit from an opportune moment or whether this time it will be possible for the Estates-General to enable France to enjoy a more solid and permanent fruit.

Section III. The Estates-General Is Able to Make the Result of Its Deliberations Permanent and Independent of Any External Sanction

Order has been restored to the finances. The ministry, the burden of necessity now being lifted, no longer needs to show restraint. The National Assembly has separated. What now will be the fate of those of its statutes that displeased the executive power? Will the representatives of the people have given any thought to the unhappy possibility that the fruits of their zeal and the hopes of the nation might wither and die after they retire?

Such fears would be chimerical if we were talking about a well-constituted society. To give the laws the degree of solidity and authority that they need, all that the legislator would need to do is to entrust their execution to the public establishment. In a well-ordered society, the public establishment would be organized in such a way that it would attend to its duties as a matter of necessity and would be utterly incapable of ever turning its force against its constituents' interest. But we are not in that happy position. Since we are obliged to inhabit a political order in which nothing is in its proper place, it is necessary therefore, and with the deepest regret at not being able to put that great public instrument to its proper use, to find an alternative means for consolidating the laws made by an authentic legislature.

Here I am entitled to assume that while under the salutary safeguard of necessity, the Estates-General was deliberating freely and without fear or danger was enacting all the laws that it adjudged to be necessary to the people's interest, it had not failed to give France a *constitution*. It would indeed be inconceivable that it would not have felt that this was how to begin and that a constitution has to be the basis of every reform, all order, and every good.

My first reply therefore would be to say that during the intervals between successive national assemblies, the constitution will preside over the laws that an assembly has made, that its presence alone will be enough to preserve them, and that it will even be enough to ensure that regular meetings of the nation's representatives will take place.

But if the constitution is to be the guarantee of the nation's statutes, who will guarantee the constitution? This is the moment to reply: *the new tax law*. Here we are not talking only about a law limiting grants of subsidies to fixed periods of time. As will soon be shown, that means will not in itself provide a sufficient guarantee in the present state of affairs. What is at issue here is a tax law that will in itself be a constitutional law. To give a general idea of what this might be before dealing with its implications would involve clearly identifying all the component parts of the constitution and giving each of them a function related to a tax, so that at every point the constitution and the fiscal system would be so tightly connected that they could not be separated from one another. It would then be certain that all the parts of our constitution would enjoy the most solid existence and the most active authority. If the only power to be feared is unable to do without tax revenue, it will have to respect the constitutional laws making it possible for that tax to be levied.

To clarify the question, it is necessary to deal separately with the work of the Assembly as it pertains to taxation and then as it pertains to the constitution without, however, forgetting that the objective is not to deal with these matters exhaustively but simply to outline the steps to be taken by the Estates-General in those of its operations whose purpose, from its very first session, will be to set the seal on a matter of great and durable utility, so that it will have the merit of having laid down unshakable foundations both for liberty and the regeneration of France.

An Outline of the Assembly's Work concerning the Finances

It is clear that this work will not be concluded until the Assembly has reached its very last sitting. A vote of subsidy can be no more than its very final act. But the scale of the preliminary work of gathering information and all the details of the order to be established in this area will make it unavoidable for the Estates-General to start to deal with the subject from its very early days. It is not particularly important how the work will be conceived and arranged provided that from the outset everyone is well aware of the double necessity to manage expenditure and take hold of income. To give these ideas some fixed form, it has to be supposed that the Estates-General will nominate three quite distinct and separate committees.

The first of these will have been made responsible for examining and authenticating *the accounts* and will draw up an exact statement of income and expenditure as they presently stand.

The work of the second committee will have as its object the task of drawing up a speculative but full account of *expenditure* in a country like France without, however, paying attention to what prevailing practice has been up to now. In this plan, the various parts of the public establishment will be reduced to their basic number and each part to its just measure, while estimates of the costs will be frugal. There should be no difficulty in finding sufficiently well informed views in Paris to meet this triple objective, and it should be clear that the committee ought to be authorized to examine and consult whomsoever it feels it should, in every class of the administration and among private citizens.

The third committee will be selected to draw up a conjectural model of a *tax* to be levied according to that method that will be most equitable to the tax payer and least harmful to national prosperity.

If it is right for the Estates-General to rely on committees drawn from its own ranks to draft the subject matter of its deliberations, it is equally certain that this method has to be subject to a set of unvarying, clearly understood rules. Thus it should not be forgotten that the work of the committees and bureaus should be limited to examining and clarifying a subject, to drawing up draft points of view, and to bringing the whole matter, in the most instructive way, before the Assembly, which alone has the power to judge and decide. However respectable a judgement by an individual committee member might be, his words alone cannot be a sufficient motive for a decision by the other deputies. The people entrusted the Estates-General as a body, not some of its members, with their confidence. An assembly cannot inform itself, deliberate, or legislate by delegating its powers. No one with the power to vote in a deliberation can under any circumstance be separated from the general representation. It is therefore the right and duty of every one of its members to inform themselves personally of every subject of deliberation so that he can make his views known in full knowledge of the issues. Committees exist to support and to facilitate this individual work, not to replace it. Nor should it be thought that these reflections are too simple to need to be made. It will be necessary on more than one occasion to remind the Assembly of the fundamental—and so fertile—principle that legislative power cannot be sub-delegated and that it belongs, inalienably and untransferrably, to the body of representatives.

In the ordinary course of deliberation, a report by a committee that has gone about the work with which it was entrusted with zeal will be enough to enlighten most voters. But this will not be the case with some more complicated matters, such as, for example, the present state of the finances, where factual proof will require a large amount of documentary evidence. However perfect might be the report by the Committee of Accounts (the first of the three committees listed above), it will still have to supply documentary proof. This is why it is important to observe that this committee will be given a special order to divide its work into as many different parts as can then be separately and fully examined and verified, and whenever it has to submit a partial report to the assembly, it will deposit all its paperwork at the registry for detailed inspection by those members who might want to examine it more closely. It is easy to appreciate the great importance of a method of this kind without there being much need here to develop the reasons that favor its adoption. Note, however, that the Assembly will hear the various parts of the Committee of Accounts' report without taking any measure to deliberate on anything to do with their substance until it no longer has anything more to learn on this matter. It will hear the reports of the other two finance committees in the same way.

Here, before proceeding further, it may now be of interest to nominate a fourth committee, responsible for considering the three reports pertaining to the accounts, future expenditure, and taxation. By studying, aligning, and comparing the three images they contain, a number of infinitely useful results should emerge. Thus this fourth committee will be responsible for drafting a complete system of income and expenditure, suitable for the harshness of present circumstances and fit for presentation for discussion by the general assembly.

I am not unaware that the ministry has, on its side, been drawing up a new financial plan. I know it intends to present it to the Estates-General in order to excite its attention and consent. It will certainly be a heartening sight to see an administration that up to now has known no more than how to ruin and wreck and having brought the political machine to the point of breakdown has found itself in such a tangle that it has had, contrary, certainly, to its own inclinations, to call for help from the nation's representatives as the only power able to remedy the disorder. It will certainly be a bizarre and wondrous spectacle to see an administration present itself boldly to the Estates-General and pretend to offer it the fruits of its enlightenment, to serve as its guide and teacher, and to instruct it, paternally, in the art of justice and rightful order.

It is to be hoped that the nation's finest men will know how to give this ridiculous presumption the treatment that it deserves and that it will be all the more attentive and resolute in ensuring that it carries out its duties itself by entrusting the preliminary work of going through and preparing materials only to its own committees. What would be people's astonishment and scandal if they were to see their representatives disown the office with which they had been entrusted and abandon it to the goodwill and enlightenment of the ministry? But an assumption like this has to be a chimera.

When the report of the fourth, *conciliatory*, committee brings the Estates-General, already enlightened by the reports of its first three financial committees, back to a consideration of this important matter, and after it has satisfied all its views concerning the constitution, etc., it will proceed to draw up a detailed regulation of all the various objects of public expenditure. It will assign to each of these objects that portion of the public revenue that should belong to it and by doing so will come to have a measure of the total amount to be raised by taxation. It is impossible that this entirely simple method of fixing the general amount of tax contributions, the only equitable one that there is, will lead it to fix these at a higher level than the enormous subsidy paid by people today.

Once the amount of public revenue has been set, it will be a matter of raising the tax under the inviolable aegis of distributive equity and national prosperity. But it is easy to see that the Estates-General will not be able to reform so ill assorted a fiscal system and put it on a proper foundation in a matter of days or even a whole session. Public opinion will have to change before it will be willing to accept changes that might otherwise be too great. This, it might be said in passing, is one more reason for abolishing all obstacles interfering with the dissemination of enlightenment.

But whatever the sources from which different parts of the national revenue will be obtained, whether before or after establishing a better order, there will always be a long series of operations involved in ensuring that the amounts of which it consists can be *equitably assessed*, *levied*, and *distributed* to their various final destinations. This is the sequence of operations that we propose should be bound inseparably to the hierarchical arrangement of the constitution. But before presenting an image of that tight connection, it is necessary to see how the Estates-General will have conducted itself to give France a constitution.

Of the Assembly's Deliberations Concerning the Constitution

First of all, what is a constitution? Even if the plan of this work does not include a detailed examination of this subject, it is still necessary to be sure of understanding the proper meaning of terms.

As was said above, every human association has to have a common aim and public functions. To carry out these functions, it is necessary to separate out a certain number of members of the association from the great mass of citizens. The more a society progresses in the arts of trade and production, the more apparent it becomes that the work connected to public functions should, like private employments, be carried out less expensively and more efficiently by men who make it their exclusive occupation. This truth is well known.

The salaries of these agents and administrators and, in general, all the expenditure of the public establishment is met by annual tax revenue. Thus citizens who pay taxes should be considered to be shareholders in the great social enterprise. They supply its capital; they are its masters. It is for their benefit that it exists and is able to act. It is they who will enjoy all its benefits.

If these mandated agents and administrators were to be left to their own devices, if they were not accountable, if they were to free themselves from their dependence upon the body of shareholders, they could not but make themselves into a separate interest, an interest that would live at the expense of the general interest. They would be its masters.

What would then come to be seen would be what happens almost everywhere. Public functions would stop being seen as a duty and instead become a right. The power and authority entrusted to administrators would stop being seen as a commission and become instead a prerogative, a property.

At this point, the political body would be disordered. It would be dead. There would be no more association, no more society. The two terms, by virtue of their intrinsic meaning, would no longer represent the true state of affairs: *societas quia inter socios* (a society exists only among associates). As soon as citizens are no longer associates, they cease to be citizens. Some other language has to be used. And since it is impossible to identify anything social arising between a number of masters and a mass of slaves busying themselves with serving them and paying for their own chains—because there is no more than domination on one side and subjugation on the other—human aggregations of this kind should renounce the word society and adopt the title of political servitude.

It follows from this that, in forming its public establishment, the first concern of every association must be to organize it in such a way as to ensure that while it is always able to reach the goal it was created to reach, it cannot dispense itself from doing so, and above all it cannot deviate from its path and attack its trustees, using the very same arms with which it was entrusted for their utility. Here then is one part of the social constitution: this is the constitution or organization of the *active* power. What remains is to identify the constitution of the *legislative* power.

The agents and legislators of a political body should be no more conflated with one another than would the head and hands of an individual body. If whoever is responsible for executing the law could also make the law, he would do so in keeping with his individual interest. Citizens would be defenseless, and society would degenerate into servitude.

Similarly, if whoever makes the law can, without having anything in common with the active power, give themselves an interest distinct from the common interest of the great body of citizens, the social order will be equally upset and soon there will be no more than despots and slaves.

It is necessary, therefore, for the legislature to be constituted in such a way as to ensure that it cannot ever have intentions contrary to the general interest of the associates. It is exactly this form of organization that has to make up the other, and most important, part of the political constitution, namely, the *legislative constitution.*

Enlightenment on this subject is quite widely disseminated among us. Few individuals able to reflect upon the social mechanism can be unaware that in a very small society the legislative power has to be exercised by the very body of shareholders in the republic itself and in a more populous nation, by a body of proxy-holders or representatives, freely chosen for a very short period of time, whose powers will remain revocable at the will of those who entrusted them with those powers. But we will still have reason to return to this subject a little further below.

We still have a right, in keeping with our plan, to suppose that the Estates-General will not have diverged from the principles of genuine social order. It represents the nation. It can do whatever it can do. It is therefore entirely up to the Estates-General to consult the highest end of every society and to arrange the two essential parts of the general constitution in a manner that meets this unique goal.

But we should not blind ourselves to the fact that all the branches of the active constitution are not all equally easy to grasp. Not all of them will lend themselves readily to national organization and a national life. But if a constitutional order cannot be established all at once, nothing must be neglected. Progress can still be made when opportunities arise.

Unless I am mistaken, the bodies responsible for exercising the judicial power want nothing more than to adopt the mantle of institutional legality and to receive an authentic title to their important functions from the very hands of the nation itself. This is both in their interest and ours.

When the nation was deprived of its rights, despotism would have invaded everything irretrievably if resistance were not somewhere to be found. But where could this have been? In a body expressly created for the purpose of balancing arbitrary power? But it must be obvious that a body created solely to resist would soon have been destroyed. The system of the balance of powers, a vicious idea to begin with, would be almost absurd if each of the weights in the balance did not have some necessary ability to last, drawn from elsewhere, attached to itself, making it impossible to push it entirely to one side. This has been the case with the judicial power in France. In the absence of a constitution, we have been only too fortunate that the Parlements were available to offer a final barrier against the devastating torrent of unlimited executive power.(*)

In future, the nation itself will exercise all its rights, rights that it will entrust to its representatives and that its representatives cannot entrust to anyone else. This does not mean that during their absence every citizen, every collective body, and every man will not be expected to do their duty as much as they can to prevent any usurpation of power.

The Parlements, happy no doubt to have contributed to bringing about a state of affairs where the country will need no more than their ordinary zeal, will be restored to their judicial functions. They will become what they should be: collective bodies endowed with a national foundation, independent of all other authority, since it is self-evident that judges responsible for telling citizens the law can stand only in a relationship of dependence upon the legislature alone. With time and the work of enlightenment, the Estates-General will come to adopt the principle of *judgement by one's peers* and will give France a new civil and criminal code, so that along with the power of enforcing the law, the high judiciary will have laws more worthy of enforcement for a civilized people.

But—and it is worth taking note of this—even though the sovereign courts will no longer need to go beyond their judicial functions, it will still be the case that in doing no more than this they will still be keeping up a special relationship between themselves and the national legislature. The power of dispensing justice is, from a political point of view, still a power to resist, at least indirectly, political excess of every kind by the collective bodies charged with the other functions of the executive power. A constant readiness to give the rope to the first official who takes it upon himself to execute an arbitrary order or tries to levy an illegal coin is worth as much as any act of direct resistance. Now for an act to be illegal or arbitrary and a genuine and punishable offence, it is enough for it to involve attacking a citizen in his real or personal property without the backing of the law. This ought to be enough to show how much of an interest the National Assembly will have in the zeal of the judges in carrying out their duties courageously.

The judicial body will be perfectly constituted only when the bonds between citizens have been simplified, only when the laws have been simplified and procedure improved. Then it will be time to choose that form deemed suitable for dispensing justice. Until then, the Estates-General will have taken an immense practical step forward by solemnly declaring where the true origin of the judicial power has to lie and as the nation's representative, by exercising its right to entrust this power to all the sovereign courts of the kingdom. Finally, that part of the public force responsible for executing court rulings and sentences can then be given a legal constitution without delay. This last point is highly important and we will return to it either in this work or another.

Beyond this great opportunity, which seems to have arisen all by itself, there are, in the plan of a complete and properly ordered executive power, parts that have either not yet been established in France or whose dispersed fragments do not amount to a proper system and that the ministry has neglected up to today. By this I mean public education, a powerful and essential means for promoting prosperity, liberty, improvement, and happiness.

In the order of great national needs, the empty space that is public education is far too obvious for the Estates-General not to hasten to attend to it efficaciously in one of its earliest sittings.(*) What I suggest here is that it should deal with this part of the active power with the intention of connecting it to the constitution. If this important branch of the administration, at which the ministry has barely bothered to throw an indifferent glance, were to come to owe its existence and constitution to a true legislator, then no more than a short lapse of time would be needed to create real men and a social state of a kind barely hinted at by centuries past, so that something which even the meditations of the philosopher might have foreseen as arising in no more than an indefinite future will become the shared inheritance of the generations who are our immediate posterity.

Despite their apparent activity, some of the other parts of the active establishment either were not designed for or are inadequate to their purpose. The rural police administration, the authentication of civil deeds, the management of public territory, the various other functions of a truly tutelary, enabling authority either have yet to be born or are still far removed from the proper state they ought to have reached among a civilized people. The ministerial administration has never paid serious attention to the public establishment as it should be properly understood. Taxes, the court, and war have been its sole preoccupations. It is undoubtedly high time, therefore, to consider public affairs with respect to the popular interest. From this perspective, it will be up to the Estates-General to establish a new system of administration, giving ministerial authority less and less to do with those national affairs which it deemed so unworthy of its views and interest.

Gradually it will be possible to see the various parts of the active constitution rising up on genuinely national foundations, independent of the sole power able to place obstacles before our liberty. That power itself will not always be foreign to constitutional order. Sooner or later it will be improved and, like every other part of the public establishment, will be guided towards the great goal of social union. Ah! If those who presently hold it as if it were a property could see their true interest, what would be their haste in calling, themselves, for a constitutional existence!

But we need to deal with what, above all else, ought to interest us at the present moment. The other branch of a public constitution is, as has been said, the *legislative* constitution. It is, in the order of the needs and rights of every political society, the first and most important of them all, and for France in particular at the present moment, it is still the sole means and sole guarantee of her restoration.

It has been proved that a national legislature can be exercised only by a body of representatives. This means that it is simply a matter of establishing a good system of *national* representation to get a good *legislative* constitution.

To begin with the basis of representation, the Estates-General will have recognized that it cannot be drawn from anywhere other than the total number of parishes. At this, I can already hear the sound of a dangerous opinion on municipal assemblies in the countryside.(*) These, it will be claimed, are incapable of undertaking the work required of them, and some, it would seem, would be only too pleased to find reasons to abolish them. But if the work looks as if it might be beyond them, then the fault lies with those who ordered it and, above all, with the way in which these municipalities were constituted. They need to be reformed and improved, not abolished. If you wreck the foundations of a building, how will it be able to stand up? Instead of a popular mandate, you will never have anything more than a chain of ministerial proclamations hanging down from a single individual's will, however many provincial assemblies, regional estates, or affiliated bodies you assume there will be and however much you might bring their forms nearer to that of a proper representation, unless the whole representative edifice is the unobstructed work of parish-based elections.

It is to be supposed, therefore, that the Estates-General will indicate to all the parishes what it takes to be the most suitable *form* for holding an assembly that it will be right to call *fundamental.* Definitions, according to age and tax payments, of the conditions that will have to be met to be an *elector* and to be *eligible* for election will have been made. It will also have been borne in mind that a citizen cannot have any influence in the legislative side of the constitution for as long as he plays any part in the active or executive side of the constitution. Finally, the *municipal bureau,* elected to manage the internal affairs of the parish, will have been given a clear idea of the extent and limits of its functions.

It is well known that there will be a larger or smaller number of *degrees* of representation according to whether the nation is more or less populous. In a community made up of a small number of citizens, they themselves will be able to form the legislative assembly. Here, there will be no representation, but the thing itself.

If we suppose a confederation of fifty to a hundred parishes, their common legislature could be taken to form a first level of representation, because the parishes would nominate deputies and their meeting would be the country's legislative body.

If, instead of a hundred parishes, we were to suppose two thousand, the legislative body could exist only at a second level of representation, meaning that the parish deputies, instead of meeting to decide upon common affairs, would have a mandate only to nominate legislative representatives and to give them such advice as they deem to be suitable. In this case, the parish deputies will meet in electoral circumscriptions (*arrondissements*) each made up of about forty parishes or so, so that fifty circumscriptions of that size, covering the total number of parishes, would then nominate the legislative deputation.

If we increase the number of parishes up to 40,000, we will need to increase legislative representation of the initial primary constituencies by only one extra level. If the parish deputies were to assemble in circumscriptions of twenty parishes, and if forty circumscriptions of that size were to form a province, and if fifty provinces encompassing the total number of parishes were to elect the national legislature, then it would stand at a third level of representation.

We recommend that this number of levels of representation should never be exceeded. Every legislature has a continuous need to be refreshed by the democratic spirit. It should not therefore be placed at too great a distance from its primary constituents. Representation is made for those it represents. It is important therefore to ensure that with a large number of intermediaries, the general will does not get lost in harmful aristocratism.

We have just referred to *territorial* divisions in talking about the levels of representation. We have already had occasion to say something about the *dependence* of deputies on their constituents. As for the duration of a deputation, sound politics indicate that it should be limited to three years and that no one should be eligible for reelection until after an interval of three years in the first instance and six years for any subsequent term, in other words, after the passage of time has increased the number of enlightened citizens, since public affairs, in the sense used here, ought to be the business of as many people as possible, and it is especially important to ensure that a small number of families cannot either control a deputation or acquire legislative influence. In this way a third of the membership of the assemblies will be renewed at a time. The most senior third will have been in office for two years, the second third for a year, and the new third will be able to take advantage of the experience of its more senior colleagues and, in turn, be of service to them by making them more aware of more recent popular wishes and desires.

I would not be keeping faith with the plan of this work if I were to allow myself to give further development to all these questions. It is time to finish off this simple indication of the main points that apply to a representative constitution. The *proportion* that parishes of different sizes, fertility, population, wealth, and tax contributions should have in nominating deputations to the assemblies representing a number of parishes will be very difficult to decide. That proportion has to be based not only on general and easily verifiable characteristics but also on characteristics that will make it possible to vary the relationships determining the number of deputies as and when circumstances cause changes in their terms, without needing to have continuous recourse to a particular decision by the legislature. This is a subject that deserves a separate work.

Since in a great political body a national deputation represents what an individual will is to any individual, it should go without saying that it would be absurd to ask for how long the Estates-General should be convoked. How easy is it to go wrong by relying on ancient prejudice to study any sort of subject instead of its nature! Forget idle French chatter and so-called English profundity. Could anyone with any sense ever imagine that it might be the mark of the highest wisdom only to allow a man the use of his will and intelligence at intervals, as if a brain is *intermittent*? Would anyone even dare to claim that an individual ought to be able to do without exercising his moral faculties, despite the most urgent necessity, simply because someone strongly subject to a very contrary interest will not give him permission?

The legislative body must be no less *permanent* than the active bodies. A legislator is made for giving life, movement, and direction to everything connected to public affairs. It is up to the legislature to watch over the common needs of the society and to meet them faithfully, surely, and fully. It is up to it to assess the exigencies of current affairs and decide how much time it can give to its *vacation*. It is up to it to decide when to *adjourn* until its annual reopening, to foresee circumstances when it might find it necessary to resume its sittings before the agreed term, and to decide in advance on the manner by which it will notify every deputy. By means of such simple arrangements, your legislature will not have to offer the strange sight of a body that periodically dies, only to be resuscitated again when it pleases an interest different from its own to restore it to life.

The costs of a general assembly are no obstacle to its permanence. It is enough to allow its members not to receive a salary or an indemnity to reduce these costs to a trifling sum. Each province, moreover, can be left to provide for the costs of its own deputies. It is up to electors to make such arrangements as they please with those bearing their mandates.

Any other plan than one involving a permanent legislative body will have unending difficulties and dangers. Suppose that you were to agree to have an *interim committee* made up of a small number of members elected by the Estates-General itself and charged with reporting to a future general assembly. I, in my turn, might then ask whether it might not be possible (1) for a small number of committee members to be won over by the ministry, and (2) whether that committee, far from guaranteeing the future return of the Estates-General, might not rather be the best resource that you could ever give to the ministry to get rid of it for ever.

Why be afraid, it will be said, that the Estates-General will not be reconvened at fixed periods of time? If it has granted a subsidy for no more than a fixed period, then is it not certain that it will have to be called back?

I would not deny that after five or six sessions this would be the case. By then, a representative assembly in France would be as much a part of the necessary and habitual cycle of events as it is in England and would be protected so strongly by manners and public opinion that the ministry would no longer be able to dispense with recalling it when the term fixed for raising a tax had expired. But allow me not yet to believe in the certainty of any periodic recall. In France, faith in absolute authority is still the prevailing social belief, and one initial session of the Estates-General will not be enough to make spirits imbibe the need for a national assembly outside times of great disorder in the public finances. The ministry will need only to avoid the enormous depredations responsible for bringing about the present situation to have nothing more to fear. If, to your great satisfaction, it were to establish an interim committee, it would then be able—as has been pointed out—to use that same instrument to start raising *provisional* taxes. Doubtless it would not neglect to acknowledge and to proclaim loudly that such taxes would be no more than provisional or were simply a prorogation of existing taxes and that the pressure of events—and events can be arranged—had made it impossible to consult the nation. The most formal promises would be made to convoke the nation at the earliest opportunity, but both the promise and the provisional nature of the tax could still last for a hundred years. In the meantime, a thousand and one different ways will be used to change the course of public opinion. Writers and journalists, the pulpit and the theatre, favors, privileges, and exemplary punishments would all be put to use, and they would be enough to bind anew an already docile nation to the yoke. Or suppose, on the other hand—and it is entirely possible—that raising public revenue continued to be called raising the *royal* revenue and that it was carried out by *royal* officers, under *royal* agents, acting for the *royal* treasury. How much hope of resistance can you expect to see from a taxpayer who, at the end of the term fixed by the Estates-General, will not be able to notice any change in the ordinary course of affairs and will still see the same tax collectors, the same formalities, and the same tax burden. He will carry on paying as he did before, and the nation will revert to, or remain, what it was.

These thoughts bring us back naturally to the project of riveting taxation to the constitution and the constitution to taxation.

A Constitutional Law of Taxation

It being supposed that all the parts of the national representation have been established and are fully active,[2] a vote of subsidy should be made on the following conditions and in the following form:

1. It will be for only one year.
2. The annual allocation of the amounts to be paid by each province cannot be made by any other body than the Estates-General itself.
3. The second level of allocating the amounts to be paid by the districts or arrondissements will be the work of the provincial assemblies.
4. The third level of allocating the amounts to be paid by each parish will be the work of their representatives assembled into districts or arrondissements.
5. The final level of allocating the amounts to be paid by individual property owners or citizens will be made by the parish assembly.
6. All those parts of taxation that cannot be allocated in this way cannot be administered or farmed out by anyone other than by the Estates-General itself if it cannot devise a way of administering them, or by the lower assemblies if the Estates-General is able to entrust them with separate local management.
7. Collection of public revenue, regulations concerning it, and generally everything pertaining to it will be the responsibility of the representative assemblies alone.
8. According to a general allocatory law, parish revenue will be divided into local revenue, which will remain at the disposal of the parish, and national revenue, which will be transferred upwardly from the treasuries of the arrondissements to those of the provinces and thence to the great national treasury.
9. Beforehand, all administrative posts and all payments made by the lower divisions will be carried out under the direction of the appropriate assembly subject to the decisions of the Estates-General as the supreme regulator.

---

[2] If it had been possible to redraft the plan of this work in time, it might perhaps have been possible not to limit its considerations to the *executive means* and to leave more room, not for the principal *objects of deliberation* in general, but at least for the one which we take to be the true foundation of everything worth doing in a political society. But we dare to believe that the *legislative constitution*, which is that fundamental object, will be sufficiently apparent to an attentive reader both in the preceding considerations and in those that now follow.

10. All the parts of general expenditure regulated by the Estates-General will be carried out by the national treasury or by lower treasuries for the account of the national treasury, always under the orders of the National Assembly.
11. Public revenue, being no more than the nation's revenue, will belong to it at every level at which it may circulate, to the point of final payment. Until that moment, it can neither be withheld from inspection nor be subject to the control exercised by the representative assemblies.
12. Finally, all agents and officials involved in public finance will, without distinction, be chosen by and subject to the orders of these same assemblies, etc., etc.

The advantage of being able to do without financiers is not what should strike us the most about this project. The motivation underlying this work is of a different order. It is about being able to be sure—yes or no—of a free constitution for France. People cannot guarantee to themselves a sure enjoyment of their rights with charters and ancient recognizances. This kind of guarantee lies where there is force. With power there is no need for charters. And one still has nothing, even with the most detailed and authenticated charter, if one does not have power. Just as despotism does not consist exactly in governing badly but in *being able* to govern badly, so political liberty does not belong to a people simply because it is able to enjoy all its rights on the basis of a promise by someone else but because it has the power not to lose them.

I do not understand how nations, after so many harsh lessons inculcating incredulity, can still be willing to trust in the promises of their leaders and, proud of having been granted a signed recognizance or a ridiculous oath, calmly offer up the power to break them as soon as it suits their masters.

People need no more than to be able to enjoy their rights. It cannot be supposed that they will want to usurp the functions of those they have mandated, because those functions themselves form part of their rights and were entrusted by them only so that they were able to enjoy those same rights. But those who have been mandated may well form an interest apart and may well then tend ceaselessly towards usurping the rights of citizens. It is therefore entirely impolitic to confer any kind of power upon those exercising a mandate rather than keeping it under the nation's continued control.

Among modern peoples there are only two patently constant kinds of power: money and the army. It has just been shown how the first of these powers can be merged with and, so to speak, made to be identified with the nation so that it can never serve anything other than the general interest. By way of the constitutional law on taxation, representation will be solid and durable. Is it possible to doubt this when it is so disposed that no collective body, no power, will be able to attack even its smallest part without, in an instant, causing everything to start collapsing all around it?

It is equally possible to constitute military force in such a way that it can never become a threat to the body of citizens, and it has to be the case that the means to do so lie in the nature of things. Unless it does, it would be necessary to give up on the object of a political union, and the social order would be no more than a chimera. But this object will be dealt with elsewhere, and it is better here to keep to our plan. It is enough to have shown that the forthcoming Estates-General is able to give us a national representation that will bear all the characteristics of having a genuinely popular mandate and a legislature that will always express the general will, and to have further proved that it will be up to it to endow this great work with a solidity enabling it to rise above any event. On this unshakeable foundation, it will then be possible to see the gradual elevation of the edifice of a human society designed at last for the utility and well-being of the members who compose it.

This brings to an end the task that we set ourselves in beginning this work or, rather, this memorandum. Like so many other citizens distinguished by a desire to be free, our thoughts turned towards the Estates-General, to the force of circumstance, to the obvious necessity to give the nation a solid guarantee against a return to the disorder to which she has presently fallen victim. Like everyone else, we thought that a national assembly could do a great deal of good. Like a much smaller number, we also thought that there could not be any solid guarantee against even a half- or a quarter-measure of public disorder, because every evil that has not been reformed will come to serve as a counter-guarantee against any good that that might be done. We came to think, therefore, that there could not be any good laws or any good institutions if they remain at the mercy of an unlimited power that is different from the power of the nation.

Turning next to the means which might possibly produce some good, we then asked whether it would be possible to draw any real benefit from scattered views that could not be made to form a unified whole. According to the point of view adopted here, it is wrong to imagine that doing a little good today, a little good tomorrow, and a bit more later on will bring us nearer towards the establishment of good order in the long term. Nothing can be done by considering a system in the light of only one of its parts. What you establish on one side, you will destroy on the other. Today, you may take a couple of steps towards some useful goal, but tomorrow you will have to start out again in a different direction. This is how laws, declarations, etc. begin to mount up. A thousand times more ground comes to be covered than is ever actually needed to get to the end of the road. And all that effort is a pure waste, because it is impossible to assume that a fluctuating ministry will ever be able to inject any consistency either into its views or into its sentiments.

It is instead necessary to take legislative operations as a whole. Doubtless everything cannot be reformed or restored at once. But within a general system of what makes for a proper and rightful order, one ought to be able to identify its most fundamental part and begin with it. On the road leading towards the right destination it should be possible to identify in advance a number of staging posts and move towards them by covering the distance between them in one whole stride rather than by taking small, hesitant steps immediately followed by several others in the opposite direction, thus making it possible to avoid the disagreeable need to retrace one's steps either because some measures were taken only by half or because they were not linked together by a general concordance.

Armed with these ideas, we then set out to show what the forthcoming Estates-General could do to be useful to the nation in a solid and permanent way, by turning first to what is most urgent and of most interest to people. A *constitution* has become a kind of rallying cry for the twenty-five million men who make up the kingdom. A constitution, therefore, is what they will have to have. Of equal force is the need to prevent any eventual return of the kind of disorder that has been displayed in the finances. There has, therefore, to be an acceptance of the simple, natural, effective principle that the public treasury should be in the hands of those who pay and not at the disposal of those who spend.

We have assumed that the Estates-General will not fail to follow what has been dictated so clearly both by national need and by the general will of its electorate. We then turned, in particular, to deal with how to combine the executive means. As my eyes began to see the possibility of regenerating France in a stable manner, without using any other means than those which the forthcoming Estates-General will have freely at its disposal, I opened my heart to a great hope and felt the joy of seeing our country at the moment when it will be born in freedom.

Further Developments on the Subject of a Bankruptcy, Related to Page 23 (Page 24 of this Edition)

Question One: Is the Nation the Debtor?

First of all, there has to be a reply to those aiming to profit from principles recently proclaimed about taxes and loans, who have argued that the nation cannot have any obligation towards those who lent their funds because, they say, no one asked it to give its consent to any of the loans floated by the king.

It is certainly the case that taxes, loans, civil and political laws, and, in general, everything pertaining to the legislature should not emanate from any part of the executive power. But if this is so, tell me how, in return, in the absence of the Estates-General, the nation could have gone about raising taxes or loans when public needs required them or how it could have made laws of any kind when circumstances seemed to call for them? Did the nation have any other representative to fulfil the functions of its legislature than the king himself, subject only to the formalities of registration by the Parlements? We are only too aware that this is not genuine representation, because the term itself necessarily includes the idea of a free election by those who are represented; but who, before the present time, set out to proclaim the eternal truth of those great principles? Did the Estates-General itself, in 1614, or any of its predecessors, display any awareness of its rights? Did it make them known to the people; did it show any inclination towards exercising them freely? No. Up to now, the only representative of the nation seems to have been the king. Everything that might have been done by a collective body of genuine representatives was done by the king. Almost all the laws by virtue of which the acquisition of property, the transmission of inherited goods, and, in general, every relationship between persons and things has come to be decided originated with kings, and it is certain that they did not always ask for the nation's consent before making them. Thus if you want to revise the past, if it is really necessary to break engagements made in the name of the state, if you want to remove the legal sanction guaranteeing transactions between individuals, if you want to reform and nullify everything that was not established by the true legislator, then you will have to resolve to overturn everything and bring down upon France the chaos that preceded the formation of the universe. The twenty-five million people who make up the kingdom will turn into so many isolated individuals, unsure of their title to their possessions and almost reduced to natural right. The same will apply to taxes that, up to now, have been paid. Not having been given any proper legal sanction, every taxpayer will have a right to object to them or to take back what could have been extorted only by force.

You may prefer not to accept all these consequences. But it will then be necessary to draw a line of demarcation between the past and the future. Everything that up to now has been issued by the only representative that the nation seems to have had will have to be ratified on condition that everything in the future will be done differently. It is for the future alone that it is important to establish true principle. *Communis error facit jus* ("shared error makes law") will suffice for the past. Error has now been dissipated. Since the nation has to exercise its legislative power itself, it can now be stated that starting from this moment no engagement made in its name will be valid unless it is contracted by the nation itself.

If there had been two ways of borrowing money when the nation needed funds and sought financial support from anyone with capital, and if it had then been possible to see an unlimited pledge of the national faith coming from the nation on one side and the king on the other, there would not have been a moment's hesitation about which borrower to choose. But in the absence of true representatives, there was only the king. There was only the king to be seen, and his title to do so was not entirely unblemished. If his invitation was a trap, what tutelary law could offer citizens a guarantee? The magistrates of the Parlements, accustomed to speaking in the name of people and the law, ought to have been able to warn those lending funds of the danger that, under the appearance of legality, they were falling into, or else their conduct would have had the character of culpable connivance. Everything would then have been combined to entrap and bring good faith towards the precipice. Since an assumption of that kind cannot be allowed, there has to be a different conclusion, namely that one can decide to follow a better system in the future without having to fall into the absurdity of going back to the very establishment of the monarchy, abolishing and overturning everything on the way, and assuming that we have absolutely no positive law. But private contracts cannot be separated from public contracts. The same tutelary law presided over them both. Someone, for example, who had bought a plot of land sold under the terms of a ruling by the Châtelet would have no more of a right to be maintained in possession of his property than would the purchaser of an annuity sold under the authority of an edict registered by the Parlement.

Second Question: Can the Debt Be Considered Usurious?

Since it is not possible to deny the legality of the national debt in terms of its origin, attempts have also been made, in the light of the maneuvers often involved in its formation, to claim that it must, at least in part, be usurious. And, it is then said, it is always permissible to revise a usurious engagement.

I am not sure where this kind of talk is supposed to lead. Is the aim to return the capital to the lender? But, it is said, the capital sums supplied are not always what they seem to be. Most recently, for example, public effects have lost up to thirty percent of their nominal value. Does this mean that those who have bought them have made a usurious profit? No. The public funds are like every other income-producing asset whose price goes up or down according to circumstances. If they are bought above par, the purchaser does not demand compensation from the government. By the same token, if he buys them below par, he does not owe the government anything. If the purchaser's profit was huge and he was required sooner or later to pay a supplementary price, it would not be the ministry that would be entitled to have a right to it. It would not have lost anything. It would be to the unfortunate seller that reimbursement should be made. His loss in selling his paper at thirty percent below par was the work of the ministry. It would be extraordinary then to give it a title, based on the disorder it had introduced into the public finances, to an indemnity that it ought rather to owe to the unhappy victims of its operations.

Agreed, it might be said. There is no need to bother with relations between individuals dealing on the bourse. But may not usury sometimes be found in dealings between the king and subscribers to a loan? No. Under no circumstances. Every legal public loan was floated by way of a law registered by the Parlement. Its rate of interest was fixed. If the law itself has set the rate of interest, it cannot be usurious. If the amount of paper issued was extended beyond a specified amount, this was an abuse of the most criminal kind, but the lender was never in a position to be able to distinguish between the extension and the loan itself.

The abuse that you hold to be usury was not a product of the public relationship between the state and its creditors. It grew up out of the ill-judged arrangements adopted by a ministry that, to maintain the nominal price of the paper it issued, offered brokers substantial discounts. We should not mix up the rate of interest with the surtax, or commission, granted to financiers to make a loan succeed. These onerous and private side-conditions have to be assigned to the class of ministerial depredations and wild expenditure. It was, literally, doing bad business. Would you like to restore to the royal treasury everything that all this dissipation could have cost the state? So would I. But who would you ask? Obviously all those who in hundreds of ways ran down cash reserves, or the brokers of public loans—very different kinds of individuals from the ultimate lenders, the real lenders, whose only intention was to acquire a fixed and stable annuity. But of what might these latter be guilty? And if some of them actually were, how would you find an expedient able to single them out from the immense mass of innocent annuitants?

The highway robbery perpetrated by speculators on the funds offends me as much as it offends you. But pay attention to the fact that they are still no more than intermediaries between the king and the annuitants.

Speculators buy in order to sell and sell in order to buy. They scarcely consume this kind of merchandise at all, meaning they do not acquire it to keep and to enjoy. They speculate on prevailing rates in the light of whether the state of the finances is good or bad. They make a profit out of the needs of forced sellers, and it has just been pointed out that their gains are not a lesion affecting the government but a wrong done by the government affecting the owners of royal paper, who are forced to find additional funds to meet their usual financial requirements. The immoral activities of speculators have nothing to do with the present question. To reform speculation, or rather to keep it within the bounds of trade in general, there is absolutely no need to dishonor the nation and ruin those of the state's creditors who do not speculate. All that is needed is to maintain good order in the public finances and to keep that order under constant public view.

Third Question: Who Will Have to Shoulder the Burden of the Debt?

Doubtless it should not be surprising that blind egoism, always fecund in unjust talk, has suggested that what is at issue here is at bottom no more than a combat between the landowners and the capitalists. Faced, it is said, with the unhappy alternative of having to strike a blow against either the one or the other, a bankruptcy that fell upon no more than a small number would surely be preferable to an additional impost affecting the generality of citizens.

To this, the reply has to be

1. that there are many more annuitants now than there were twenty years ago;
2. that an immense mass of citizens belonging to the toiling classes are accustomed to receiving from the outlay of the capitalists their entitlement to what they need for subsistence—the wages of their labor—and that these relationships cannot be subject to sudden change without the most appalling disadvantages;
3. that a chain of private bankruptcies will bring misery and terror even to families who believe themselves to be furthest removed from the common misfortune and the least exposed to its effects;
4. that draining capital from the hands of the annuitants will dry up the source of a multitude of commercial ventures and inflict sterility upon most of the manufacturing and other productive enterprises that they support and promote;

5. that it would be a very strange reversal of ideas to have the gall to transform the public debt into a subject of conflict between the landowners and the capitalists—as if all that a debtor wanting to be rid of a burden of this kind needed to do was to treat his creditor as his enemy.

It would better, you say, to ruin a hundred thousand men than twenty five million. But whatever the proportions might be, I would first reply that a burden capable of crushing a hundred thousand men could be born more easily by twenty five million. Above all, however, I would reply that it is in the nature of things for a debt to be the responsibility of the debtor and not the creditor. Someone who lends money has deprived himself of its use. By selling its use to you at a rate of interest, he has supplied your needs, while you, the borrower, have avoided having to go short and, by purchasing the use of the capital, have put yourself under an obligation to pay an annuity for its use. Did you, in borrowing the money, ever think that one day all you would need to do to be rid of the cost would be to weigh up how much of a burden it would be to you or your creditor? There is talk of ruining the state's creditors, as if it is the case that the nation ought to hold them to account for the new taxes with which it believes it has been threatened. Why not rather attack the unprecedented level of depredation and the abuses of every kind that swelled the state of expenditure? These were certainly not the work of those who entrusted their money to the royal treasury, but those who pillaged it. It has to be said again that if a debt is to be a burden for anyone, it is just that it should be a burden for the one who owes, not for the one who is owed.

It is a strange sight, one that gives much pause for thought, to see in the unhappy state of the public the creditors of the state on the one side, fearful for their fortunes and for their very existence, and on the other the mass of taxpayers, fearful of a ruinous surcharge, both trembling like criminals facing the death penalty; and then to see the ministry, the sole cause of all the disorder, calmly looking on as a spectator to the debate, waiting impassively, without the slightest qualm of doubt, either to be granted a new impost or to be authorized to carry out a bankruptcy! Can anything more revolting be conceived?

Fourth Question: Neither a Bankruptcy nor a New Impost

There seems to be a will to make it a necessity to choose one or other of these two options. But this is to confuse the imperious law of necessity with both want of courage and lack of the energy needed to give up a thousand costly habits as well as with a failure of good sense or morality, making the most simple rules of natural enlightenment seem unfamiliar and foreign. How can anyone be allowed to say that a people currently paying six hundred million ought to pay more? Even if half of that sum, huge as it is, was needed to cover the debt and a new plan for repaying it, who, with a freestanding tax revenue of three hundred million, could dare to call for new subsidies? Are there any other states with so large a revenue? Is it the case that other states simply neglect the upkeep of all the parts of their public establishments? The emperor has more extensive territories under his domination, and because of their absence of unity they are more difficult to manage. His military establishment is infinitely larger than yours, and yet in terms of ordinary subsidies, including the public debt, he does not have a fortune equal in size to the sum you have at your free disposal.

It has to be said to the ignorant or cowardly councilors of the French government that it is time to give up functions that are beyond your strength. You cannot, you claim, cover all expenditure. But what does your expenditure matter if it is too much, or irrelevant, or even harmful to what ought to be necessary for the public? It is only too true that there is no end to that expenditure in sight. Ah! What kind of treasury could ever suffice for so many depredations, for so much neglect, for that multitude of ridiculous or pointless posts? Pointless! Yes, yours was the privilege of creating posts of such a kind. Can there ever be any treasury able to satisfy the insatiable avarice of that highborn mendicancy that has laid siege to and that prides itself in honoring the throne? Yet you can still talk about raising new taxes! No. They have reached the highest point they can go. The nation cannot and must not make any further sacrifice.

The needs of an empire, like those of private individuals, do not amount to much if one takes the trouble to examine nature and the laws of a wise economy. Our representatives will know how to take a useful lesson from them. They will learn that to restore order to the finances, there can be no question of surcharging the people but, instead, of freeing them from abuse. And if these are the options, can it be difficult to make the choice? They will be sure to feel the worth of that particular truth and will be convinced of the people's great interest in ensuring that the Estates-General bases public expenditure solely upon real public needs and fixes all the parts to which that expenditure will be put. In this way, the court will no longer be able to use a surplus that it does not have the power to use, or to use an ordinary income which henceforth will be diverted no longer from its proper destination to subsidize the tools of its pleasures, its power, and our servility. It is still possible to talk about increasing the public revenue at the ministry's request without seeing that its financial embarrassment has opened a door for us to have a constitution and that the limits to which the ministry will be confined are, precisely, the preconditions of our liberty.

If peoples' tax payments ever do produce a surplus, there can be no doubt that it would still be better to lavish it thoughtlessly upon the most useless citizens than to leave it at the disposal of a ministry which was taken off its leash. Even if it is to be supposed that a foreign treasury might be willing to offer to pay for every sort of caprice entirely freely, it would still be the duty of the Estates-General to prevent it from doing so, because one way or another every abuse comes to find its victim and every disorder comes, ultimately, to smite the nation.

AN ESSAY ON PRIVILEGES

Sieyès' Essai sur les privilèges *was published in November 1788 and reprinted with additions in 1789. This translation is based on the contemporary English translation of that later edition, published as* An Essay on Privileges and particularly on Hereditary Nobility written by the Abbé Sieyès, a Member of the National Assembly; and Translated into English, with Notes by a Foreign Nobleman now in England *(London, 1791). That contemporary translation contains some minor inaccuracies that have been silently corrected, but the vividness of many of the eighteenth-century terms used by the translator is still striking. I have also restored both the arrangement of the original French paragraphs and the italicized words or passages of the original. The punctuation and spelling of the translation have been modernized, and a sentence attacking Edmund Burke's* Reflections on the French Revolution *of 1790 (not, unsurprisingly, to be found in Sieyès' own pamphlet) has been omitted. As the unwarranted subtitle of the eighteenth-century translation suggests, the translator tended to use the word "nobility" as an English equivalent of Sieyès' word* privilégiés. *I have reinstated "the privileged orders," "the privileged," or "the privileged class" as more in keeping with the original French, unless it was obvious that Sieyès was actually referring to nobles or the nobility.*

An Essay on Privileges

Privilege has been defined to be "*a dispensation or exemption in favour of him who possesses it and a discouragement to those who do not.*"(*) If this then be the case, it must be allowed that privileges are a very poor invention indeed! Imagine a society the happiest and best calculated that can be devised. Can anything be more evident than that to destroy this society, nothing more would be necessary than to exempt one party from the proper duties of society and to burden and discourage the others?

I could have wished to examine privileges according to their origin, their nature, and their effects, but this arrangement, methodical as it is, would have reduced me to the necessity of recurring too frequently to the same ideas. But independent of this inconvenience, an examination of their origin would have involved me in a tiresome and endless detail of facts and precedents. What is there indeed so absurd as not to be supported by facts and precedents in the manner they are sometimes applied? I would rather, then, at once allow the purest possible origin to exclusive privileges, if that would satisfy their admirers. And, in reality, what can they desire more?

Every privilege, without distinction, has certainly for its object, the *dispensing* with the law of the land; or the giving an *exclusive right* to something that is not prohibited by the law. It is the essence, the characteristic, of privilege to place the possessor of it beyond the boundaries of common right, and it is only in one of these two modes that this can be effected. In placing the subject in this double point of view, it must be allowed that all privileges whatever will be equally involved in the decision which will result from our present enquiry.

In the first place, let us only ask, what is the object of the laws? It is doubtless to preserve the liberty and property of every individual from assault and violence. Laws are not made merely for the amusement of making them. Those which have no effect but to harass the citizens, or to abridge them of their liberty would be diametrically opposed to the ends of civil society and ought to be abolished.

There is one *supreme* law which ought to be the parent of all others, and that is, *"Do wrong to no man."* It is this great natural law which the legislature distributes, as it were, piecemeal in applying the principle case by case to the various private orders in society. All patriotic laws derive from that source. Those which prevent injury from being done to any person are good; those which neither directly nor indirectly contribute to this end, even if they did not manifest a malignant intention, are bad, because, in the first place, they are so many needless restraints upon liberty and, in the next, they occupy the place of good laws.

Beyond the limits of the law all is free. Everything belongs to every man, except what is assigned to any individual by the law.

Such, however, is the deplorable effect of long servitude on the human mind that the people of every nation, far from knowing their real value in the scale of society, far from feeling that they have even the right of repealing bad laws, are induced to suppose that nothing is their own, except what the laws, good or bad, condescend to grant them. They seem to be ignorant that liberty and property are paramount to every thing else, that men in uniting themselves in society, could have no other view, but that of placing their rights under a permanent safeguard against the enterprises of bad men, and of indulging themselves in the mean time under the shelter of this protection in the full exercise of their physical and moral qualities, more extended by these means, more energetic and more abundant in the fruition. They seem ignorant that their property, thus increased, with all the additions which a new spirit of industry has been able to accumulate in a social state, is in reality their own, and could never be considered as the gift of an extrinsic power; that the tutelary authority is established by themselves, not to give them what is their own, but to protect it; and in fine, that every citizen has an inviolable right not only to all which the laws permit, but to all which they do not prohibit.

By means of these elementary principles, we are already enabled to form some judgment with respect to privileges. Those whose object is to exempt them from the law cannot be defended. Every law, as we have already observed, expressly says, "Do wrong to no man." Where then any class of citizens enjoys an exemption from any particular law, it is directly saying to those citizens, "You are permitted to do wrong." There is no power on earth which should be authorised to make such a concession. If a law is good it ought to bind every individual; if bad it ought to be abolished. It is an assault upon liberty.

Upon the same principles it cannot be just to grant any person an exclusive right to any thing which is not prohibited by law. This would evidently be plundering other citizens of their right. All which is not prohibited by law, as we have already remarked, is a part of the domain of civil liberty and is free to the whole community. The grant of any exclusive privilege to any person with respect to that which belongs to all would be to wrong the whole community for the sake of an individual; which is an idea at once the most unjust and the most absurd.

All privileges, then, from the very nature of things, are unjust, odious, and contrary to the supreme end of every political society.

Honorary privileges cannot be exempted from the general proscription, because they fall immediately under the definition which we have just stated, that of giving an exclusive right to something which is not forbidden by the law, without taking into the account besides, that under the deceitful title of honorary there is scarcely a place of profit which these honorary privileges do not invade. But, as there are even found amongst men of good sense many who declare themselves in favour of this species of privilege, or who are, at least, disposed to think that they are entitled to some indulgence, it will be necessary to examine whether in reality these privileges are more excuseable than others.

For my own part, I freely acknowledge that I find this species of privilege a vice beyond the rest, and that vice seems to me enormous. It is that they tend to degrade the great body of citizens. And certainly to debase the mind of man is not to be considered as a slight injury. Can it be conceived that a nation could ever consent to humble, in this manner, 25,850,000 inhabitants for the sake of ridiculously complimenting 200,000? Can the most artful sophist point out, in a combination so anti-social, a single circumstance which contributes to the general interest?

The most favourable claim for a concession to an honorary privilege would be that of having rendered some peculiar services to our country, that is, to the nation, which can be no other than the generality of the citizens. In such an instance, let that member who has deserved well of the whole community be rewarded; but let the absurd folly be avoided of humbling the whole community to one of its members. The entire body of citizens is the principal object. It is that which is served. Ought it then in any sense to be sacrificed to a servant who is only entitled to a reward for having rendered it a service?

So palpable a contradiction ought to have been more generally felt, and yet our conclusion will probably appear novel, or at least singular, since there exists among us an inveterate superstition which repels the beams of reason, and is even offended at a doubt. Some savage tribes are delighted with ridiculous deformities and render them that homage which ought to be the prize only of natural beauty. Amongst the northern nations, political excrescences much more deformed, and still more noxious (as they undermine the foundation and dissolve the fabric of society), are worshipped with the most prodigal respect. But this superstition is passing away and the body which it has long degraded is emerging in all its native strength and beauty.

It may perhaps be objected, would you then refuse to reward services rendered to the common wealth? No, far from it. But I would not make the rewards of a nation consist in any thing which is unjust, or humiliating. We must not recompense one person at the expense of another and especially at that of almost all the rest. Let us not confound two things so entirely different as privileges and rewards.

Are we speaking of ordinary services? To requite such, there are ordinary salaries or gratifications of the same nature. If a brilliant action or an important service is performed, let it be followed by a rapid advancement in the service or a distinguished employment in proportion to the talents and services of the person; or, if necessary, let a pension be added. But this last ought to be recurred to in very few cases and under certain circumstances only, such as old age, wounds, etc., when the other means of reward may not be found adequate.

But this, it will be said, is not enough. We must also have obvious distinctions; we must attract the eye and catch the attention of the public.

For my own part I must answer that the services themselves, which are rendered to the community and to mankind, constitute the most lasting distinction; and that the public regard and attention will always follow where this kind of merit is found to exist.

Leave it to the public then freely to dispense the marks of its esteem. For when, with a philosophic eye, you regard this esteem as a species of moral coin, potent in its effects, you are right; but when you wish that the solid distribution of it should be vested in the prince, you then contradict your own principles. Nature, a better philosopher than you, has placed the real source of respect in the hearts and feelings of the people. It is among the people only that real wants exist. *There* is the country; *there* men of superior abilities are called to consecrate their talents; there ought of consequence the treasury to be placed, whence the recompense should be drawn to which they aspire.

Blind chance and bad laws which are blinder still have conspired against the multitude. They have been disinherited, deprived of every thing. They have nothing left but the power of honouring with their esteem those who have rendered themselves worthy of it. They have no other means left of exciting the emulation of men worthy of serving them. Will you rob them then of this last valuable possession, this last reserve, and in doing this, render their most peculiar property of no use to their happiness?

The generality of statesmen having ruined and degraded the great body of the citizens, have accustomed themselves to neglect them. They scorn and despise, almost deservedly, a people who can never become despicable but by their own fault; and if they give themselves any concern about them, it is only to punish their crimes. Their resentment flows in torrents upon the people. It is only for the privileged class that they reserve their affections. But even in that class, virtue and genius, the dictate of nature, a secret voice continually and internally speaks to the pure and energetic spirits in favour of the weak. Yes, the sacred necessities of the people will be perpetually the object of meditation to the independent philosopher; the point to which, publicly or secretly, the virtuous citizen will direct his whole attention, to which he will sacrifice every selfish view. The poor repay their benefactors only with blessings; but those rewards how superior to all the favours of power! Ah, leave the reward of public esteem to flow freely from the bosom of the nation! Leave them to discharge their debt to genius and virtue. Let us guard from violation the sublime principles of humanity which nature has been attentive to imprint in the bottom of our hearts. Let us applaud this admirable commerce of benefits and respect, which she has established for the consolation of human kind, between the wants of the grateful and the great, abundantly repaid for all their services by a simple tribute of gratitude. In this amiable interchange all is pure, fruitful in virtuous actions, powerful in goodness as long as it runs uninterrupted in its natural channel.

But if the Court seizes upon it, it can then only regard the public esteem as an adulterated coin, debased by the alloy of a shameful monopoly. From the abuse which is instantly made of it, the most audacious immorality proceeds and in its impetuosity overflows on every class of citizen. The ensigns of distinction are bestowed unworthily, and they confuse and distract the sentiment. This sentiment, indeed, becomes completely corrupted by the alliance into which it is forced. For how is it possible that it should escape the poison of those vices with which it becomes commonly connected? Amongst the small number of enlightened people, this sentiment of esteem and respect retires to the bottom of the heart, indignant at the disgraceful character which it is required to assume. There is but one species of real esteem, and yet its language, its character, its appearance are still employed in society for the purpose of prostituting false public honours to court sycophants, to favourites, and but too often to the most flagitious of mankind.

In this disorder of manners, genius is persecuted and virtue is turned into ridicule; and, on the other hand, a heap of ensigns, ribbands, decorations, strangely figured, imperiously command respect and homage to be paid to mediocrity, to meanness, and even to crimes. How is it possible that dignities conferred in this manner should not extinguish the sparks of real honour, corrupt the public opinion, and degrade the mind?

In vain would you pretend that being virtuous yourself, you will never confound the artful quack or the profligate courtier with the good servant that prefers just claims to public rewards. Experience in this respect evinces your numerous errors. And after all you must confess that those whom you have enrolled in your parchment honours, may, in the course of time, degenerate in sentiment and esteem. They will continue, however, to exact and attract the homage of the multitude. It will be then for some unworthy citizens, marked, perhaps, by our just contempt, that you have irrevocably alienated a portion of the public consideration. It is not so with respect to the esteem which flows from the public, and which is necessarily free. This retires as soon as merit ceases, still purer in its sources, more natural in its motions, and also more certain in its course and consequently more salutary in effect. It is the only prize proportioned to the soul of the virtuous citizen, the only one proper to inspire good actions and not to inflame the thirst of vanity and pride; the only one that may be sought, that may be attained, without meanness.

Once more, permit the citizens to distribute their respect according to their feelings and give themselves up to that expression, so flattering, so encouraging, that they give it as by inspiration and you will then see in the free concourse of all those men who are possessed of energetic minds, efforts multiplied in every species of good, which ought to conduce to the advancement of social perfection, the great source of public esteem.[1]

But your insolence and your vanity are better pleased with privileges. It is then but too plain that you wish rather to be distinguished *from* your fellow citizens, than *by* your fellow citizens.[2] Here then is manifested this

---

[1] I speak particularly of a nation which is free or one that wishes to become so. It is certain that the distribution of public honours cannot be vested in a nation of slaves: amongst people who are slaves, the moral coin is always adulterated, be the hand what it may that distributes it.

[2] Should even this distinction be accused of being rather metaphysical, a word which of late has become so alarming to inattentive minds, I will, however, assert that the distinction marked by the word *from* is a real difference; it belongs indeed to both the terms at the same time, because if A is distinguished from B, it is clear, for the same reason, that B will be distinguished from A; consequently A and B are upon an equal footing. All individuals, all beings, must need be different, one from the other; there is no great matter of pride where every person would have an equal title. In nature, superiority and inferiority are not matters of right but of fact; this advantage supposes, in truth, greater power on one side than on the other, but if we enquire into the original claim and title, to whom do you imagine

secret sentiment, this unnatural appetite, so full of vanity, and yet so mean in itself that you are endeavouring to conceal it under the appearance of public interest. It is not the esteem or the love of your fellow citizens to which you aspire. On the contrary, you are only alive to the sentiments of a culpable vanity which is so hostile to mankind, with the natural equality of whom you are offended. You are offended in the inmost recesses of your heart. You are reproaching nature that *she* has not placed your fellow citizens in some inferior classes destined for your service only, methinks I hear you exclaim. Why does not all the world share with me my indignation? Truly, you are very far from having any personal interest in the question which now occupies our attention and which treats of the rewards due to merit and not the punishments, which, in a well-regulated state, ought to be inflicted only on the enemies of social felicity.

From these considerations, let us proceed to the *effects* of honorary privileges, whether involved in the public interest, or the interest of the privileged themselves.

From the moment that ministers imprint the character of privilege on a citizen, they open his mind to a particular interest and close it more or less against the common good. The idea of country shrinks in the heart of the privileged and becomes limited to the class into which he is adopted. All his efforts, hitherto employed in the service of the common weal, are turned against it. The professed intention of the privilege was to incite him to better actions, but it has succeeded only in depraving him.

His heart is then agitated with a desire of being first, with an insatiable thirst of domination. This desire, unfortunately too agreeable to human nature, is a true antisocial malady, and, from its very nature, it must always be detrimental. Judge then of its ravages, when opinion and the laws of a country conspire to lend it their power and support.

For a moment inspect the sentiments of a person newly privileged. He looks on himself and his colleagues as forming a separate order, a chosen nation within the nation. He considers in the first place what he owes to his own caste. He imagines that he is devoted to his own particular party;

---

that this superiority ultimately belongs? To the body of citizens, or to the few privileged persons? The distinction marked by the word *by*, on the contrary, is the most social principle, the most fruitful in good actions, and good morals, but this distinction must be enthroned in the soul of those that grant it and not placed in the hand of one individual that pretends to the distribution. If it is a sentiment on their part, it cannot be any thing else without ceasing to be true. It must be avowed, also, that this sentiment is essentially free, and that there must be extreme folly in any person whatever to pretend to dispose of my esteem and veneration without my consent.

and if he continues to trouble himself about others, it is about such as no longer deserve to be termed *others*. They are his own friends, connexions, and companions. The people is no longer that body of which he was a member. It is nothing but the *people,* the people who in his heart and in his language are "nobody," a class of men, created on purpose to serve him, whilst he himself is born solely to command and to enjoy.

It is an absolute fact that the privileged class look upon themselves as another species of beings.[3] This opinion, in appearance so exaggerated, and which does not seem included in the notion of privilege, insensibly becomes its natural consequence, and in the end establishes itself in all minds. I shall put this question to some frank and liberal nobleman, as such it must be confessed there are, when he sees a common man near him who does not come for his protection, does he not generally feel an involuntary motion of repulse ready to break out upon the slightest pretext, either by some injurious expression, or some offensive gesture?

The false sentiment of personal superiority is so dear to the privileged class that they wish to extend it to all transactions with the citizens. They *are not made* to be *confounded,* they are not fit to *mix* together; it would be *wanting* to one's self essentially to dispute, or seem to be wrong when one is wrong, it is *compromising* one's self, even when in the right, etc., etc.

Nothing is more curious in this respect than the scene exhibited in countries remote from the capital. It is there the noble sentiment of superiority feeds and fattens unmolested by reason and the commotions of crowded cities. In the ancient castles, the noble baron learns to respect himself much better. He may indulge his ecstasy for a longer time before the portraits of his ancestors and intoxicate himself at more leisure with the honour of being descended from men who existed in the thirteenth or fourteenth century, for he never suspects that a similar advantage can be common to all families. In his opinion it is a characteristic peculiar to a certain race.

He frequently presents with all possible modesty to the adoration of strangers this train of ancestry, the sight of whom has so often filled him with the most delightful visions. But he does not rest long upon his father or grand-father. The most distant ancestors are the most esteemed. In proportion to his vanity, they are nearest to his heart.

I have seen some of these large galleries of family pictures. They are not absolutely valuable on account of the paintings, nor yet from the sen-

---

[3] As I do not wish to be accused of exaggeration, the reader may consult at the end an authentic paper, which I have extracted from the journals of the order of nobility at the Estates General, in the year 1614.

timents of filial affection, but they are indebted for their sublimity to the antiquity and manners of the good feudal times.[4]

In these castles it is that the true effect of a genealogical tree with unfolded leaves and expanded branches is felt. It is there that we discover, even in the most trifling circumstance, what is the value of a man of birth, *un homme comme il faut,* and the rank[5] in which every man ought to be placed.

---

[4] Who has not heard on those occasions the gentleman who exhibits it, make some charming reflexions upon this man who was, in the twelfth century, a fine dog. His vassals had not a fair chance with him? Another (taking care the ancient name is predominant) who, having incautiously engaged in a conspiracy paid for it with his head; but all in the twelfth century. On this subject I must relate an anecdote of a lady, who, in a genteel party, violently exclaimed against the conduct, really criminal, of a gentleman of one of the first houses in the kingdom. All on a sudden, she interrupted herself, and in a tone difficult to be described, added, "But I don't know why I should speak so ill of him, because I have the honour to be related to the family."

[5]It is impossible to catch with accuracy the shades, the subtleties of the language used among the privileged orders; for this purpose a dictionary would be necessary, which would at least have novelty to recommend it, because instead of giving the direct or metaphysical meaning of the words, the object on the contrary would be to detach them as far as possible from their natural signification, to leave nothing beneath the sound, but a complete vacuity of sense and the most unlimited scope for absurdity and prejudice. In this dictionary we should find what it is to be of nobility which never had a beginning. Persons of this species are of the right sort; they are by the *grace* of God, very different from the herd of new nobility, that are so by the grace of the prince. Those citizens are never taken into the account, who, without sufficient interest to be promoted by the prince's mercy, are reduced to the necessity of distinguishing themselves by their personal qualities. These are nothings, they are only the nation! We should learn from this new dictionary that none are to be accounted really of a noble birth but those who have no origin. Those made nobles by the prince have only half a family; the rest of the nation have none. It would be superfluous to observe here that the birth and family in question is not that which comes in a natural way from a father and mother, but that which the prince bestows by virtue of a patent, signed with his sign manual; or still better, that which comes from nobody knows where, which is still more valued. If, for instance, you have been so vulgar as to think that each man necessarily has a father, a grandfather, etc., you are mistaken in this case. There is nothing authentic but the attestation of Mr. *Cherin.*[(*)] To be of an old family, you must be of the right race, which has no beginning. The new nobility are men of yesterday. And as to citizens who are not noble, I don't know what to say but that apparently they are not born yet. I am astonished at the ability with which the nobility prolong to an endless length those sublime though never ceasing conversations. But the most entertaining of all, in my opinion, are those who constantly fall on their knees to worship their own dignity and laugh from their heart at the same absurdity in others. I maintain that the opinions of the privileged order are in exact correspondence with their feelings, and to give a further proof of it will now offer, according to their manner of estimating things, the real picture of a political society. It is to consist of six or seven classes, subordinate one to another. In the first rank are the high and powerful nobility, *les grands seigneurs*, viz. that part of the court, in which high birth, exalted station, and immense wealth are united. The second class includes the *présentés connus*, those

Compared with these elevated situations, how mean and contemptible must the persons and occupations of the trading part of the community appear! If we were allowed to insinuate a comparison, what is a *yeoman, a tradesman, or a merchant* compared with a nobleman of ancient family whose eyes are incessantly fixed upon the *good old times?* There he contemplates his titles, his power. He may be said to exist in his ancestors. On the contrary, the tradesman fixes his attention on the *ignoble present* and the *indifferent future.* He prepares for the one and sustains the other by the resources of his own industry. He, instead of *having been,* undergoes the labour and, what is worse, the scandal of employing his time, his talents, his continued efforts, in our immediate service. He submits to exist by his own industry, so necessary to us all. Ah! Why cannot those privileged beings return to ages that are *past,* there to enjoy their titles, decorations, etc. and leave to the stupid nation the *ignoble present?*

The self-complacency of a really ancient nobleman bears an exact proportion to his contempt for others. He caresses, he idolizes his personal dignity; and though all the efforts of this superstition are insufficient to impart the least shadow of reality to those ridiculous errors, they do not on that account engage his attention the less, or the less fill up the vacancy of his mind. He gives himself up to those delusions with as much rapture as the maniac of Piraeus evinced for his chimera.

Vanity, which is generally selfish and is gratified with being insulated, here transforms itself all at once into an *Esprit de corps,* or an incorrigible party spirit. If a member of the privileged class sustains the smallest inconvenience from any part of that class which he despises, he is instantly inflamed. His passions swell beyond all bounds; he feels himself wounded in his dearest prerogative, calls in every assistance, fans the sparks of resentment in his colleagues, succeeds in forming a dreadful confederacy, ready to sacrifice every thing for the maintenance and aggrandisement of

---

presented at court whom everybody knows (by the way, it is very common in some of the people of fashion, chiefly ladies, if they meet at any public place a number of genteel people, but not quite of the highest fashion, to say, "There was *nobody* there one knows." I have heard it a hundred times) people of quality, *gens de qualité.* In the third rank comes presented at court, that *nobody* knows, *présentés inconnus.* In the fourth class of the non-presented, *non-presentés,* are included those who, however, may be of the *right sort,* all the country nobility, *des gentillâtres,* it is their expression. To the fifth class are referred all the created nobility, a little ancient, or men of nothing, *gens de néant.* In the sixth class are packed together all the new nobility, or men less than nothing, *gens moins que rien.* Lastly, that nothing, however insignificant, may be omitted, they will condescend to thrust down in the seventh and last division the rest of the citizens, who it is not possible to characterise otherwise than by the most contemptuous appellations. This is the real social order, the prevailing prejudice, and I am sure I advance nothing new, unless to those people, who are not at all in the world.

his odious prerogative. Thus it is that political order and decency are reversed, and in their place we behold nothing but a detestable Aristocratism.

It may be said, however, that in company the privileged are as polite to the non-privileged as to one another. I am not the first who has remarked the characteristic politeness of the Gallic nation. The privileged Frenchman does not treat them with politeness because he thinks it is *due* to them, but because he believes it is *due* to himself. It is not the rights of others that he respects, but his own dignity. He will not be confounded by vulgar manners, with what he calls *bad company*. He would be under apprehensions that the object of his politeness would take him for a *common man like himself*.

Be on your guard, my fellow citizens, against these seductive grimaces. Have the good sense to draw the veil aside, and you will perceive underneath it those haughty attributes of those same privileges which we ought to detest.

To account for this ardent thirst of acquiring titles, it may be thought, perhaps, that a species of peculiar felicity has been created for the privileged at the expense of public happiness, in the supreme delight of that superiority enjoyed by a small number, to which a greater number aspire and of which the rest are reduced to revenge themselves by recurring to the resources of envy and hatred.

But can it be forgotten that nature never imposes vain or impotent laws; that she has determined to distribute happiness to man only in that state of equality; and that which is offered by vanity is a treacherous exchange for that multitude of natural sentiments which form the component part of substantial happiness?

Let us attend to our own experience.[6] Let us direct our view to that of the privileged themselves and the great mandatories, or public officers,

---

[6]Society affords to all whose fate has not condemned them to unremitting labour, an inexpressible source of pure and agreeable enjoyments; this we feel, and it is generally agreed upon: that the people who believe themselves the most civilised also boast of having the best society. Where then is the best society to be found? There, certainly, where men, who being suited to one another, can assemble freely and where those who are not suited to each other may separate without any obstacle. There, where in a given number of men there is a majority possessing the talent and spirit of society and where the choice is not compelled by any consideration foreign to the end proposed in assembling together; can it now be said that the prejudices of rank do not oppose this simple arrangement? How many women of fashion, having families, are obliged to renounce the company of men, the most agreeable, lest a mixt company should offend the pride of rank? You do well to exclaim in your societies, so select and so insipid, against this equality of which you cannot help feeling the absolute necessity. It is not in a short space of a few moments that men can seriously

whose department in the provinces enables them to enjoy the fancied charms of superiority, which spreads all her charms for them in it. They, however, soon find themselves alone, their minds fatigued and exhausted with littleness. And thus the violated rights of nature are avenged. Observe the impatience with which they return to meet with *equal* society in the metropolis. How absurd then is it continually to sow and cultivate the seeds of vanity, to reap only the thorns of pride and the poppies of *ennui!*

We are far from wishing to confound, with the absurd and chimerical superiority, which is the effect of exclusive privileges, that legal superiority which divides mankind into two classes, the governors and the governed. This is real and necessary, it neither fills one party with pride nor debases the other. It is a superiority of employments, not of persons. Now, since even this superiority cannot compensate for the enjoyments of equality, what must we think of the chimera with which the privileged persons delude themselves?

If men consulted their own interest, if they knew how to pursue their proper happiness, if they would consent at least to open their eyes to the lamentable imprudence which has taught them to prefer the senseless privileges of servitude to the rights of free citizens, how would they hasten to abjure the numerous vanities in which they have been trained up from infancy! How would they mistrust an order of things so aptly calculated to combine with despotism! The rights of citizens embrace all. Privilege destroys everything valuable and affords nothing in return, except amongst slaves.

Hitherto I have made no distinction between the different kinds of privileges, between those that are hereditary and those obtained by the person himself who possesses them. It is not but that they are all equally pernicious, equally dangerous in the social state. If there are degrees in the order of evils and absurdities, then hereditary evils ought certainly to be placed in the first rank. And I shall not degrade my reason to prove a truth which is self-evident in itself, viz., that to make a privilege a transmissive property is to take away the feeble pretexts by which it is attempted to be supported. It is an overturning of all principle and of all reason.

Some additional observations will reflect fresh light on the pernicious effects of privileges. But before we proceed, let us remark a general truth, which is that personal interest, supported by the example of ages, is all that is necessary to give force and effect to any false notion. In the perni-

---

mould themselves so as to become society for one another, which they certainly would be if equality was the daily practice of our lives rather than the sport of a few moments. This matter presents itself in so many points of view that I have only instanced a few.

cious process of corrupting the understanding from one prejudice to another, we fall insensibly at length into a system which exhibits the last extreme of folly. And, what is still more mortifying, it becomes impossible to produce the least alteration in the credulous superstition of nations.

Thus we behold (without the smallest effort on the part of the nation to reclaim its own imprudent concessions) innumerable swarms of the privileged race daily arise under a strong and almost religious persuasion that they have acquired, by birth alone, a right to public honours; and, by the continuance of their existence, a claim to a portion of homage from the people. And these circumstances constitute in their eyes a sufficient title.

It is not enough, in effect, that the nobility look on themselves as another species of men. No, they actually consider themselves and their descendants as a something of which the nation stands absolutely in *need.* They would not be content with being considered as the agents or officers of the *common-wealth.* For, in this respect, they would be debased to the situation of the generality of the public mandatories or servants of the state, from whatever class they may be taken. It is in the capacity of a privileged or noble class of personages that they look on themselves as necessary to the existence of society under a monarchical government. If they speak to the monarch himself, they never fail to represent themselves as the prop of the throne and his natural champions against the people. If, on the other hand, they condescend to address themselves to the nation, they exhibit themselves as the true defenders of the people who, but for them, would be immediately crushed by the weighty hand of royalty.

With a little better information, government might see that all which is wanted in society is that the citizens should merely live and act under the protection of the law and a tutelary authority whose duty it is to watch over and protect the state. The only gradation of rank necessary exists among those who administer the public affairs. It is there the gradation of power should be sought; it is there the relation of superior and inferior should be found, because the public machine can only be moved and directed by means of this correspondence.

Except those who are immediately engaged in the functions of government, all are citizens equal in the eye of the law; all dependent, not one class upon another, for that would be an useless and intolerable servitude, but on the authority that protects, judges, and defends them. The man who possesses immense property is no more than he who lives by his daily labour. If the rich man contributes more to the exigency of the state, he has more property to be protected. But, should the *little all* of the poor man be the less precious, and ought not his person to repose under the shade of at least an equal protection?

It is by confounding these notions, so simple in themselves, that the privileged still speak of the necessity of a subordination, foreign to that which subjects us to government and law. The military spirit would exalt itself into the judge of civil relations and consider a nation only as an extensive barrack. In a late publication the writer has even presumed to establish a comparison betwixt the officers and privates on one side and the privileged and non-privileged on the other. If you consult the monastic spirit which has much analogy with the military, you will immediately hear that there can be no order or government in a nation until it has been submitted to that mass of regulations by the aid of which the numerous victims to monasteries are held in subordination. The monastic spirit, under a more specious and more respectable name, has greater influence in society than is generally imagined.

Let us speak out plainly and at once. Such narrow, contracted, miserable views of things can only belong to men who neither respect nor feel the real bonds that connect men in the social state. A citizen, whoever he may be, who does not fill a public office, is entirely at liberty to apply himself to the melioration of his lot in life and to the enjoyment of his natural rights, provided he does not infringe the rights of another, that is, provided he commits no breach of the law. All the relations between citizen and citizen are founded on the basis of freedom and equality. One gives his time or his merchandise, the other in return his money. There is no subordination, but a continual exchange.[7] If, in your narrow policy,

---

[7]It will probably facilitate the communication of our ideas on this subject to distinguish the two species of hierarchy of which we have now been treating, by the names of *real* and *false*. The gradations between the governors and the obedience of the governed, to the various degrees of legal authority form the *true* hierarchy which is necessary in all societies. That of the governed amongst themselves is *false,* useless, odious, and the unenlightened remains of the feudal system. To form an idea of subordination among the governed, we must imagine an armed troop possessing themselves of a country, becoming the sole proprietor of it, and preserving for the common security the relative habits of military discipline. In this situation government is melted away in the civil estate. It is not any longer composed of a people—it is an army. With us, on the contrary, the different branches of the public power exist separately and are organized, including a great armed force, in such a manner as to require from simple citizens nothing but contributions to defray the public expence. Let us not be deceived in the midst of all these phrases of *subordination, dependency,* etc. which the nobility so loudly claim for themselves. It is not the interest of true subordination to which they are attending; they only think of the *false.* It is that which they want to exalt on the ruins of the *true.* Hear them when they speak of the ordinary agents of government; observe with what contempt a really old nobleman thinks proper to treat them. What do they see in a *lieutenant de police,* a justice of the peace, a man of no importance, a mere nothing, established only to frighten the people and who has not a right to intermeddle with *persons of rank*? The example which I have just recited falls within the observation of all. Let it be plainly declared whether there is any nobleman who thinks himself under the jurisdiction of

you distinguish a body of citizens by placing them between the government and the people, either this body will share the functions of government, and then it is not the privileged class of which we are speaking, or it will possess none of the essential functions of public power. And then I wish they would explain to me what this intermediate body can be, other than a pernicious excrescence. Pernicious either by intercepting the direct communications between the governors and the governed, pressing on the springs of the public machine; or, at best, becoming, by all that distinguishes it from the great body of citizens, an additional burden upon the community.

All classes of citizen have their functions, their particular tasks, employments, which collectively form the general movement of society. If there is any class that pretends to exempt itself from this general rule, it is easy to perceive that is not likely to remain content with being useless, but that it must of necessity exist at the expense of the rest.

What are the two great principles of action in society?: *Honour* and *emolument*. It is from the desire that we have of the one or of the other that society is maintained. These two springs of action should not be separated in a nation where the value of good morals and manners is known. The ambition of being found worthy of the public esteem (and every profession may be entitled to a portion of it) will be found to operate a necessary check on the inordinate love of wealth. Let us now examine how these two different sentiments are modified in the privileged class.

In the first place *honour* is assigned to them as their inheritance, or *appenage*. All other citizens are entitled to it only as the reward of their conduct, but to the nobility it is enough to *be born*. It is not enough for them to feel the necessity of acquiring honour, and, as they are born with it, they may renounce the pursuit of it, and leave it to others to obtain it by merit; they may resign it with safety to all that press forward to merit it.[8]

As to *money*, the privileged, it is true, feel the greatest want of it. They are ever more exposed to the influence of this passion because the false opinion of their superiority continually urges them to enlarge their expenses. And in grasping at every thing that may contribute to that end,

---

a lieutenant of the police? In what manner do they look upon the other ordinary agents of government, except the military commanders? Is it uncommon to hear them say, "I am not made to submit myself to the minister; if the king had done me the honour of giving his orders, well, etc.?" I leave this subject to the imagination or rather to the experience of the reader. But it was necessary to observe that the real enemies of subordination and true hierarchy are those very men who urge submission with so much ardour to the *false one*.

[8]Here it must be understood that we do not confound *honour* with the *point of honour*, which has sometimes been obtruded as its substitute.

they are not restrained like other men by fear of losing all their honour and consideration.

But, by a singular contradiction, while the prejudice of rank continually impels to the derangement of fortune, it imperiously cuts off all the honest means by which it might be repaired.

What modes then are left to the privileged of gratifying this love of riches, which must necessarily influence them more than others? *Intrigue* and *solicitation*. Intrigue and mendicity will constitute the whole *industry* of this class. In the exercise of these two employments, they resume, in some measure, their place among the active and labouring part of society. If they dedicate themselves entirely to these pursuits, they will excel in them. Consequently you may be sure, whenever this double talent may be practised with success, that privileged families will qualify themselves in such a degree as to exclude all competition on the part of the non-privileged.

They will fill the Court, besiege ministers, monopolize all favours, pensions, church-preferments. *Intrigue* will cast at once an usurping eye at the church, the sword, and the law. In them it discovers a considerable revenue or a power which leads to it. This power, which is attached to a multitude of places, immediately causes those places to be considered as lucrative sinecures established, not for the purpose of exercising talents or industry, but merely to insure *comfortable settlements* for privileged families.

These experienced men will not depend entirely on their superiority in the art of intriguing. But, as if they dreaded that the love of the public welfare should, in some moment of infatuation, seduce the minister from their party, they will resolve to profit in time by the incapacity or treachery of ministers till in they end they obtain a sanction to their monopoly by some secure edicts, or by a system of administration equivalent to an exclusive law.

Thus it is that the state becomes devoted to principles destructive of all public economy. It may well have a right in all things to prefer the most able and the least expensive servants. But monopoly commands the choice of the most extravagant and the least able, since it is well known that the effect of monopoly is to stop the exertions of ability, which, in a free state, would be ever active in the public service.

Privileged beggary is less fraught with inconveniency to the commonwealth. In every view it is a parasitic branch that absorbs all the juices, but does not at least pretend to replace the useful boughs. Like very other species of mendicity, it stretches out the hand in order to excite compassion and to receive gratuitously. It is only the posture which is less humble. It seems rather to dictate a duty than to implore relief.

It has been sufficient to impart a kind of false dignity to intrigue and beggary. They have been particularly practised by privileged personages.

Thus almost every man is found to boast of his success in these so really despicable arts. They inspire emulation; they excite envy, but never contempt.

This species of begging is principally exercised at Court, where the most powerful and the most opulent make the best advantage of it.

From that fountain of corruption the contagious example winds its way to the most distant recesses of the provinces and imparts to all the *honourable* and *virtuous* desire of living in idleness at the expence of the public.

It is not enough to obviate these objections, to assert, that beyond all comparison, the privileged order is the most opulent in the kingdom; that the bulk of the land and all the overgrown fortunes belong to the members of this class. The love of expense and the pleasure of ruining themselves are superior to all the riches of the world, and there must, of course, be at least some privileged beggars.

The word *poor* is never heard united with that of *privilege* but a cry of indignation is immediately raised. A member of the privileged order without an estate to support his name and his rank is a disgrace to the nation! We must hasten to remedy this public disorder. And though supplies be not publicly demanded for that express purpose in the budget of the minister, it is but too true that if the national accounts were but nicely inspected, a considerable part of the public expenditure would be found to have been distributed in this way.

It is not for nothing that the administration is chiefly composed of persons of considerable families. No, this administration thus composed watches, with a paternal solicitude over all the interests of the privileged. Here we have even pompous establishments (vaunted, it is said, all over Europe) for the education of the *privileged poor* of both sexes. It is in vain that the order of Providence, by its freedom, reproaches the folly of your institutions. It would bring back those who are in want to the general law of nature, that of labouring for their bread. But you discern nothing in this wise order but an error of destiny. And you take care not to give to your pupils the habits of a laborious profession capable of yielding a subsistence.

In your admirable system you proceed even so far as to inspire them with a sort of pride in having so early subsisted on the bounty of the public, as if it was more glorious and honourable to have been maintained by alms than to have been above the necessity of receiving them.

You reward them, besides, with pecuniary gifts, pensions, and ribbands for having been reduced to the necessity of receiving this first pledge of your tenderness.

Whilst even in a state of infancy the privileged young claim rank and appointments. And, if they happen to be poor, their penury is loudly lamented. Look amongst the non-privileged of the same age destined for professions which require ability and study; look if there be any one of them who, though trained to a laborious employment, does not cost his parents a considerable sum before he can be admitted to the uncertain chance of deriving even a necessary subsistence from his long labours.

Every door is thrown open to the solicitation of the privileged. It is sufficient for them just to appear, and every one imagines he does himself an honour of interesting himself in their advancement. Each member of the administration looks on their fortunes as inseparably connected with his own. Yes, government has secretly contributed a thousand times to the settlement and aggrandisement of their families.

Even their own treaties of marriage are considered as affairs of public importance. Places are created on purpose for them; exchanges are negotiated to accommodate them; and this has sometimes been effected by considerable, though secret, disbursements from the public treasury.

Those members of the privileged orders who cannot aspire to these high favours find abundant resources elsewhere: in religious institutions for both sexes; in a multitude of military ranks and orders without use or object or, if they have any object, such as is pernicious and unjust, in pensions, prebends, governments, and honourable sinecures. And, as if the errors of our ancestors were not enough, government has been occupied for some years past with redoubled ardour in augmenting a number of those brilliant but useless employments.[9]

It would be an error to suppose that the privileged beggars despise little opportunities or petty assistance. The funds set apart for the royal alms are in a great measure absorbed by them. And to say that a privileged person is poor is not intended to convey an idea that he has not enough to supply all his natural wants but that his vanity suffers, and that is enough. Thus the real indigence of each class of citizens is sacrificed to the insatiate cravings of vanity.

In reviewing the earlier pages of history, we observe the privileged orders in the habit of usurping by force whatever they pleased. Violence and rapine, conscious of impunity, were doubtless sufficient without soliciting alms. This privileged begging, of course, could only have commenced with the first dawn of public order, which evinces that it is

---

[9]A strange contradiction is manifest in the conduct of government. On the one hand it declaims most vehemently against the wealth which is consecrated to the worship of the divinity, which at least exempts the national purse from the discharge of this branch of the public service but at the same time endeavours with all its might to appropriate that wealth and more to the privileged orders, who render no public service at all. It is curious to read the list of chapters lately created or devoted to the use of the *noblesse* of both sexes, and it would be still more curious if we could develop the secret motives which have shamefully led to the corruption of ecclesiastical foundations, which, if they are to be modified, ought to be so for an interest truly national, and by the nation itself alone.

different in its nature from beggary by the people. This last species of poverty grows with the corruption of the government. But the other increases in proportion as the government is improved. It is true that after some further progress in the arts of government both of these social evils will probably cease. But this can never be effected by cherishing and feeding them, and much less by honouring that which is by far the most inexcusable of the two.

It cannot be denied but that there is considerable address in obtaining from compassion what cannot at present be wrested from weakness and in profiting sometimes by the audacity of the oppressor, and sometimes by the sensibility of the oppressed. The members of the privileged orders have certainly distinguished themselves in both ways. From the instant that rank could no longer obtain what it wanted by force, it adopted a new plan and lost no opportunity of imploring the liberality of the king and of the nation.

The minutes of the ancient Estates General, those of the old assemblies of the Notables, are loaded with petitions in favour of the *poor privileged class.*[10] The *pays d' états* have been employed a long time, and always with an additional zeal, in every thing that can augment the number of pensions which they have assigned to the privileged poor.(*) The provincial administrations already follow these honourable steps. And the three orders in common, because they are still entirely composed of members of the privileged orders, on every occasion attend with the most respectful approbation to all the advices which are sent to them relative to the needy class of the privileged. The Intendants of provinces have procured particular funds for this purpose.(**) And to ensure their own success in every thing, nothing more is necessary than to show themselves warmly interested in the distresses of the *privileged poor.* In short, in books; in pulpits, academies, and discourses; in conversations, if you wish to interest your hearers, it is only to speak of the *poor privileged class.* When we observe this general infatuation and the innumerable methods which superstition (to which nothing is impossible) has taken to relieve the needy member of the privileged orders, it is difficult to assign a reason why there has not yet been fixed on the church door a box for the *poor distressed privileged class.*[11]

---

[10]Now that the principles of general justice are more diffused and that the assemblies of the *bailliages* will have objects of great magnitude to discuss, it may undoubtedly be hoped that they will not sully their instructions with what might formerly be called the *beggarly couplet.*

[11]I expect this to be taken as a sign of *bad taste.* That is as it should be. The power to proscribe, under this guise, forms of words which are quite simply exact is still a right belonging to the privileged orders.

It may be necessary in this place to notice an inexhaustible kind of traffic which has been carried on by the privileged. It is founded in the one part on the superstition of names and in the other upon a species of covetousness, which still more powerful than vanity. I speak of what is impudently termed *misalliances,*[12] though this expression has not been sufficient to discourage the stupid citizens who pay so dear for an insult immediately offered to themselves.

As soon as any of the lower order, by the mere effort of industry, have made a fortune; as soon as the agents of public revenue have accumulated treasures by easier means, the privileged immediately set their hearts on those riches. It appears indeed that our unfortunate nation is condemned to work, to toil, and exhaust themselves without ceasing to gratify the insatiable avarice of the privileged class.

Agriculture, manufactures, and the arts attempt in vain either to support or aggrandize themselves. In vain would they dedicate to the property of the public a portion of the immense capitals to which they have contributed. The rapacious privileged class devours all. All is devoted without any return to the barren and ungrateful region of privilege.[13]

The subject-matter of privileges is as inexhaustible as the prejudices which conspire to support them. But let us quit this topic and spare ourselves the reflections which it suggests. The time will come when our indignant posterity, amazed at the perusal of our history, will stamp our unparalleled insanity with that opprobrium which it justly deserves. In our younger days we have seen men of letters distinguish themselves by their courage in attacking opinions, equally strong and equally disgraceful to humanity. At this day their successors repeat in their writings and conversation antiquated reasonings against prejudices which no longer exist. The prejudice which supports privilege is the most pernicious that ever affected the earth. It is more intimately connected with the social organization than any other. It corrupts it more deeply and it interests a far greater number in its defence. How numerous are the motives which concur in this subject to excite the zeal of true patriotism and to abash and confound the indolence of our contemporary writers!

---

[12]It would be proper, at least for the decency of language, to make use of another word to design the action of giving the hand to the rich offering of stupidity; there ought to be a word which would mark more clearly on which side the misalliance lies.

[13]Honour is said to be the principle of monarchy. It must be acknowledged at least that France has for a long time made dreadful sacrifices to fortify herself in principle.

Extract from the Minutes of the Order of Nobility to the Estates General in 1614, Page 113

Tuesday 25th of November, having had an audience, M. de Senecey[14] addressed the king in the following manner.

Sire,

The goodness of our kings has at all times granted a liberty to their nobility to report to them on every occasion, their elevated rank approaching so near to their persons as to make them always the principal executors of the royal will.

I should never have dared to relate to Your Majesty what antiquity teaches us, that *Birth* has given pre-eminence to this order. And that so great is the difference between this order and the rest of the people, that it never could so much as think of suffering any kind of comparison.

I could dwell on this subject, Sire, a considerable time but so clear a truism does not stand in need of any greater proof than what is acknowledged by all the world. Besides I am speaking before a king, whom we hope to find as jealous of maintaining to us all that we share of his splendour as we should be to supplicate and entreat him. We are much concerned that so extraordinary a novelty should open our lips to pour forth our complaints rather than to offer up the most humble supplications for which we are assembled.

---

[14]The baron de Senecey was the President of the Nobility.

Sire, Your Majesty has been graciously pleased, to assemble the Estates General of the three orders of your kingdom, destined and separated amongst themselves in functions and qualities. The church, devoted to the service of God and the cure of souls, holds the first rank. We honour the prelates and ministers as our fathers and as the mediators of our reconciliation with God.

The nobility, Sire, holds the second. It is the right arm of your justice, the support of your crown, and the invincible power of the state.

Under the happy auspices and valorous conduct of kings, at the price of their blood, and by the employment of their victorious arms, public tranquillity has been established; and by their pains and labours the *Tiers-Etat,* the people, is about to enjoy the convenience and happiness which result from that peace. This order, Sire, which holds the last place in this assembly, is an order composed of the people, both of the town and of the country. The last are almost all the vassals of the first orders. The citizens are made up of burgesses, shopkeepers, artisans, and a few officers; these are they who, forgetful of their duty, without the sanction of their constituents, dare to compare themselves to us.

I am ashamed, Sire, to repeat the terms by which they have offended us. They compare your kingdom to a family composed of three brothers; they call the clergy the eldest, the nobility the second, and themselves the youngest.[15]

Into what a miserable situation are we now fallen! If this be true, how does it come to pass that so many services rendered to the country since time immemorial, so many honours and dignities acquired by their labours and hereditarily transmitted, instead of elevating should be looked on as the means of sinking them into the most intimate society with the vulgar or into the lowest kind of society amongst men? And, not content with calling themselves our brethren, they ascribe to themselves the restoration of the kingdom to which, as all France can bear witness, they have not in the least contributed. It must therefore be evident to all that they cannot in any manner compare themselves to us; an enterprise so ill founded cannot be endured.

---

[15]This was the offence against which the nobility demanded redress. The day before, the civil lieutenant at the head of a deputation from the Third Estate, had dared to say, "Treat us as your younger brothers and we will honour and love you." All this chicanery should be read in the minute itself, beginning with the speech by the President Savaron, which occasioned it. In the reply by the baron de Senecey to the deputation by the Third Estate, on 24 November, one will be able to find expressions even more outrageous than those making up the speech to the king.

Sire, give your judgement in this point, and by a declaration founded in justice, cause them to return to their duty and to acknowledge what we are and the difference betwixt us. And for this, we most humbly entreat your Majesty in the name of all the nobility of France (whose deputies we are) to the end that, supported in their natural pre-eminence, they may devote, as they always have, their honour, and their life, to the service of our Majesty.

Ecquid sentitis in quanto contemptu vivatis? Lucis vobis hujus partem, si liceat, adimant. Quod spiratis, quod vocem mittitis, quod formas hominum habetis indignantur.

Liv. lib. 4, c. 56.(★)

WHAT IS THE THIRD ESTATE?

This translation is based upon the third edition of Sieyès' pamphlet, published, like the first two, in 1789. Sieyès' italicization of certain words has been retained, but his capitalization of words like "Nation," "Legislator," or "People" has been dropped unless the word is used to refer to a proper noun: e.g., the King, for Louis XVI, or the Nation, for the French nation.

What is the Third Estate?[1]

"For as long as the philosopher does not stray beyond the bounds of truth, do not accuse him of going too far. His function is to mark the goal; he has, therefore, to reach it. If he were to dare to raise his standard while still on the road, the signal might mislead. The duty of the administrator, on the other hand, is to measure and adjust his step according to the nature of the difficulties. . . . If the philosopher has not reached the goal, he does not know where he is. If the administrator cannot see the goal, he does not know where he is going."

[1]This work, composed at the time of the Assembly of Notables in 1788, was published early in January 1789. It can be taken to be a continuation of the *Essay on Privileges*.

The plan of this work is quite simple. There are three questions that we have to ask of ourselves:

1. What is the Third Estate?—*Everything.*
2. What, until now, has it been in the existing political order?—*Nothing.*
3. What does it want to be?—*Something.*

First we will see whether these answers are correct. Meanwhile it would be wrong to brand truth as exaggeration until all the evidence has been seen. Next we will examine the measures that have been tried and those that should be taken to ensure that the Third Estate really does become *something*. Thus, we will show:

4. What ministers have *attempted* to do and what the privileged orders themselves now *propose* to do for its benefit.
5. What *ought* to have been done.
6. Finally, what *remains* to be done for the Third Estate to take the place which is its rightful due.

Chapter One
The Third Estate is a Complete Nation

What does a nation need to survive and prosper? It needs *private* employments and *public* services.

All the different kinds of private employment can be grouped into four classes:

1. Since land and water supply the primary materials for meeting basic human needs, the first class, in logical order, consists of all those families engaged in work on the land.

2. Between the initial sale of these materials and their final consumption or use, a new kind of handiwork, which may be either simple or complex, adds further amounts of additional value to these primary goods. Human industry thus has an ability to perfect the gifts of nature and increase the value of total production by double, tenfold, or a hundredfold. These form the activities of the second class.

3. Between production and consumption—as well as in the different stages of production—stand a mass of intermediate agents, useful to both producers and consumers. These are the merchants and dealers. Merchants, continually comparing variations in needs according to time and place, speculate on the profitability of storage and transportation. Dealers

sell either wholesale or retail directly to their customers. This kind of useful activity distinguishes the third class.

4. In addition to these three classes of industrious and useful citizens whose prime concern is with *objects* of use and consumption, a society also needs different kinds of individual activity and specialized services that are *directly* useful or agreeable to the *person*. This fourth class encompasses everything from the most distinguished liberal and scientific professions to the least esteemed domestic services.

These are the activities that support society. But who undertakes them? The Third Estate.

Public services can also, in present conditions, be grouped under four well-known headings: the army, the law, the church, and the administration. It would be superfluous to analyze them in detail to show that nineteen out of twenty of those employed in them are members of the Third Estate. The difference here is that they are also required to bear the whole burden of all the genuinely hard work, namely, all the things that the privileged order simply refuses to do. Lucrative and honorific offices alone are filled by members of the privileged order. Did they deserve them? If this was so, then the Third Estate must have been either unwilling or unable to fill them. We, however, know the real answer. Nonetheless, the privileged order has presumed to place an embargo upon the Third Estate. "However useful or talented you may be," the Third Estate has been told, "you will go so far and no further. Honors are not for the likes of you." Rare exceptions, noticed as they are bound to be, are no more than a mockery, and the language used on such occasions serves only to add insult to injury.

If this exclusion is a social crime, a veritable act of war upon the Third Estate, could it not at least be said to have some public utility? Ah! But surely we know the effects of monopoly? Besides discouraging those it excludes, does it not also ruin the abilities of those it favors? It is surely well enough known that the absence of free competition in work of any kind means that it will be done badly and cost more.

When any sort of public service is made the prerogative of a distinct order of citizens, has nobody considered that it is not simply the man who works who has to be paid but all those of the same caste who do not as well as the whole families of both those who work and those who do not? Has nobody noticed that as soon as a government becomes the property of a particular class, it swells beyond all measure, creating posts to meet the needs not of the governed, but of those who govern? Has nobody considered that although we basely—and, I would dare to say, *stupidly*—respect this state of affairs at home, we find it despicable, monstrous, destructive of all industry, inimical to social progress, degrading to the human race in general, and intolerable to Europeans in particular (etc. and so forth), when we encounter it in histories of ancient Egypt or in reports by travelers to India?[2] But we need to set such considerations aside. Although they might broaden and clarify the question, they will nonetheless slow the pace of the argument.[3]

Here it ought to be enough to have shown that the so-called utility of a privileged order for performing public service is no more than an illusion; that with no assistance from that order, everything arduous in providing that service is done by the Third Estate; that without a privileged order, the higher-level posts would be infinitely better filled; that they ought to be the natural prize and reward for recognized talent and service; and that if the privileged have succeeded in usurping every lucrative and honorific post, this is both an odious iniquity towards the generality of citizens and an act of treason towards the state.

Who then would dare to say that the Third Estate does not, within itself, contain everything needed to form a complete nation? It resembles a strong, robust man with one arm in chains. Subtract the privileged order and the Nation would not be something less, but something more. What then is the Third Estate? Everything; but an everything that is fettered and oppressed. What would it be without the privileged order? Everything, but an everything that would be free and flourishing. Nothing can go well without the Third Estate, but everything would go a great deal better without the two others.

But it is not enough to have shown that the privileged, far from being useful to the Nation, can only weaken and harm it; it is also necessary to prove that the noble *order*[4] simply has no place at all in the organization of society—it may be a *burden* upon the Nation, but it cannot be part of it.

---

[2]On the subject of the Indian castes, see the *Histoire philosophique et politique des deux Indes*, Bk. 1.(*)

[3]We might, however, be allowed to point out the sovereign absurdity of claiming on the one hand that a nation is not made for its head and, on the other, of wanting it to be *made* for the aristocrats (namely, those of its members who disdainfully refuse to take any part in the useful work of other citizens or anything tiring in public affairs. A class of men like this is certainly a heavy burden to impose upon a nation! The countless abuses in public order, the poverty, distress, and servility of twenty-five million men amount to irrefutable factual proof of this).

[4]Here, I make no reference to the clergy. If it is taken to be a body entrusted with a public service, it belongs to the social organisation since every public service forms part of the government. When it is said that the clergy is a *profession*, not an *order*, clerics of the eleventh century and those who, for reasons of calculation, feign to be so, complain that this is to deny them their status. They are wrong. It is precisely because the clergy is a profession that it counts for something among us. If it was no more than an *order*, it would have no genuine status. The more progress that is made in the science of morality and politics,

Firstly, it is not possible to identify a place for a *caste*[5] of nobles anywhere among all the elementary components of a nation. I know that there are individuals (all too many) whom infirmity, incapacity, incurable laziness, or the tide of moral dissolution have made strangers to all the activities involved in society. There are always exceptions to, and abuses of the rules, especially in a vast empire. But we ought to be able to agree that the fewer the abuses, the better ordered a state might be supposed to be. The most poorly-ordered state of all must be one in which not just a few isolated individuals but a whole class of citizens glories in remaining inert in the midst of the general movement and contrives to consume the better part of the product without contributing in any way to its production. A class like that is surely foreign to a nation because of its *idleness.*

The noble order is no less a stranger in our midst by virtue of its *civil and political* prerogatives.

What is a nation? It is a body of associates living under a *common* law, represented by the same *legislature*, etc.

But is it not obvious that the noble order has privileges and exemptions—which it dares to call rights—that are separate from those of the great body of citizens? As a result, it stands apart from the common order and the common law. Its own civil rights make it a people apart within the greater nation. It is truly an *imperium in imperio.*

As for its *political* rights, it also exercises these apart from the Nation. It has its own representatives, who are certainly not entrusted with any

---

the easier it is to see that a society contains only public or private professions. Beyond these, there is no more than nonsense, or dangerous illusions, or pernicious institutions. Thus, by asserting that the clergy should not be an order, the intention is not to place it below the nobility. It should not amount to an *order* because there should be no distinction of *orders* in a nation. If orders are to be allowed to exist, it would doubtless be better to grant that privilege to men who can show proof of sacerdotal election, rather than men whose only proof of their entitlement is a birth-certificate. One can, in the end, prevent someone with no talent or probity from joining the clergy, but it is rather more difficult to prevent someone from being born.

[5]That is just the word to use. It refers to a class of men who, having no function or any utility, nonetheless enjoy the privileges attached to their persons simply by dint of their existence. From this point of view, which is the true point of view, it may well be true that there is no more than one privileged caste, that of the nobility. It is quite genuinely a people apart, but it is a false people that, not being able to exist by itself, since it has no functioning organs, attaches itself to a real nation like one of those parasitic forms of vegetation that live off the sap of the plants that they exhaust and desiccate. The clergy, the law, the army, and the administration amount to four classes of public officials needed everywhere. Why, then, should they be accused of *aristocratism* in France? It is because the noble caste has usurped all the best positions, turning them into a kind of patrimonial property to be exploited, not in the spirit of social law, but for its private profit.

mandate from the people. The body of its deputies sits apart from them and, even if it were to gather in the same hall as the deputies of the ordinary citizenry, it would still be an essentially distinct and separate representative body. It would be foreign to the Nation first, by virtue of its *principle*, because its mandate did not come from the people, and second, by virtue of its *object*, because this consists in defending, not the general interest, but a particular one.

The Third Estate thus encompasses everything pertaining to the Nation, and everyone outside the Third Estate cannot be considered to be a member of the Nation. What is the Third Estate? EVERYTHING.[6]

Chapter Two
What Has the Third Estate Been until Now? Nothing.

We will not examine the state of servitude in which the people have suffered for so long, any more than the condition of constraint and humiliation to which they are still confined. Their civil condition has changed and ought to change still more. It is absolutely impossible for the whole body of the Nation, or even one of its particular orders, to be free unless the Third Estate is free.

---

[6]A worthy author has aimed to be more precise.(*) He has said that "the Third Estate is the nation *less* the clergy and the nobility." I must confess that I would never have found the force of intellect to have announced that great truth. Someone might come along and say, "the nobility is the nation *less* the clergy and the Third Estate; the clergy is the nation *less* the Third Estate and the nobility. These are, to be sure, geometrically demonstrable propositions. I must beg your pardon; but if your aim was to do more than express a naïve truism; if you had already conceived of what a nation is, what its integral parts might be and how these consist of no more than public and private activities, and how the Third Estate is all that is needed for the performance of all these tasks; if you had been able to see that the benefit that the state is able to draw, in this regard, from a privileged caste, is excessively ruinous; if you had seen that all the errors and misfortunes which afflict—and will continue to afflict—the French nation are connected to these wretched privileges; if you know that a monarchy, like every other kind of political regime, needs no more than rulers and subjects; that a caste which the most stupid of prejudices has allowed to usurp every post and live off its privileges will soon give us no more than rulers governing despotically and subjects obeying rebelliously; and that this will be the heaviest burden that Heaven in its wrath might ever have imposed upon a people; and that it will become an almost insurmountable obstacle to any project for restoring justice and any progress towards social order; if, I repeat, your mind had quickly grasped all these truths, and thousands of others of equal relevance to our subject, why then have you not been able to come out and say clearly that the Third Estate is everything? How could you have been able to conclude a sequence of steps like that with the cold corollary, "the Third Estate is the nation *less* the clergy and the nobility"?

Freedom does not derive from privilege but from the rights of the citizen, rights which belong to all.

If the aristocrats were to try to keep the people in a state of oppression, even at the price of that liberty of which they would have shown themselves unworthy, the people will still dare to demand why they might be entitled to do so. If, in reply, they were to invoke a right of conquest, it would have to be conceded that this amounts to wanting to go back a little far.(*) But the Third Estate should not be afraid of going back to such distant times. All it needs to do is to refer to the year before the conquest, and since it is strong enough now not to be conquered, its resistance would doubtless be effective enough. Why not, after all, send back to the Franconian forests all those families still affecting the mad claim to have been born of a race of conquerors and to be heirs to *rights of conquest?*

Thus purged, the Nation might, I imagine, find some consolation in discovering that it is made up of no more than the descendants of the Gauls and Romans. Indeed, comparing lineage for lineage, might there not be some merit in pointing out to our poor fellow citizens that descent from the Gauls and the Romans might be at least as good as descent from the Sicambrians, Welches, and other savages from the woods and swamps of ancient Germania?(**) "Yes," some might say, "but the conquest disrupted all relationships, causing hereditary nobility to be transferred to the descendants of the conquerors." Well and good! We shall just have to transfer it back again. The Third Estate will become noble again by becoming a conqueror in its turn.

But if all lines of descent are mixed, if the blood of the Franks (hardly worth more in its pristine separateness) is indistinguishable from the blood of the Gauls, and if the ancestors of the Third Estate are the fathers of the whole Nation, can we not hope one day to see an end of that long-drawn-out parricide proudly carried out every day by one class against all the others? Why should not reason and justice, which may one day be motives as strong as vanity, press the ranks of the privileged, moved by a new, more true, and more social interest to seek their *rehabilitation* within the order of the Third Estate?

Let us pursue the object of the argument. The Third Estate has to be understood as the totality of citizens belonging to the common order. Whoever has a legal privilege of whatever kind has deserted the common order to form an exception to the common system of law and consequently does not belong to the Third Estate. As has been said, a nation is made *one* by virtue of a common system of law and a common representation. It is only too true, however, that a man is a *nobody* in France if he has no more than the common system of law to protect him. Without some sort of connection with privilege, one has to resign oneself to scorn, injury, and every kind of harassment. To avoid being entirely crushed, what can an unfortunate non-privileged person do? He has to attach himself to some magnate by every sort of base means; to buy, for the price of his values and human dignity, the capacity to call, when necessary, upon the protection of a *somebody*.

But we need to consider the order of the Third Estate less in relation to its civil state than in relation to the constitution. Let us see what part it stands to play in the Estates-General.

Who have been its so-called representatives? Men who have been ennobled or were granted temporary privileges for a term. These spurious deputies have not always even been freely elected by the people. At some meetings of the Estates-General and almost every meeting of the provincial estates, representing the people has been regarded as a right attached to certain offices or duties.(*)

The old nobility abhors new nobles. It allows them to sit among them only if they can prove, as the phrase goes, four generations and a hundred years.(**) In this way it pushes them back towards the order of the Third Estate to which, obviously, they no longer belong.[7]

But in the eyes of the law, all nobles are equal—those made so yesterday just as much as those who have been more or less successful in concealing their origins or usurpation. All of them have the same privileges. Opinion alone makes a distinction between them. But if the Third Estate has to put up with a prejudice sanctioned by the law, it has no reason to submit to one that is contrary to the letter of the law.

Let new nobles be treated in any manner of different ways. What is certain is that once a citizen acquires privileges contrary to the common system of law, he no longer belongs to the common order. His new in-

---

[7]The vanity of old has here given way to a more considered interest. In the parts of the kingdom without estates, the nobility of the bailiwicks has come to see how unwise it might be to irritate the new nobles and force them from spite to side with the Third Estate. Those parts of the kingdom with estates adopted this clumsy tactic, and experience has shown that it was a mistake.(***) So there has been a change of course. It has now been decided to allow all those whose nobility is *transmissible* to be admitted to the nobility, so that several of those who would have been placed among the Third Estate in areas with estates and in the provincial assemblies will be admitted to the order of the nobility in the bailiwicks and the Estates-General. But what meaning can this distinction between nobles who can and cannot *transmit* possibly have? What it actually means is that if they cannot *transmit* nobility, then this will affect their children. But it is hardly a question here of whether we should allow children whose fathers have not transmitted nobility to them to deliberate in our assemblies. All that is at issue here is the fact that their fathers were able to acquire, by virtue of a patent, what they have not as yet been able to acquire for their progeny. Their *persons* are noble. Their *persons* should therefore be admitted to the nobility.

terest is opposed to the general interest. He is unfit to vote in the name of the people.

This irrefutable principle also entails excluding the holders of temporary privileges from representing the Third Estate. Their interest is also more or less inimical to the common interest, and even though opinion might place them in the Third Estate, and the law is silent as far as they are concerned, the nature of things, stronger than both opinion and the law, incontrovertibly sets them outside the common order.

But suppose it was to be said that wanting to remove temporary members of the privileged order from the Third Estate as well as those with hereditary privileges is tantamount to wanting to weaken that order by light-heartedly depriving it of its most enlightened, courageous, and valued members?

The last thing I wish to do is to diminish the strength or dignity of the Third Estate because to my mind the Third Estate is always identical to the idea of a nation. But whatever our motives may be, can we act as if the truth were not the truth? If an army has had the misfortune to see the best of its soldiers desert, should it still entrust them with the defense of its camp? It cannot be said too often that every privilege is the opposite of the common law. As a result, all those endowed with privileges, without exception, constitute a class that is separate from and opposed to the Third Estate. At the same time, I must point out that this truth need not alarm the Friends of the People. On the contrary, it brings us back to the higher national interest, because it emphasizes the need to suppress at once all temporary privileges[8] that serve to divide the Third Estate and seem to condemn it to place its destiny in the hands of its enemies. This remark should not, moreover, be separated from the following. The abolition of privileges within the Third Estate should not mean that it should loose those exemptions which some of its members enjoy. These exemptions are no more than the entitlements of common right, and it has been a sovereign injustice to deprive the main body of the people of them. Thus what I am calling for is not the loss of a right, but its restitution;[9] and if it is claimed that it would become impossible to meet a public need by making some privileges common to all—by, for example, making

---

[8]Some municipal officials, the procurators attached to the *présidial* court of Rennes, etc., have already set a fine example by renouncing all exemptions and privileges that set them apart from the people.(*)

[9]It is certain that a community of privileges is the best way to bring the three orders closer together and prepare the most important law of all—the one which will convert the three orders into *one* nation.

everyone exempt from going into the ballot for the militia[10] —I can only reply that every public need ought to be everybody's responsibility, not that of a particular class of citizens, and that one would have to be entirely unacquainted with both reason and equity to be unable to find a more national way of adding the final detail to, and maintaining, whatever kind of military establishment one might wish to have.(*)

Thus, either because they were not elected at all; or because they were not elected by the general membership of the Third Estate of the towns and the rural areas entitled to be represented; or because, since they held privileges, they were not even eligible; the so-called deputies of the Third Estate who put in appearances at past Estates-General had no true mandate from the people.

Occasionally some seem to be surprised to hear complaints about a threefold aristocracy, made up of the army, the church, and the magistracy. They would rather prefer to insist that this is no more than a figure of speech. But it ought to be taken quite literally. If the Estates-General really is the interpreter of the general will and has possession of the legislative power, then it is surely the case that you will have a genuine aristocracy if the Estates-General is no more than a *clerico-nobili-judicial* assembly.

Add to this horrifying truth the fact that in one way or another every branch of the executive power has fallen into the hands of the caste from which the church, the magistracy, and the army are recruited. A sort of fraternity or spirit of *connivance* makes nobles give preference to one another on every issue over the rest of the Nation. Usurpation has been consummated. They really do reign.

If you study history to check whether the facts agree or disagree with this assertion, you will discover, as I did, that it is a great mistake to believe that France is, or has been, subject to a monarchical form of government. Take away a few years under Louis XI, under Richelieu, and a few moments under Louis XIV, when all that can be seen is undiluted despotism, and you will find yourself reading the history of a *palace* aristocracy. It is the court that has reigned, not the monarch. It is the court that makes and breaks careers, that summons and dismisses ministers, that creates and distributes offices . . . . And what is the court if not the head of that immense aristocracy that has spread itself over every part of France,

---

[10] I cannot avoid expressing some astonishment at the fact that gentlemen are exempt from the ballot for the militia! It seems to show a very haughty disdain for the only reason given in support of so many antiquated pretensions. It is hardly usual to expect payment as the price of *blood shed for the king*. M. Cérutti's remark has managed to mark that eternal refrain with an indelible scorn: "Was, then, the blood shed by the people mere water?"(**)

whose limbs touch everything and perform every kind of essential public function? This is why the people, in their complaints, have grown accustomed to distinguish between the monarch and the agents of power. They have always held the King to have been so completely misled and so utterly defenseless against an active and all-powerful court that they have never thought to blame him for all the evil done in his name. Is it not enough simply to open our eyes to what is happening at this very moment? What can we see? The aristocracy on its own, simultaneously fighting against reason, justice, the people, the minister, and the King. The outcome of this terrible struggle is still uncertain. Can it still be said that an aristocracy is no more than a chimera!

To sum up: Until now, the Third Estate has never had genuine representatives in the Estates-General. Thus its political rights are null.

Chapter Three
What Does the Third Estate Want? To Become Something.

The Third Estate's demands are not to be measured in terms of the isolated observations made by the small number of authors who are more or less acquainted with the rights of man. The Third Estate is actually still remarkably backward in this respect, not only in comparison to what has come to be envisaged by those who have studied the social order but even to the mass of ordinary ideas that have come to form public opinion. Any evaluation of what the Third Estate has actually been calling for has to be based only upon the procedurally authenticated demands addressed to the government by the great municipalities of the Kingdom.(*) What do they reveal? That the people would like to become *something,* but in truth, not very much at all. It would like to have (1) genuine representatives at the Estates-General, namely deputies *drawn from its own order,* entitled to interpret its will and to defend its interests. But what would be the point of attending the Estates-General if the interest that is contrary to the Third Estate is to remain predominant? All that its presence would do would be to set a seal of legality upon the oppression to which it will remain eternally victim. Thus it is very obvious that any delegation by the Third Estate should not go to vote in the Estates-General unless it has *an influence at least as great as that of the privileged orders.* Therefore, the Third Estate has also demanded (2) a number of representatives equal to that of the two other orders together. Finally, since equality of representation of this kind would be entirely illusory if each chamber is to vote separately, the Third Estate has demanded (3) that votes should be taken *by counting heads, not by counting each separate order.*[11] This, in substance, is all that is to be found in claims that seem, nonetheless, to have thrown the privileged orders into a state of alarm. On the strength of no more than this, the great municipalities have imagined that the reform of abuse will become inevitable.

The Third Estate's modest aim is to have an influence *equal* to that of the privileged orders in the Estates-General. I repeat, can it demand anything less? It ought to be clear that if its influence is less than equal, it cannot expect to emerge from its present state of political nonentity and become *something*.

But what is really lamentable is that the three articles forming the Third Estate's demands are simply not enough to give it that equality of influence that it genuinely cannot do without. It may well obtain an equal number of representatives drawn from its own order, but that equality will be quite vain for as long as the influence of the privileged orders has a presence and an ability to be predominant even in the sanctuary of its own chamber. Where are the gifts of office, position, and benefices to be found? Who is in need of favor and protection, and who has the power to bestow them? The mere thought is enough to make every Friend of the People tremble.

Is it not the case that those commoners whose talents seem to make them most apt to defend the interests of their own order were raised with an enforced or superstitious respect for the nobility? It is well known how generally inclined men are to adopt habits to suit what is of use to them. Man's constant concern is to improve his lot, and when individual industry cannot proceed by using honorable means, it will stray quite readily from the right path. We have all read how among some of the peoples of the ancient world, children learned not to expect a meal until they had performed some violent or skilful exercise. This was the way to teach them how to excel. In our case, the most able members of the Third Estate have been forced to earn their keep by learning flattery and by devoting themselves to the service of powerful men, a less honorable or social sort of education than antiquity supplied but one that is every bit as effective. This wretched part of the Nation has come to inhabit a kind of vast antechamber, where, constantly on the alert for what its masters might say or do, it is always ready to sacrifice everything to the fruits

[11] According to the decisions made in the Royal Council of 27 December 1788, the second of these demands has been *granted* even though no clarification has been given on the third, and the first has simply been rejected.(*) But it must be obvious that none of these demands can be met unless all three go through together. They amount to a whole. Nullifying one amounts to destroying them all. Further below, we will say who is entitled to decide everything affecting the constitution.

promised by the happy coincidence of being able to find favor. In the light of manners like these, is it groundless to fear that the qualities most needed for the defense of the national interest have been prostituted to the defense of prejudice? Aristocracy's boldest supporters may well be found within the Third Estate, among men born with much wit and little merit, as incapable of feeling the value of liberty as they are avid for fortune, power, and the favors of the great.

In addition to the empire exercised by an aristocracy that, in France, disposes of everything and the one generated by a feudal superstition that is still capable of debasing most minds, there is also the influence of property. This last is natural, and I would not wish to have it proscribed. But it has to be admitted that its influence still favors the privileged orders and that it is right to fear the power which that influence is likely to give them against the Third Estate. The municipalities have believed all too readily that the influence of privilege could be eliminated simply by excluding privileged persons from the people's representatives. But where in the countryside, or anywhere else for that matter, is there not a seigneurial landowner with even a modicum of popularity who does not have a large number of the commoner sort of people at his disposal? Think about the consequences and repercussions of this initial degree of influence, and then try to reassure yourself, if you can, about its possible impact upon an assembly that may well be far removed from these primary electoral assemblies but will still consist of a combination of those initial elements.(*) The more thought one gives to the subject, the more inadequate the three demands of the Third Estate begin to seem. Yet, such as they are, they have still been attacked with great violence. The pretexts for such malevolent hostility call for some examination.

§ 1
The Third Estate's First Demand

That the representatives of the Third Estate are to be chosen only from citizens who truly belong to the Third Estate.

We have already explained that it is necessary either to be untainted by any kind of privilege or to be completely and immediately purged of any such blemish to belong truly to the Third Estate.

The robe nobility, having acquired noble status by way of a door that, for mysterious reasons, they have decided to close,[12] would very much

[12]They say that henceforth they would like to be *well-assorted* and, to this end (one that leads to pride by way of humility, since it presupposes that they were once *badly-assorted company*), they have adopted a measure making every judicial and administrative office be-

like to take part in the Estates-General.(*) Their reasoning runs as follows: "Since the nobility wants no part of us, while we want no part of the Third Estate, it would be better by far to form a separate order. But we cannot. What then can be done? The only course is to preserve the ancient abuse allowing nobles to represent the Third Estate. Doing this will enable us to satisfy our desires without losing our pretensions." Every new noble, whatever his origin, has rushed to repeat the same view, namely, that the Third Estate should be able to elect gentlemen. The old nobility, which calls itself the true nobility, does not have the same interest in preserving this abuse. But it knows how to calculate. "We (it reasons) will be able to put our children into the commons; all in all, entrusting us with the task of representing the Third Estate is an excellent idea."

It is always possible to find a reason for what one has already decided to do. So it is now apparently necessary to maintain ancient *usage,* that excellent usage that until now positively excluded the nobility from representing the Third Estate! But the order of the Third Estate has political as well as civil rights. It ought to exercise both the one and the other all by itself.[13] It is quite extraordinary to make a *distinction* between the three orders to promote the utility of the first two and the misfortune of the third and then to make a demand that they should be *conflated* as soon as this looks useful to the two privileged orders and detrimental to the Nation. What kind of usage is being preserved if it is possible for clerics and nobles to lay claim to the chamber of the Third Estate! Could they in good faith claim to be represented if the Third Estate were to usurp the delegation representing their orders?

To show what is vicious in a principle, it is allowable to take its consequences to their furthest extreme. By using this method, I could say that if all the members of the three estates were allowed to give their proxy to whomsoever they pleased, it would be possible for the assembly to be made up of the members of no more than a single order. But would it be acceptable for the clergy alone to represent the whole nation?

I could go further. After entrusting the confidence of all three estates to a single order, why not give the mandate of all the citizens to a single individual? Is it possible to claim that a single individual could replace the Estates-General? If a principle entails such absurd consequences, it has to be vicious.

Another argument is to claim that restricting the electorate's choice is to violate its freedom to select whomever it prefers. There are two answers to this so-called problem. The first is that it is a difficulty that has

---

long almost exclusively to the families that possess them now. Recall what was said above about the aristocratic avidity for power.

[13]This principle is of the highest importance. It will be developed below.

been raised in bad faith and this can be proved. Nobody is unaware of a seigneurial landowner's ability to dominate the peasants and other country dwellers; everybody knows about the possible or habitual intrigues of their numerous agents, including the officers of their manorial courts. Any seigneur with a mind to influence a primary election can generally be sure to be elected to a *bailliage* assembly, where the choice will be purely among nobles themselves or among those deemed to merit their entire confidence.(*) It is hard to believe that keeping this power to surprise and abuse the people's trust is designed to secure its liberty. It is disgraceful to hear the sacred word "liberty" profaned when it is used to conceal designs that are the most opposed to it. The electorate should undoubtedly be free. That is why it is necessary to rid the primary electoral assemblies of all those privileged individuals who are all too accustomed to their imperious domination of the people.

My second reply is direct. Freedom and rights can never be unlimited in any area whatsoever. In every country, the law specifies the character of those entitled to be electors and to be elected. Thus, for example, the law determines the age below which it is impossible for anyone to be able to represent his fellow citizens. Everywhere too, women are deemed, for better or worse, to be ineligible for this kind of mandate. It is equally certain that a beggar or a vagabond cannot be given a people's political trust. Are domestic servants, or anyone dependent on a master, or non-naturalized foreigners ever to be found among the representatives of a nation? Like civil liberty, political liberty also has its limits. The question here is simply whether the requirement of non-eligibility demanded by the Third Estate is as essential a stipulation as all those just mentioned. Comparison between them actually serves to favor the claim, because a beggar or a foreigner may well have no interest opposed to the interest of the Third Estate, while nobles or clerics will, by virtue of their estate, be bound to incline towards the privileges they enjoy. Thus of all the conditions that the law should apply to the choice of representatives, the condition of non-eligibility demanded by the Third Estate is the one which is the most important and the most in keeping with equity and the nature of things.

To make the force of this argument clear, imagine this hypothesis: Suppose that France is at war with England and that everything to do with the conduct of hostilities is handled, as far as we are concerned, by an executive directory made up of elected representatives. Would we, in these circumstances, allow any of our provinces to choose their deputies to this directory from among members of the English ministry under the specious pretext of not wanting to violate their liberty? But it is obvious that the privileged orders have shown themselves to be no less of an enemy of the common order than the English have been to the French in time of war. Here is another conjectural image, drawn from the many crowding into my mind. If there were a general diet of all the maritime peoples to establish freedom and security for navigation, do you think that Genoa, Leghorn, or Venice would choose their plenipotentiary ministers from among the Barbary pirates or that the law allowing rich foreigners to buy or acquire a vote at Genoa was a good one? I do not know whether this last comparison is exaggerated, but it serves the purpose of my argument. In any event, like everyone else, I hope that, since the light of reason cannot exist for long without having some effect, the day will come when aristocrats will cease to show themselves to be the Barbary pirates of France.

As a consequence of these principles, those members of the Third Estate who are too closely connected to members of the first two orders should not be entrusted with the commons' confidence. It has already been established that their dependent position makes them ineligible. But without a formal exclusion, the influence of the seigneurial landowners, having become useless for themselves, cannot but be used to favor those they have at their disposal. It is particularly important to pay careful attention to the large number of agents of feudalism.[14] It is to the odious remains of that barbarous regime that, to the continuing misfortune of France, we owe the existing division of the country into three orders, enemies to one another. All will be lost if the mandatories of feudalism were to usurp the common order's delegation. Everyone knows that servants are harsher and more enterprising in defending their masters' interests than their masters themselves. I am well aware that this proscription encompasses a large number of people, because it concerns all the officials of the seigneurial courts,[15] etc. But here necessity has to command.

Here the province of Dauphiné has set a notable example.(*) It is essential to do as it has done and divest tax officials and their guarantors, to-

---

[14]The countryside is still being ravaged by the numberless vexations of these agents. One could say that the privileged order has a tail that is as noxious as itself. People are no less burdened by it than by the many arms of the fiscal system, all of which suggests that it is not beyond the bounds of possibility for the aristocrats to dare to make a show of so much misery by suggesting to the people that its true enemies are in the Third Estate, as if the lackeys of feudalism and anyone attired in livery of any kind and living in dependence on the aristocracy truly belongs to the Third Estate. It is only too true that the most dangerous of the people's enemies are to be found among those classes that have no attachment to the national interest, even though it is not by invoking the name of an *order* that the defenders of privilege normally use them for hire. There are terrible examples, in France, Holland, and everywhere else of the natural coalition between the lowest class in society and the privileged orders. To be plain, the mob belongs to the aristocracy in every country in the world.

[15]It is hard to imagine anything more opposed to sound politics than *patrimonial jurisdictions*. We owe it to scholars of jurisprudence for raising them as high as they could from the wreckage of feudal anarchy, for dressing up this sinister scaffolding with the appearance

gether with administrative officials, etc. of eligibility to represent the Third Estate. I also think that the farmers of land belonging to the first two orders are, in their present condition, too dependent to be able to vote freely in favor of their own order. But am I not entitled to hope that legislators will one day be sufficiently enlightened towards the interests of agriculture, *citizenship,* and public prosperity to be able to stop confusing the work of government with fiscal rapacity? Then every farmer will hold, and be encouraged to hold, a *life tenancy,* and we in turn will come to see these precious farmers as simple freeholders who will certainly be eminently fit to uphold the nation's interests.[16]

---

of legal forms, and, perhaps, for setting yet newer traps. One has to have a singular idea of *property* to conflate it with a *public function* and be able, in a country which is said to be so monarchical, to see without astonishment the royal sceptre shattered into a thousand pieces and thieves transformed into legitimate owners. It surely ought to have been possible to see how far something quite the opposite of genuine property, namely the *right* to do harm to someone else, could have insinuated itself under the guise of that indeterminate word "property." Can any kind of possession, however long it may have been, legitimate such disorder? Here, we are no longer talking about public functions that can certainly never become the property of any individual nor be disassociated from sovereign duty. I am rather talking about manifest usurpations of *common* liberty and property. I would like to have it explained to me what something called a *seigneur* is and why such an entity has to have *vassals.* Can such metaphysical relationships (here I am not concerned with real or monetary obligations) have anything to do with a proper political association? It is certainly possible that the term *proprietary* ward can encompass genuine acts of theft—thefts which cannot be covered by prescription. Imagine that in the absence of any system of police, Cartouche had made himself master of a high road.(*) Would he be entitled to exercise a genuine right of toll? If he had had the time to sell this kind of monopoly which was once quite common to a purchaser acting in good faith, would his so-called right be any the more respectable in the hands of the purchaser? Why is it the case that restitution is usually seen as something less just or more difficult than theft? There are, in the third place, possessions that do have a legal origin but that can nonetheless be said to be harmful to the public establishment. The owners of these may well be rightly entitled to expect an indemnity, but they should still be abolished. Once this entirely necessary and just work of political sifting has been done, we will then be able to fall to our knees before the sacred name of *property*, and do not imagine that he who has the least is less interested in this than he who has the most. Above all, do not imagine that denouncing property which is false amounts to attacking true property.

[16]Any aristocrat wanting to joke about what he calls the pretensions of the Third Estate always affects to confuse that order with his saddlemaker, shoemaker, and the like, adopting a language that he imagines is most likely to inspire scorn for the people he is referring to. But why should the most humble of trades dishonour *the order of the Third Estate* when they do not dishonour a *nation*? . . . . On the other hand, when attempts are made to sow division within the Third Estate, they are all too ready to point out differences between its various component classes. They would love to excite and set the one against the other, the inhabitants of the towns against those of the countryside. They seek to set the poor against the rich. How many stories could be told about the elegant features of refined hypocrisy, if it was allowable to say everything! But try as you can, men are not divided by differences of profession, or fortune, or education, but by interest. And as far as the present

To magnify the problem that we have just destroyed, it has been said that the Third Estate does not have enough enlightened or courageous, etc. members to represent it. This ridiculous assertion does not deserve a reply. Consider the *available* (*disponible*) classes within the Third Estate (and like everyone else, I take available classes to mean those with the kind of ease that enables a man to be given a liberal education, to cultivate his reason, and to take an interest in public affairs). These classes have no other interest than that of the rest of the people. Look and see whether they do not contain a sufficient number of educated and honorable citizens, all eminently well-qualified to be good representatives of the Nation.

But what if a *bailliage* is determined to give the Third Estate's mandate to a noble or a cleric if, it claims, it only has confidence in him?

I have already said that there cannot be any unlimited freedom and that, of all the conditions to be imposed upon eligibility, the one demanded by the Third Estate is the most essential of all. But there is also a more direct reply. Suppose that a *bailliage* is absolutely determined to harm itself. Should it then have a right to harm the others? If I alone have an interest in the actions of my authorized agent, it might indeed be possible to say, "So much the worse for you, why did you make such a bad choice?" But here the deputies of a district are not only the representatives of the *bailliage* that elected them. They also have to represent the generality of citizens and vote for the entire Kingdom. There has, therefore, to be a common rule and a common set of conditions, however displeasing they may be to some electors, to offer reassurance to the totality of the Nation against the vagaries of a few electors.

§ II
The Third Estate's Second Demand

That the number of its deputies is equal to those of the two privileged orders.

I cannot avoid repeating that the timid inadequacy of this demand is still too redolent of a bygone age. The Kingdom's great cities have not paid enough attention to the progress of enlightenment or even that of public opinion. They would have met with no more substantial resistance if they had demanded two votes for every privileged vote, and perhaps some haste would then have been made to offer them that equality which is now being opposed with such vigor.

---

question is concerned, there are but two: the interest of the privileged classes and that of the non-privileged. All the classes making up the Third Estate are bound together by a common interest against the oppression of privilege.

To determine a question like this, it is not enough, moreover, to be satisfied, as is often the case, with taking one's desire, or will, or usage for a reason. Recourse has to be made to principles. Political rights, like civil rights, must belong to those endowed with the qualities of citizenship. The ownership of legal entitlements of this kind is the same for everyone, irrespective of the different amounts of real property making up every individual's fortune or the assets they enjoy. Every citizen able to meet the requisite conditions to be an elector has a right to give himself a representative, and his own representation cannot be a fraction of someone else's representation. The right in question is indivisible. It is exercised equally by all, just as everyone is equally protected by the law they contribute to make. How then can it be possible to claim, on the one hand, that the law is the expression of the general will (meaning the majority) and, on the other, pretend that ten individual wills can balance a thousand others? This must amount to running the risk of leaving a minority to make the law, something that is obviously contrary to the nature of things.

If these principles, however well founded they are, seem to be a little too far-removed from ordinary ideas, I could draw the reader's attention to a more recognizable comparison. Is it not true that everyone agrees that it seems right for the huge *bailliage* of Poitou to have a larger number of representatives at the Estates-General than the tiny *bailliage* of Gex? Why is this so? Because, it is said, the population and tax-contribution of Poitou are much bigger than those of Gex.(*) So, there do seem to be principles that can be applied to determining the proportion of representatives. Should the tax contribution be the determining principle? Although we have no exact knowledge of how much each order pays, it leaps to the eye that the Third Estate bears over half of the tax burden.

As far as population is concerned, it goes without saying that the third order is enormously larger than the first two. Like everyone else, I do not know what the real proportion may be. But, like everyone else, I can be allowed to make my own estimation.

First, take the *clergy*. We know that there are 40,000 parishes, including their annexes. This immediately gives the number of parish priests, including those serving the annexes:	40,000
On average, there is one vicar to every four parishes, i.e.,	10,000
The number of cathedrals is the same as the number of dioceses. With an average of twenty canons per diocese and including the 140 bishops or archbishops,	2,800
The number of collegial canons can be estimated to be about double this, or	5,600

After this, it should not be assumed that there remain as many ecclesiastical heads as there are abbeys, simple benefices, priories, and chapels. It is well known that simony, or pluralism of benefices, is not unheard of in France. Bishops and canons are often also abbots, priors, or chaplains. To avoid double-counting, I estimate that, excluding those already enumerated, the number of beneficiaries is 3,000

Finally, I suppose a total of 3,000 ecclesiastics in holy orders without any kind of benefice: 3,000

All that remains are the monks and nuns, whose number has fallen at an accelerating rate over the past thirty years. I do not believe that there can be more than seventeen thousand today: 17,000

Total number of ecclesiastical heads: **81,400**

Nobility. I know only one way to arrive at the number of individuals in this order. This is to take the province where the number is best known and to compare it to the rest of France. Brittany is the province in question, and I ought to say at the outset that it is more fecund in nobles than the others, both because derogation does not occur there and because of the privileges that serve to keep families resident in the province.(*) In Brittany there are 1,800 noble families. I suppose that there are 2,000, because some do not yet have a right to belong to the provincial estates. Assuming that each family consists of five persons, there are 10,000 nobles of every age and both sexes in Brittany. Its total population is 2,300,000 individuals. That ratio of that total to the population of France is of the order of 1: 11. This implies multiplying 10,000 by 11 to give a total of 110,000 nobles at the most for the entirety of the kingdom: **110,000**

Thus, in total, the first two orders contain no more than 200,000 privileged individuals.[17] Compare that number to twenty-five or 26,000,000 souls and then decide.

---

[17]To make a further comment, if one deducts the monks and nuns but not the convents from the total number of ecclesiastics, it can be estimated that there is a remainder of about 70,000 genuine taxpaying citizens qualified to be *electors*. As for the nobility, if you deduct the women and the non-taxpaying children as non-*electors*, there remain barely thirty to forty thousand citizens with the same quality. It follows that, in terms of the representing

To reach the same conclusion by following other equally indisputable principles, imagine that the relationship between the privileged orders and the great body of citizens is like the relationship between exceptions and the law. Every society has to be ruled by common laws and to be subject to a common order. If there have to be exceptions, they should also be rare, and in no case should an exception have the same weight or influence in public affairs as the common rule. It is utterly insane to set exceptional interests alongside the great interest of the national mass, as if there can be any kind of balance between the two. This will suffice for

---

the nation, the clergy amounts to a more substantial mass than the nobility. The point of making this comment is that it runs directly against the flood of contemporary prejudices. I cannot genuflect before an idol. Even if the Third Estate, moved by blind animosity, were to applaud an arrangement by which the nobility was to obtain twice as many representatives as the clergy, I would still have to tell it that it has failed to consult either reason, justice, or its own interest. Is the public truly incapable of seeing anything except through the prism of prevailing prejudice? What is the clergy? A body of mandated officials entrusted with responsibility for the functions of education and worship. Change its internal administration; reform it in one way or another. But in one form or another it will still be necessary. As a body, it is not an exclusive caste but is open to any citizen. Its establishment costs nothing to the state. It is enough to work out how much it would cost simply to pay the parish priests to be horrified by the additional tax burden that the despoliation of ecclesiastical goods would entail. As a body, moreover, it is one that cannot avoid having a corporate nature because it is part of the hierarchy of government. The nobility, on the other hand, is an exclusive caste that is separate from a Third Estate that it affects to despise. It is not a body of public officials. Its privileges apply to individual persons independently of any office. Nothing other than the law of the strongest can justify its existence. While the clergy is losing privileges by the day, the nobility is preserving its own. In fact, it is adding to them. Is it not the case that we have witnessed in our own time that ordinance requiring *proof* to enter the army—*proof*, that is, not of talent or a favourable inclination but *proof on parchment* excluding the Third Estate from being able to serve! The parlements may well look as if they were created deliberately to maintain and uphold the people against seigneurial tyranny, but the parlements seem to have decided to change their role. Just recently, without any justification, they have made a gift in perpetuity of every office of councillor or presiding magistrate to the nobility.[*] At the time of the Assembly of Notables of 1787, the nobility also obtained a right to share in presiding over the provincial and any other assemblies with the clergy, and by demanding that the right to preside be shared, it succeeded in excluding the Third Estate that had, however, also been invited to do so by the Ministry. To add insult to injury the Third Estate was compensated by being given an exclusive right to elect presiding officers from the first two orders! In the last analysis, which of the two orders does the Third Estate have most to fear? One that is growing weaker by the day, nineteen-twentieths of whose members are made up of its own order? Or one that, at a time when privileged individuals seemed to want to revert to the common order, is aiming instead to distinguish itself even more strongly from that very same common order? When parish priests come to play the part in the clergy's affairs that will be entailed by the nature of things, the Third Estate will come to see how essential to its interest reducing the influence of the nobility rather than the clergy should have been.

now, but we will have more to say on this subject in the sixth chapter. In a few years time, when the objections now being made to the all-too-modest demands made by the Third Estate come to be remembered, there will be astonishment at both the specious character of the pretexts that were invoked and, even more, at the bold iniquity which dared to invoke them.

Those who seek to invoke the authority of facts to oppose the Third Estate can, if they are in good faith, readily read about facts that ought to guide their conduct. All that was needed to form a chamber of commons in the Estates-General held under Philip the Fair was the existence of a small number of boroughs (*bonnes villes*).(*)

Since that time, feudal servility has disappeared, and the countryside has yielded up an increasing population of *new citizens*. Towns have increased and grown in size. There, trade and the arts have, so to speak, created a multiplicity of new classes, including a large number of opulent families, rich in well-educated and public-spirited men. Why has this twofold increase, greater by far than the original weighting in the national balance that the boroughs once had, not been matched by an undertaking by the same royal authority to create two new chambers in favor of the Third Estate? Equity and sound policy join together to demand it.

No one would dare to appear to be so unreasonable when dealing with another kind of increase that occurred to France, namely the new provinces added to the kingdom since the last Estates-General. Nobody has dared to say that these new provinces should not have their own representatives over and beyond those represented at the Estates of 1614. But it is surely the case that, like additional territory, manufacture and the arts also create additional wealth, taxes, and population. Why, since it is so easy to make a comparison between an increase of this type and an increase of territory, refuse also to give the former a number of representatives over and beyond the number dispatched to the Estates of 1614?

But this is to reason with people able only to listen to their own interest. Better, rather, to present them with a more immediate consideration. Is it still right for the nobility to keep to the language and attitude that it used in a gothic age? Is it still right, at the end of the 18th century, for the Third Estate to keep to the abject and cowardly manners of ancient servility? If the Third Estate knew how to prize and respect itself, the other orders would undoubtedly respect it too! Remember that the old relationship between the orders has changed on both sides. The Third Estate, once reduced to nothing, has re-acquired, by means of its industry, a part of what was stolen from it by injurious force. But instead of retaking its rights, it has agreed to pay for them. They have not been restored; they have simply been sold back, and the Third Estate has been willing to buy them. But one way or another, it is now in position to take possession of them. It cannot be ignorant of the fact that where once it was no more than a shadow, it is now the real nation and that over the course of this long transformation, the nobility has ceased to be that monstrous feudal reality that once was able to oppress with impunity and instead has become no more than its shadow. It is now quite vain for that shadow to try to overawe an entire nation unless that nation wants to be regarded as no more than the lowest nation on earth.

§ III
The Third Estate's Third and Final Demand

That the Estates-General vote by head and not by order.

The question can be approached in three ways: from the point of view of the Third Estate; according to the interest of the privileged orders; and finally, according to true principles. It is useless, to take the first point of view, to add anything to what has already been said. From the Third Estate's point of view, this demand is a necessary consequence of the two others.

The privileged orders are afraid of the third order having an equality of influence and declare it to be unconstitutional. Their conduct is all the more striking because there are two of them against one, but they do not seem to have found anything unconstitutional in this unjust superiority. They are very convinced of the need to maintain a *veto* over anything that might be contrary to their interest. I do not want to repeat the arguments used by a score of writers to defeat this claim and its basis in an appeal to ancient constitutional forms. I have but one remark. There are certainly abuses in France. These abuses are to somebody's advantage, but they are hardly advantageous to the Third Estate. They are, rather, particularly damaging to it. Now in these circumstances will it be possible to destroy any abuse for as long as those benefiting from it have been left with a *veto?* Justice will have no force at all on its side. Everything will depend on the pure generosity of the privileged orders. Is that the right idea to have of a social order?

If we now consider the same subject independently of individual interest and instead deal with it on the basis of the principles that are intended to throw the most light on it, namely, those that form the science of the social order, or social science, the question begins to look quite different. I maintain that it is not possible to accept either the demand of the Third Estate or its rejection by the privileged orders without overturning the most obvious notions. I certainly do not mean to accuse the loyal boroughs (*bonne villes*) of the kingdom of having had any such intention. Their aim was to get nearer to attaining to their rights by calling for at least a balance between the two influences. They have, moreover, set out some excellent truths, because it is certain that a *veto* by one order over the others is a right that is able to paralyze everything in a country in which interests are so opposed. It is equally certain that by not voting by head, it will not be possible to identify a genuine majority and that this will be the greatest of all drawbacks, because the law, at root, will be null. These truths are absolutely indisputable. But could the three orders as now constituted join together to vote by head? This is the real question. The answer to it has to be no. In the light of true principle, they cannot vote *in common;* they cannot vote either by head or by order. Whatever the proportion adopted between them, it will not be able to meet the required objective, which is to bind and engage the totality of representatives by *one* common will. This assertion undoubtedly needs explanation and proof. I propose to reserve these for the sixth chapter. I have no wish to offend those disposed towards moderation who are always inclined to be afraid that the truth will come out at the wrong moment. But first it is necessary to make them see that the present state of affairs has come about solely through the fault of the privileged orders, that it is time to choose, and time to say what is true and just in all its force.

Chapter Four
What the Government Has Attempted to Do, and What the Privileged Orders Have Offered To Do to Favor the Third Estate

The government was led to imagine that it could obtain blind assent to all its projects by offering to do something for the Nation, not for reasons that were likely to produce a feeling of gratitude but because of its blunders and its realization that it could not correct them without the help of the Nation. With this in mind, M. de Calonne produced the plan for the provincial assemblies.(*)

§ I
The Provincial Assemblies

It was impossible to pay a moment's attention to the interest of the Nation without noticing the political nullity of the Third Estate. The Minister even seems to have realized that the distinction between the three orders was incompatible with any hope of a successful outcome and was probably aiming to make that distinction disappear in the fullness of time. This at least appears to have been the spirit in which the initial plan for the provincial assemblies seems to have been conceived and drafted. It needs only to be read with a little attention for it to be clear that it had no concern with the *personal* status of citizens. Its only concern was with their property or their *real* status. It was to be as a property owner and not as a priest, a noble, or a commoner that one was to be summoned to attend these interesting assemblies. They were interesting not only in the objective that they were supposed to serve, but even more so because of the way that they were to be convoked. It amounted to the establishment of a genuinely national representation.

Four kinds of property were distinguished. The first consisted of seigneurial domains. Those possessing them, whether nobles or commoners, ecclesiastical or lay, were to form the first class. Ordinary property, as against seigneurial property, was to be divided into three classes. A more natural division would have consisted of no more than two, namely, rural and urban property, given by the nature of the employments associated with them and the ensuing balance of interests. All the trades, arts, manufacturing industries, etc. could then have been included in the latter class, along with the houses. But it was doubtless thought that the time was not yet ripe to merge ordinary ecclesiastical property with either of these other two categories. Thus it was deemed to be necessary to leave the clergy's ordinary, non-seigneurial property as a separate class. This formed the second kind of property. The third included rural property, while the fourth consisted of property situated in towns.

Note that since three of these various types of property could be owned indistinctly by citizens in any of the three orders, three of the four classes of representatives would have been made up indistinctly of nobles, commoners, or priests. The second class itself would have contained knights of Malta or even laymen representing hospitals, parish charitable trusts, and the like.

It is natural to believe that had public affairs come to be dealt with in these assemblies without any regard to personal status, a community of interests between the three orders would have come to be formed and that this would have been the general interest, so that the Nation would have ended up by being what every nation ought to have been to begin with, by being *one*.

All these good ideas did not impinge on the Principal Minister's much vaunted mind.(*) It is not that he did not have a very clear view of the interest that he sought to serve, but rather that he had absolutely no understanding at all of the real value of what he went about damaging. He revived the politically inept division into orders based on persons, and although this change alone ought to have led to a need to make a new plan, he remained content with the old one in everything that did not seem to be at odds with his aims and was then astonished by the scores of problems arising daily from the lack of compatibility between the two. The nobility above all could not understand how it could possibly regenerate itself in assemblies where no provision had been made for a supply of genealogists. Its anxieties on that score were amusing to observe.[18]

Of all the vices involved in establishing this edifice, the greatest was to begin, so to speak, with the roof instead of with the natural foundation on which it ought to have been based, namely, free elections by the people. But at least the Minister, as a gesture of homage towards the rights of the Third Estate, announced that its order would have a number of representatives equal to those of the clergy and nobility combined. This, at any rate, is the positive wording of their founding articles. But what, in fact, happened? Deputies of the Third Estate were nominated from among the privileged orders. I know of one assembly in which only one of its fifty-two members is not a member of a privileged order. Thus has the cause of the Third Estate been served, even after it was proclaimed publicly that justice would be its rightful desert!

§ II
The Notables

The Notables deceived the hopes of both ministers. In this respect, there is no more fitting portrait than the excellent sketch provided by M. C[erutti]:

> The King assembled them twice to consult them over the interests of the Throne and the Nation. What did the Notables of 1787 do? They defended their privileges against the Throne. What did the Notables of 1788 do? They defended their privileges against the Nation.(*)

Instead of consulting those whose *privileges* made them notable, those who should have been consulted ought to have been those who were notably *enlightened*. Even the most ordinary private individuals are not mistaken about where to seek council either for their own affairs or for those people in whom they have a genuine interest.

---

[18]See the minutes of the provincial assemblies.

M. Necker was duped.(*) But how could he have guessed that the very same men who voted to accept an equal number of representatives from the Third Estate in the provincial assemblies would reject that very same equality in the Estates-General? Whatever the case, the public has not been duped. It had always disapproved of a measure (namely convening the Notables) whose outcome it could foresee and which, at best, it held to be responsible for delays that can be prejudicial only to the Nation. This might suggest that now is the time to investigate some of the motives underlying the majority decision in the most recent Assembly of Notables. But this is not the moment to anticipate the verdict of history. That verdict will still come all too quickly for men who, in the best of circumstances and with all the ability to dictate all that would have been just, fine, and good for the benefit of a great nation, chose instead to prostitute that superb opportunity to a miserable vested interest and, by doing so, gave posterity yet another example of the way that prejudice can maintain its empire over every sense of public spirit.

As can be seen, the ministry's efforts have not yielded any fruits that have been favorable to the Third Estate.

§ III
The Patriot Writers of the First Two Orders

It is noteworthy to see that the cause of the Third Estate has been taken up with more speed and vigor by noble and ecclesiastical writers than by those who themselves have no privileges.

I am inclined to explain the slowness of the Third Estate in terms of the habits of silence and fear that are the hallmark of the oppressed and, as such, amount to additional proof of the reality of oppression. Is it really possibly to reflect seriously about the principles and purpose of the social state without, in the depths of one's soul, feeling a revulsion towards the monstrous partiality of human institutions? I am not at all surprised that the first two orders were the first to defend justice and humanity. If the *talents* are connected to the exclusive use of intelligence and long-standing habit, and if the members of the Third Estate may have had an abundance of reasons for distinguishing themselves in this area, an *enlightened* concern for public morality is more likely to be found among men who are better placed to grasp the nature of the great bonds of society and whose original impulses are usually less likely to have been cut short. It has to be recognized that there are some sciences which have as much to do with the soul as with the mind. Once the Nation is free, it will not be able to avoid gratefully remembering those patriotic writers of the first two orders who were the first to abjure encrusted error and to prefer the principles of universal justice to the murderous combinations of vested interests against the national interest. In anticipation of the public honors to be bestowed upon them, let them not refuse the tribute of a citizen whose soul is aflame with love for his country and who adores every effort made to free it from the wreckage of feudalism.

It is certain that the first two orders have an interest in restoring the Third Estate to its rights. There is no reason to disguise the fact that the only guarantee of public freedom is to be found where real force resides. We can be free only by and with the People.

If a consideration of this importance is likely to go over the heads of the frivolousness and egoism of most French people, they will still at least be struck by the changes that have taken place in public opinion. Reason's empire is growing by the day. Increasingly it requires the restoration of rights that were usurped. Sooner or later every single class will come to be bound by the limits of the social contract, the contract that concerns and obliges every associate, one to another.[19] Will that fundamental principle then be used to obtain its innumerable benefits or to sacrifice them to despotism? This is the true question. True human bonds may have been destroyed during the long night of feudal barbarism. Every notion of right may have been overturned and justice corrupted. But as light begins to dawn, gothic absurdity will have to take flight, and the last vestiges of ancient ferocity will fall and be annihilated. This much is certain. The question is then whether we will simply substitute one evil for another or whether true social order in all its beauty will come to replace ancient disorder. Will the changes that we are about to undergo be the bitter fruit of civil war, which will be disastrous in every respect for all three orders and advantageous to ministerial power alone, or will they instead be the natural, long-foreseen and well-managed effect of a just and simple vision, of happy cooperation, favored by propitious circumstances and freely promoted by every interested class?

§ IV
On the Promise to Shoulder the Burden of Taxation Equally

The Assembly of Notables expressed a formal wish that the three orders should all be subject to the same taxes. But they were not asked to offer this opinion. The question at issue was the manner in which the

---

[19]There is no other way to conceive of the social contract. It binds the associates to one another. To assume that there is a contract between a people and its government is a false and dangerous idea. A nation does not make a contract with those it mandates; it *entrusts* the exercise of its powers.

Estates-General was to be convoked, not the content of the deliberations that that Assembly might undertake. This wish has, therefore, to be set alongside those issued by the Peers, the Parlement and the many private associations and individuals who are all now rushing to agree that the richest should pay as much as the poorest.

I cannot conceal the fact that so new a turn of affairs has frightened a part of the public. It might, perhaps, be said that is encouraging to see so much good-hearted willingness towards an equitable distribution of the tax burden in advance of the moment when it will be settled by the law. But what is the cause of this new zeal and of so much haste and willingness to cooperate now shown by the nobility? By offering to make a voluntary donation, could they not be hoping to forestall the need for the law to perform an act of justice? Might this excessive concern with anticipating what the Estates-General might do not be designed simply to make it easier to do without the Estates-General altogether? I would not wish to accuse the nobility of wanting to tell the King: "Sire, you need the Estates-General only to restore your finances. So, we propose to pay, just like the Third Estate. Consider this small surplus and see whether it might not rid you of an assembly that is a cause of more alarm to us than it is to you?" Surely no one could ever possibly think that.

One might, instead, suspect the nobility of wanting to bathe the Third Estate in illusions, of wanting, by making a gesture of equity in advance, to offer a *quid pro quo* for its current demands and distract it from its need to be *something* at the Estates-General. It seems to be saying to the Third Estate: "What do you want? That we pay like you. Which is just; so we'll pay. But leave the old state of affairs—where you were nothing, and we were everything, and it was so easy for us to pay no more than what we wanted—as it was." It would be so useful, merely by paying the price of a forced renunciation, for the privileged classes to maintain all the abuses and still hope to be able to add a few more! If to strike so excellent a bargain, all that was needed was to excite a little enthusiasm among the people, would it be so hard to find a way to move it and even arouse its tenderness by talk of relieving its suffering and by filling its ears with the sonorous *words* of equality, honor, fraternity and the like?

The Third Estate might reply: "It is high time that you shouldered the burden of taxes that are much more useful to you than to us. You have well been able to see that this monstrous inequity cannot last much longer. If we are to be free in what we offer as taxes, it is clear that we cannot, nor should not, nor will not, give anything more bountiful than you. This simple resolution on our part serves to make us more than a little indifferent to those acts of renunciation that you continue to vaunt as a rare kind of gesture, one befitting what honor and *generosity* would command to *French chivalry*.[20] Truly, you will have to pay, not from generosity, but from justice; not because you choose to, but because you ought to. All that we expect from you is a sign of obedience to the common law and not an insulting sign of pity towards an order that you have treated without pity for so long. But the whole matter is one for the Estates-General to deal with. What is at issue now is how it will be constituted. If the Third Estate is not represented, the Nation will be dumb. Nothing it undertakes can be valid. Even if you were to find a way to establish a rightful order everywhere without our assistance, we cannot allow you to dispose of us in our absence. Long and bitter experience has made it impossible for us to believe that any good law can be sound if it is merely a *gift of the strongest*."

The privileged orders do not tire of saying that, from the moment that the three orders jointly surrender their purely monetary exemptions, everything will be equal between them. But if everything will be equal, why then should they be afraid of the demands of the Third Estate? Is it to be supposed that the Third Estate would want to harm itself by attacking a common interest? If everything is to be equal, how can one explain all those efforts to prevent the Third Estate from escaping from its political nullity?

But where, I ask, is the miraculous power able to guarantee France from the possibility of any abuse of *any kind* as soon as the nobility begins

[20] I confess that I find it impossible to approve of the great store set upon getting the privileged orders to renounce their pecuniary privileges. The Third Estate seems to be unaware that since consent to taxation is as much a matter of the constitution whether it applies to itself or to the other orders, all it will need to do is to declare that it does not intend to bear any tax which is not born by all three orders at once. I am no more satisfied with the way in which this far-too-highly solicited renunciation has been carried out in the majority of the *bailliages*, despite the show of gratitude that has filled the pages of the newspapers and magazines. It can be read there that the nobility *will retain the sacred rights of property . . . the prerogatives belonging to it . . . and the distinctions essential to a monarchy*. It is astonishing that the Third Estate has not replied, first, to the *reservation of the sacred rights of property* by saying: that the whole Nation has an interest in doing so but that it could not see who this reservation is directed against; and that if the three orders wished to consider themselves separately, history would doubtless instruct them which of the three had the most reason to be suspicious of the others; that, in a word, the claim can be regarded only as a gratuitous insult, tantamount to saying *we will gladly pay taxes on condition that you do not steal from us*. In addition, what are *prerogatives belonging* to part of the Nation when the Nation never seems to have granted them? Prerogatives which would soon no longer be esteemed if granted no other origin than the *right of the sword!* Finally it is even more difficult to understand what these *essential distinctions* in a monarchy might be, without which, presumably, a monarchy would not be able to exist. As far as we can see, none of them, not even the distinction of mounting the royal carriage, seems to be important enough to make it true that a monarchy would not be able to survive without them.

to pay its share of the taxes? If such abuses and disorder will still exist, I would like to know how everything can be equal between those who profit from them and those who suffer from them.

Everything is equal! Presumably it has been out of a spirit of equality that the Third Estate has been subject to the most degrading exclusion from every official position and every more than slightly distinguished office? Presumably it has been out of a spirit of equality that it has been forced to pay an additional financial tribute to produce that prodigious quantity of resources of all kinds, destined exclusively for what is called the *poor nobility*?

In any trial between a member of a privileged order and a man of the people, is the latter not certain to be oppressed with impunity precisely because he will have to turn to someone privileged if he dares to ask for justice? They alone dispose of every power, and is not their first reaction to regard a complaint by a commoner as a lack of subordination?

Why do the toadies of the judicial system and the police tremble in carrying out their functions on a member of the privileged orders, even when someone has been caught red-handed, while they show so much brutality towards a poor man who has merely been accused?

What is the point of all those privileges connected to legal proceedings, of those attributions, evocations, letters of suspension, etc. that serve to discourage or to ruin an opposing party? Are they for the benefit of the non-privileged Third Estate?

Who are the citizens most exposed to personal vexation by agents of the tax collectors and their subordinates in every part of the administration? They are members of the Third Estate, by which I still mean the veritable Third Estate, the one that does not enjoy any kind of exemption.

Why do members of the privileged orders, after the most appalling crimes, almost always avoid punishment, thus depriving law and order of its most effective exemplary deterrents?

What sort of absurd and ferocious scorn do you dare to display by demoting a privileged criminal to the rank of a commoner in order, as you put it, to *degrade* him and make him *fit* in such company to submit to the death penalty.(*) What would you say if, before punishing a criminal from the Third Estate, the Legislator were to grant him letters of nobility to purge his order of his presence?

The law prescribes different punishments for someone who is privileged than for someone who is not. It seems to show a fondness towards the noble criminal, honoring him to the very scaffold. In addition to this abominable distinction that, at bottom, must be thought to be worth preserving only by those projecting some sort of crime, there is then, as is well known, attached a further punishment, namely, that of infamy for the entire family of the unfortunate wretch executed without the benefit of privilege. It is the law itself that is guilty of this atrocity, but there are those who would refuse to reform it! The *duty* is the same for everyone; the *crime* is the same; why then should the *punishment* be different? Note well that as things stand you can never punish anyone who is privileged without both honoring him and punishing the Nation, which has already suffered enough for his crime.

I put it to you, is it permissible, in the light of the most superficial glance at society, to repeat that everything will be equal as soon as the nobility renounces its monetary tax exemptions? There are indeed some men who are sensible only to money. Being literally paralyzed when it is a matter of liberty, honor, equality before the law or, in a word, every social right except money, they cannot imagine that it might be possible to be anxious about anything other than paying a penny more or less. But I am not writing for men of so vile a character.

What is to be said of the exclusive privilege of appearing in arms, even in peacetime, not for reasons related to any military function and without even the uniform of that estate? If a privileged person can arm himself to protect his life, his goods or his honor, does a member of the Third Estate have less of an interest in preserving his life or his goods and is he not just as sensible of his honor? Would anyone dare to claim that the law offers additional protection to someone without a privilege and that this actually exempts him from having to arm himself for his own defense?

If everything is equal, why are there such voluminous compilations of law, all advantageous to the nobility? Has someone discovered the secret of favoring one order without prejudicing the rest? But even when you know perfectly well that all this separate legislation serves to turn the nobility into a race apart, one which appears to have been born to command and turn the rest of the citizenry into a people of helots destined to serve, you still dare to lie to your own conscience and try to deafen the Nation into dull credulity by making a clamor about everything being equal.[21]

Even those laws that are taken to be the most general and the most exempt from partiality are the accomplices of the privileged orders. Examine their spirit; consider their effects; who do they appear to have been

[21]I would very much like to know where all those numerous privileges that everyone complains that we enjoy might be, said an aristocrat. Better, rather, to say where are they not, replied a Friend of the People. Everything about a privileged person reeks of privilege, even his manner of asking a question, which, in an ordinary citizen, would be found to be quite extraordinary; even the tone of assurance he adopts in asking questions that in his own heart he has already resolved. Even if every privilege were to be reduced to a single one, I would still find it intolerable. Is it not obvious that it would multiply just like the number of privileged individuals?

made for? For the privileged orders. Against who? Against the people, etc., etc.

But the people are expected to be content and are not supposed to dream of anything more, because the nobility has *agreed* to pay taxes just like it! Future generations are expected to close their eyes to contemporary enlightenment and habituate themselves calmly to an oppressive order that the present generation can no longer endure! But it is time to turn away from an inexhaustible subject and the feelings of indignation that it is bound to reawaken.[22]

There can be no doubt that all the taxes that fall particularly on the Third Estate will be abolished. A country in which those citizens who benefit the most from the public establishment contribute the least is a strange sort of country! Even stranger is one where some taxes were said to be shameful to bear and where even the Legislator held them to be degrading!(*) What sort of a society, with even a modicum of sanity, would take work to be a *derogation* from nobility, would hold consumption to be honorable and production a form of humiliation, and would call hard physical labor *vile,* as if anything other than vice ought to be called vile, and as if there is more of this, the only real kind of vileness, to be found among the laboring classes!

In the end, all those words like hearth taxes,[23] freeholds, billets, etc. will be proscribed for ever from political language and the Legislator will no longer be able to take a stupid pleasure in obstructing foreigners,

---

[22]Here, what has been at issue has been only the question of the inequality of *civil* rights; in the two final chapters I propose to set out the correct way to deal with the monstrous inequality of *political* rights.

[23]It is worth pointing out that the abolition of the hearth tax (*taille*) will be very advantageous to the privileged orders in monetary terms if it is agreed, as seems likely, to replace it by a general subvention. (1) In regions in which the hearth-tax falls upon a *person,* it is very well known that, at bottom, the tax is paid by the landowner. The farmer, told by the landowner that he will take responsibility for the payment of his tax, simply pays a higher proportional rent. This fact is known. If a general tax common to all goods, even those not now subject to the tax, were to be substituted for the hearth tax, it is evident that the mass of goods now bearing the costs of paying the hearth tax would be relieved of that portion of the new tax which would fall on goods that are currently exempt from paying the hearth tax. Since land that has been farmed out has to pay the largest share of the tax, it is certain that the largest proportion of the relief will favour the mass of that land. But it belongs overwhelmingly to the privileged orders, so that I am right to say that the privileged orders will pay less.

(2) In areas where the hearth tax falls upon *real* property, not persons, rural land will be relieved of all of that proportion of the new tax which will affect noble land. This conversion will take place irrespective of the personal quality of the landowners. Since nobody knows which order of citizens most noble and most common land belongs to, there is no

barred by these wounding distinctions, from bringing their capital and industry into our midst.

But while setting forth this advantage and a score of others that a well-constituted assembly might be able to obtain for the people, I cannot yet see anything capable of promising a good constitution to the Third Estate. It has made no further advance in its demands. The privileged orders continue to defend all their advantages. Whatever the proportional number of deputies, they still want to form two separate chambers; they still want two votes out of three and they still insist that each of them should have a veto. What wonderful ways to make all reform impossible! Paralysis might suit the taste of the first two orders. But will it please the Third Estate? It is not all that likely to be heard repeating the fine words of that royal tax farmer who said, *Why change? We are so comfortable!*

§ V
On the Compromise Suggested by the Friends of the Ministry and the Privileged Orders

The ministry is most afraid of a form of deliberation that, by bringing matters to standstill, would also entail a suspension of any grant of the financial assistance that it expects. If agreement could only be found to cover the deficit, the rest would no longer matter. The three orders could argue as much and for as long as they liked. Indeed, the less progress they make, the more the ministry might hope to reinforce its arbitrary authority. This is what lies behind the appearance of a possible compromise that has begun to be circulated widely and that would be as useful to the privileged orders and the ministry as it would be fatal to the Third Estate. This proposal is to vote by head in granting subsidies and on anything concerning taxation. The three orders would then withdraw to their separate chambers as if to impregnable fortresses, where the Third Estate would continue to deliberate without success, while the privileged orders would continue to enjoy their privileges without further fear, and the

---

reason to assume that the nobility ought to be given all the credit for the individual advantages or disadvantages arising from the suppression of the hearth-tax.

Well-to-do owners of seigneurial domains have also calculated very well that the abolition of the hearth-tax, free-hold etc. ought to favour sales and purchases by their vassals, increasing the value of their property and, as a result, promising them a new source of monetary profit. The hearth-tax is undoubtedly badly levied when it falls on farmers. But levying it, under a different name, on the landowners themselves and all the goods that they farm out would turn it into a purely political tax, insofar as it will discourage small landowners from giving up the management of their goods and will stand in for a prohibitive tax or fine on the idleness of the great landowners.

ministry would remain the master. But can it be believed that the Third Estate would fall into so crude a trap? Since a vote on the subsidy has to be the Estates-General's very last act, it will first have had to come to an initial agreement on a general form for all its deliberations; and it cannot be doubted that this will not be far-removed from one which allows the assembly to maintain the use of all its wisdom and enlightenment.[24]

§ VI
On the Proposal to Imitate the English Constitution

Different interests have had time to develop within the noble order. It is not far from dividing into two parties. All those connected to the three or four hundred most distinguished families aspire towards the establishment of an upper chamber, similar to the one in England. Their pride has been fed on the hope that they will no longer be confused with the mass of ordinary gentlemen. Thus the high nobility would be quite happy to see the rest of the nobility relegated to the House of Commons along with the generality of citizens.

The Third Estate will take care to preserve itself from a system that aims at nothing less than filling its own house with people with an interest that is so contrary to the common interest, a system that would soon push it back towards nullity and oppression. In this respect, there is a real difference between England and France. In England the only nobles with privileges are those granted a share in the legislative power by the constitution.[25] Every other citizen is subsumed under the same interest; there are no privileges that give rise to distinct orders. If, in France, there were a desire to join the three orders together to form one, then every kind of privilege would have to be abolished first. The noble and the priest would have to have no other interest than the common interest and, under the protection of the law, would have to enjoy no more than the

---

[24]See the *Views of the executive means etc.*, pp. 87–91 [above, pp. 34–9]

[25]The lords of the upper house do not even form a distinct *order*. There is only one order in England, and that is the nation. A member of the House of Lords is a great mandatory designated by law to exercise part of the function of legislating and the great judicial functions. He is not someone endowed with privileges by right of belonging to a *caste*, with no connection with public affairs, since a peer's younger brothers have no share in the privileges enjoyed by the elder. It is true that these great functions are connected to birth, or rather to primogeniture. This is a gesture towards feudalism whose influence was still preponderant a hundred years ago. It is an institution that at one and the same time is both gothic and ridiculous. If kings became hereditary to avoid the civil disturbances that their election might occasion, there is no reason to fear anything similar in the case of the nomination of a simple lord.

rights of ordinary citizens. Without this, it would be pointless to join the three orders together under the same denomination. They would still remain three types of heterogeneous matter that it would be impossible to amalgamate. Here, I have no wish to be accused of supporting any distinction of orders, something that I hold to be an invention that is the most harmful to any social good. The only misfortune greater than this would be the even more extreme misfortune of *nominally* combining the orders while still leaving them *really* separate by maintaining their privileges. This would set the seal on their victory over the Nation forever. Public safety calls for the common interest of society to be preserved somewhere in a pure and unmixed form. On the basis of this point of view—the only good, truly national, point of view—the Third Estate will never lend its authority to admitting several different orders into a so-called House of Commons, because the very idea of a House of Commons made up of different orders is a monstrosity. It amounts to a contradiction in terms.

Its opposition will also have the support of the minor nobility because it will never be willing to exchange the privileges that it enjoys for a distinction that it would never actually have. Take note of the way that, in the Languedoc, it has always risen up against the aristocracy of the barons.(*) In general, men always have a strong liking for reducing everything superior to them to a state of equality; in this, they display themselves as *philosophers*. The word becomes odious to them only when they notice that their inferiors have the same principles.

The project to establish a two-chamber system has, however, gained so large a number of partisans among us that it has become a matter of real concern. The differences that we have presented are quite real. A nation that is split into orders can never have anything in common and can never be *one* nation. How, with such dissimilar materials, can it be possible to conceive of building the same political edifice in France as in England?

Can you possibly expect that it would be feasible to admit a part of the first two orders to the lower house? In that case, you will have to show us how to form a single common legislature out of several different orders. As has just been said, a common legislature cannot be anything other than a body of citizens with the same civil and political rights. It is a mockery to conceive of one in any other terms and imagine that one can form a common legislature by making citizens with unequal civil and political privileges sit together in the same chamber. You will not find so strange a combination in England. I should add that the part of the nobility that you propose to introduce to your so-called House of Commons would not need much time to seize control of most of the deputations. The Third Estate would lose its authentic representatives, and we would go back to the old state of affairs, where the nobility was everything and the Nation, nothing.

To avoid these difficulties, would you propose to establish a second chamber exclusively for the Third Estate? In this case, you will not have changed your present position but will have added an additional evil to it by joining the two privileged orders. By promoting this alliance, you will give them more power against the common order, but both sides will be weaker against ministerial power, which will be all-too-well aware that it will always be called upon to lay down the law to two divided peoples. Moreover, I cannot see why this new arrangement goes any nearer towards the English Constitution. You will have legitimated and sanctioned the separateness of the privileged orders; you will have divided them forever from the Nation's interest; and you will have perpetuated the hatred or, better, the sort of endless civil war affecting every people divided between those with privileges and those with none. With our neighbors, on the contrary, all the nation's interests are united in the House of Commons. The Lords themselves are careful to avoid forming any opposition to the common interest because it also happens to be their own, since it is the interest of their brothers, their children, and their whole families, who all rightfully belong to the Commons. But there are still those who dare to compare the English upper house to a house that would combine the French clergy and nobility! But, however this latter may be presented, it cannot escape from the cluster of evils that are inherent in its very nature. If it is composed of genuine representatives of the clergy and nobility drawn from the whole Kingdom, it will, as has been said, divide the two interests forever, putting an end to the hope of ever forming *one* Nation. If the aim is to create a chamber of peers, it will either have to be made up of deputies elected by a certain number of the most distinguished families, or to avoid diverging too far from the English model it will be necessary to decide simply to make the title of peer a hereditary or life privilege, relegating the rest of the nobility to the Third Estate. But all these suppositions simply add to the problems. They all entail a hybrid and, consequently, a monstrous House of Commons, etc. Moreover, when it pleases the King of England to create a peer, he is not obliged to choose someone from a single class of citizens. This is yet another difference, absolutely confounding all our own ideas about nobility.

I have a last comment to make. It follows on naturally from the supposition of an upper house made up of either hereditary or life members. It is certain that such individuals cannot, on any construction, be the representatives of the Nation, and yet they will exercise all the powers associated with that function. In good faith is it entirely impossible to foresee circumstances when, for example, convoking the Commons might become highly embarrassing? Dozens of reasons that are easy to imagine might first lead to one delay and then another. Finally, time would be so short that the upper house would be duly invited to give its assent in advance either to a loan or a law, etc. I leave the rest to the reader's imagination. It would be odd indeed to think that we might finally end up with that *plenary court* which we were once so reluctant to accept!(*) It should, it seems to me, be allowable not to be too favorably disposed toward a project capable of bringing us to the brink of a precipice that we ought to think we had managed to avoid for ever. We certainly do not need a *royal* or a *feudal* chamber. But I must also point out, before finishing this section, that I have attacked the idea of separate *chambers* only on the assumption that it would be based on a separation of *orders*. Separate these two ideas, and I would be the first to call for three chambers, equal in every respect and each made up of a third of the great national deputation. All that would remain, under this new plan, would be to adopt the means indicated on pp. 38 and 46 of the *Views of the executive means, etc.* in order to end up with a resolution amounting to the majority of votes on any occasion when the three chambers, taken as single bodies, were not in agreement with one another.

§ VII
The Spirit of Imitation Is Not Fit To Serve as a Good Guide

We would not have so much faith in English institutions if political knowledge and understanding were better established and more widely disseminated among us. In this respect, the French nation consists of men who are either too young or too old. The two ages, which are so close in many ways are also similar in this respect: namely, that neither the one nor the other is able to be guided by anything other than example. The young seek to imitate; the old can do no more than repeat. The latter are true to their own habits; the former mimic the habits of others. That is as much as they can achieve by relying on their own aptitudes and industry.

It should not be surprising, therefore, to see a nation, having barely opened its own eyes to the light, turn towards the English Constitution and want to take it as a model in everything. It would be highly desirable at this particular time for an able writer to enlighten us by addressing the following two questions: Is the British Constitution good in itself? Even if it is good in itself, is it likely to be good for France?[26]

---

[26]Since the appearance of the first edition of this pamphlet, an excellent work that in most respects fulfils the wish expressed here has been published. This is the *Examen du Gouvernement d'Angleterre comparé aux Constitutions des Etats-Unis*, a 291-page brochure.(**)

I am very much afraid that this much-vaunted masterpiece cannot withstand an impartial examination based on the principles of a genuine political order. We will perhaps be able to see that it is more of a product of chance and circumstance than enlightenment. Its upper house is obviously redolent of the period of the Revolution of 1688. We have already pointed out that it is almost impossible not to see it as a monument to gothic superstition.

In the second place, consider the system of national representation and how bad all its elements are, as the English themselves admit. But the characteristics of a good system of representation are the most essential requirements for forming a good legislature.

Thirdly, is the idea of dividing the legislative power into three parts, only one of which is taken to speak in the name of the nation, based on correct principles? If the Lords and the King are not the nation's representatives, they ought to have no part in the legislative power, because it is the nation alone that is able to will for itself and, consequently, create laws for itself. Whatever goes into a legislative body is competent to vote on a people's behalf only insofar as it is entrusted with their proxy. But if there are no free, general elections, where is the proxy?

I do not deny that the English Constitution was an astonishing piece of work at the time when it was established. But, even though there will be many who are willing to mock someone who is French but who is not inclined to prostrate himself before it, I would still dare to submit that instead of displaying all the simplicity of good order, it rather reveals a scaffolding of precautions against disorder.[27] Since everything in political institutions is connected, and there is no effect which is not, in its turn, the origin of a further sequence of causes and effects that can be extended for as far as it is possible to remain attentive, it is not surprising that thinking people take all this to be a sign of great profundity. But in the ordinary course of events it is usual for the most complicated machines to come first and, as with every other art, the same applies to the true progress of the social art. Its crowning triumph is to produce the greatest effects by the most simple means.

---

[27]In England, the government is a subject of a perpetual combat between the ministry and the aristocracy in opposition. The Nation and the King seem to be mere spectators. The King's policy consists of always adopting the strongest party. The Nation suspects both the stronger and the weaker party. For its safety, the combat has to continue. This is why it supports the weaker party to prevent it from being completely crushed. But if, instead of leaving the management of its affairs as a prize in this gladiatorial combat, the people decided to take them in hand by way of genuine representatives, can it, in all good faith, not be believed that all the importance presently attached to the *balance* of powers would not fall away, along with the order of arrangements that alone was what made it necessary?

It would be wrong to decide in favor of the British Constitution simply because it has lasted for a hundred years and looks as if it should last for centuries more. As far as human institutions are concerned, where are those that have not lasted for a very long time, however bad they may be? Is it not the case that even despotism goes on for a long time, even seeming to be eternal in the greatest part of the world?

A better proof would be to refer to *effects*. By comparing the English people to their continental neighbors with this in mind, it is difficult not to believe that they do have something better. Indeed, what the English people have is a constitution, however incomplete it may be, while we have none. The difference is considerable. It is hardly surprising that the effects are noticeable. But it is surely a mistake to attribute everything good about England to the sole power of the constitution. There is, self-evidently, at least one law that is worth more than the constitution itself. I mean, of course, trial by *jury,* the true guarantor of individual liberty in every country in the world where men aspire to be free. This way of providing justice is the only one able to offer protection from the abuse of judicial power, something so frequent and so redoubtable wherever judgment is not given by one's peers. Once it exists, all that is needed for anyone to be free is to take precautions against illegal orders emanating from ministerial power. For that, what is needed is either a good constitution, which England does not have, or a set of circumstances in which the head of the executive power is not in a position to use force to back up his arbitrary will. It is not difficult to see that the English nation is the only nation to have been allowed not to have a standing army that might be a threat to the nation. This is also why it is the only nation that is able to be free without having a good constitution. This reflection ought to be enough to make us weary of the mania for imitating our neighbors. Better, instead, to consult our own needs; they are nearer to us and will inform us rather better. If you want to try to naturalize the English Constitution here, you will have no difficulty in obtaining its defects because they will be of use to the only power whose obstruction you will have to fear. But will you obtain any of its advantages? This question is more problematic because here you will encounter a power with an interest in frustrating your desires. What, after all, is the reason for desiring an exotic constitution with such ardor? It is because it looks as if it has approached the proper principles of the social state. But if, in every sphere, there is a model of the good and the beautiful that is used to assess the amount of progress that has been made towards what is right, and if it cannot now be said that, in terms of the social art, this model is known less to us now than it was to the English in 1688, why should we spurn the very archetype of the good and restrict ourselves instead to imitating a mere copy? Would it not be better to raise our ambition directly and seek instead to become an example to every other nation?

No people, it is said, have done better than the English. But, even if this is true, does it mean that at the end of the eighteenth century the products of the political art should be what they were at the end of the seventeenth century? Just as the English did not fall below the level of enlightenment of their age, so we should not fall below the level of our own. Above all, we should not be discouraged by finding nothing in history that seems to fit our own position. The true science of the state of society is not all that old. For a long time men built huts before they were able to build palaces. This is why social architecture, the most important art of all, has been even slower to progress. It is not the sort of thing that despots and aristocrats could have been expected to encourage.

Chapter Five
What Should Have Been Done.
First Principles on This Matter

In morality, nothing can stand in for simple and *natural* means. But the more time that man has wasted on useless trials, the more he dreads the idea of beginning again, as if it can never be better to start again and get to the end instead of having to remain at the mercy of events and of those *factitious* resources which always lead to having to start again and again, but without ever getting any further.

In every free nation (and every nation ought to be free) there is only one way to put an end to differences about the constitution. Recourse should not be made to the Notables, but to the Nation itself. If we lack a constitution, then a constitution must be made, and the Nation alone has the right to do so. If we do have a constitution, as some persist in claiming and if, as they pretend, it means that the National Assembly should consist of three separate deputations drawn from the three different orders of citizens, it is still quite hard not to see that one of these orders has made such strong protestations that it is impossible to go one step further without some adjudication of its claims. But who is entitled to decide in such disputes?

A question of this kind will seem to be a matter of indifference only to those who, setting little store on just and natural means in social matters, value no more than those more-or-less invidious, complicated, and artificial expedients that serve to give what passes for repute to statesmen and great politicians. We, however, do not stray from morality. Morality is what should regulate all the ties binding men to one another, both in terms of their individual interests and their common or social interest. Morality ought to tell us what should have been done and, when all is said and done, it alone is able to do so. It is always essential to go back to first principles because these are more powerful than all the labored efforts of genius.

It will never be possible to understand the social mechanism without first deciding to analyze society as if it is like an ordinary machine, taking each part in turn and joining them together in one's mind to see how they fit together, one by one, to produce the resultant general harmony. Here, we do not need to do anything quite so elaborate. But it is still necessary to be clear. And, since it is impossible to be clear without starting from first principles, the reader is asked merely to consider the formation of a political society in terms of three epochs and to consider the differences between them as the basis of all the further elucidation that will be needed.

In the first of these epochs, one can imagine a more or less substantial number of isolated individuals seeking to unite. This fact alone makes them a nation. They have all the rights of a nation; it is simply a matter of exercising them. This first epoch is characterized by the activity of *individual* wills. The association is their work. They are the origin of all power.

The second epoch is characterized by the action of a *common* will. Here, everyone involved in the association seeks to give their union consistency. They all want to accomplish its purpose. Thus, they confer with one another and agree upon public needs and how to meet them. Here it can be seen that power belongs to the public. Individual wills still lie at its origin and still make up its essential underlying elements. But taken separately, their power would be null. Power resides solely in the whole. A community has to have a common will. Without this *unity* of will, it would not be able to make itself a willing and acting whole. It is also certain that this whole has no rights that are not connected to the common will.

Now consider the passage of time. The members of the association will have become too numerous and too widely dispersed to be easily able to exercise their common will themselves. What do they do? They will detach all that is needed for overseeing and providing for public concerns and will entrust that portion of the national will—and consequently power—to the exercise of some of their number. This brings us to the third epoch, or the period of *government by proxy*. This calls for several remarks. Firstly, the community does not divest itself of the right to will. This right is its inalienable property. All it can do is to entrust the exercise of that right to someone else. This principle is elaborated upon elsewhere. Secondly, the body of those delegated to exercise that trust cannot even enjoy the full exercise of the community's power. The community can entrust only that portion of its total power that will be needed to maintain good order. In this kind of delegation, nothing more than what is necessary is surrendered. Thirdly, it is not up to the body of delegates to alter the limits of the power with which it has been entrusted. It is easy to see that it would be self-contradictory to grant it this kind of faculty.

The third epoch can be distinguished from the second inasmuch as it is no longer a *real* common will that acts, but a *representative* common will. It has two ineffaceable characteristics and these need to be repeated. Firstly, that will, as expressed by the body of representatives, is neither complete nor unlimited; it is no more than a portion of the great common national will. Secondly, those delegated to exercise that will do not do so as a right that is their own, but as a right exercised on others' behalf. The common will is exercised as a delegation or trust.

Here, in order to get to the end, we have to set aside a mass of further considerations to which, quite naturally, this presentation might lead. What matters now is to know what should be understood by the political *constitution* of a society and how to identify its just relationship to the *nation* itself.

It is impossible to create a body for an end without giving it the organization, forms, and laws it needs in order to fulfil the functions for which it has been established. This is what is meant by the *constitution* of that body. It is obvious that it could not exist without one. It is equally obvious that any delegated government must have its constitution and that what is true of government in general is also true of each of its component parts. Thus the body of representatives entrusted with the legislative power, or the exercise of the common will, exists only by way of the mode of being which the nation decided to give it. It is nothing without its constitutive forms; it acts, proceeds, or commands only by way of those forms.

In addition to the necessity to organize the body of the government so that it can exist or act, the nation also has an interest in ensuring that public power so entrusted can never become harmful to those who entrust it. Hence the multitude of political precautions that are added to the constitution. These amount to so many essential rules of government, without which the exercise of power would become illegal.[28]

---

[28]When a constitution is simple and well made, precautions can be few in number. In countries where a constitution is complicated or, more truthfully, poorly understood, precautions increase *ad infinitum*. These become an object of study. Constitutions become a science, and their most essential feature, namely their internal organization, gets buried or lost underneath a purely accessory scientific scaffolding.

There is, therefore, a double necessity to subject a government to fixed forms, both internal and external, in order to guarantee its ability to meet the ends for which it was established and to make it incapable of diverging from these ends.

But how, in the light of this, is it possible to claim that the *nation* itself ought to have been given a constitution? The nation exists prior to everything; it is the origin of everything. Its will is always legal. It is the law itself. Prior to the nation and above the nation there is only natural law. To have a proper idea of the sequence of *positive* laws, all emanating solely from the nation's will, the first in order of precedence will be the *constitutional* laws, which will be divided into two parts. Some will regulate the organization and functions of the *legislative* body; others will fix the organization and functions of the various *active* bodies. These laws are said to be *fundamental,* not in the sense that they can be independent of the national will, but because bodies that can exist and can act only by way of these laws cannot touch them. In each of its parts a constitution is not the work of a constituted power but a constituent power. No type of delegated power can modify the conditions of its delegation. It is in this sense, and in no other, that constitutional laws are *fundamental.* The first of these, those that establish the legislature, are *founded* by the national will prior to any constitution. They form its first level. The second should also be established correspondingly, by a *special* representative will. Thus all the parts of a government are answerable to and, in the last analysis, dependent upon the nation. This is no more than a brief sketch, but it is correct.

One can then see quite easily how laws in the proper sense, laws that protect citizens and define the common interest, will be the work of a legislative body formed and moved by the provisions given by its constitution. Although laws of this type appear here as no more than second in order of precedence, they are nonetheless the most important. They are the *end* to which the constitution is no more than the *means.* They too can be divided into two parts: direct or protective laws and indirect or permissive laws. This is not the place to give further development to this analysis.[29]

We have seen how the birth of a constitution took place in the second epoch. It is clear that it was designed solely for the *government.* It would be ridiculous to suppose that the nation itself was bound by the formalities or the constitution to which it had subjected those it had mandated. If a nation had to wait for a *positive* mode of being in order to become a nation, it would simply never have had an existence. A nation is formed

---

[29]It need only be said that the best way not to make sense is to conflate all the parts of the social order and place them all under a rubric headed "constitution."

solely by *natural* law. Government, on the other hand, is solely a product of positive law. A nation is all that it can be simply by virtue of being what it is. It cannot decide by an act of its will to give itself any more or less rights than those that it actually has. In the very first epoch it had all the rights of a nation. In the second epoch, it exercised them itself. In the third, it turned all the rights needed for the preservation and the good order of the community into rights exercised by its representatives. If you stray from this sequence of simple ideas, you will simply stumble from one absurdity to the next.

Government can exercise real power only insofar as it is constitutional. It is legal only insofar as it is faithful to the laws imposed upon it. The national will, on the other hand, simply needs the reality of its existence to be legal. It is the origin of all legality.

Not only is a nation not subject to a constitution, it *cannot* and *should* not be—which amounts to repeating the point that it is not subject to a constitution.

It *cannot* be subject. From who, in effect, could it have received a positive form? Is there any antecedent authority able to have told a multitude of individuals, "I have united you under this set of laws, and you will form a nation under the conditions which I have laid down"? Here we are not dealing with brigandage or domination but with a legitimate association, one that is voluntary and free.

Can it be said that a nation could, by an initial act of will that is truly free of every prescribed form, undertake to will in future only in a determinate manner? In the first place, a nation cannot alienate or prohibit its right to will and, whatever its will might be, it cannot lose its right to change it as soon as its interests require it. In the second place, to whom might a nation thus offer to bind itself? I can see how it can *oblige* its members as well as those it has mandated and everything connected to it. But can it in any sense impose duties on itself? What is a contract with oneself? Since both sides are the work of the same will, it is easy to see that it can always withdraw from the so-called engagement.

But even if it could, a nation *should* not subject itself to the restrictions of a positive form. To do so would expose it to the irretrievable loss of its liberty. Tyranny needs no more than a single moment of success to bind a people, through devotion to a constitution, to forms which make it impossible for them to express their will freely and, as a result, to break the chains of despotism. Every nation on earth has to be taken as if it is like an isolated individual outside all social ties or, as it is said, in a state of nature. The exercise of their will is free and independent of all civil forms. Since they exist only in the natural order, their will needs only to have the *natural* character of a will to produce all its effects. However a nation may will, it is enough for it to will. Every form is good, and its will is always the supreme law. Since, in conceiving of a legitimate society, we have supposed that every purely natural, individual will has the moral power to form an association, how can we deny that power to an equally natural, *common* will? A nation never leaves the state of nature and, amidst so many perils, it can never have too many possible ways of expressing its will. There is no reason to be afraid of repeating the fact that a nation is independent of all forms and, however it may will, it is enough for its will to be made known for all positive law to fall silent in its presence, because it is the source and supreme master of all positive law.

Although they do not need further proof, there is an even stronger proof of the truth of these principles.

A nation should not and cannot subject itself to constitutional forms because, at the first conflict between the various parts of its constitution, what would become of a nation so disposed and so ordered as to be unable to act in any other way than through the provisions of the disputed constitution? It is worth emphasizing how essential it is in the civil order for citizens to find a branch of the active power readily able to exercise authority to settle their legal differences. In the same way, among a free people the various branches of the active power must have the freedom to appeal to the legislature for a decision in every unforeseen difficulty. But if the legislature itself or the various parts of this primary element of the constitution cannot agree among themselves, who is to be the supreme judge? There is always a need for one because, without one, order will give way to anarchy.

How can it be imagined that a constituted body can decide upon its constitution? One or several of the component parts of a moral body are nothing when taken separately. Power belongs solely to the whole. As soon as a part objects, the whole no longer exists, and if it no longer exists, how can it judge?[30] Thus it ought to be recognized that there would no longer be a constitution if, at the slightest dispute between its component parts, the nation did not have an existence independent of all procedural rules and constitutional forms.

In the light of these observations, it should now be possible to answer the question we posed. It is clear that that the various parts of what you take to be the French constitution are not in agreement. Who then is entitled to decide? It must be the Nation, independent as it necessarily is of

---

[30]It is said that in England the House of Commons represents the Nation. This is not right. Perhaps I have said so already, in which case I can only repeat that if the Commons alone represented the entire national will, then it alone would form the whole legislative body. Since the constitution has it that it is simply *one* part of *three*, it follows that both the King and the Lords have to be taken to be representatives of the nation.

all positive forms. Even if the Nation had held regular sessions of the Estates-General, it would not be up to this constituted body to pronounce upon a dispute affecting its own constitution. To do so would be a petition of principle or a vicious circle.

The *ordinary* representatives of a people are entrusted with exercising, according to constitutional forms, that portion of the common will that is necessary for good social administration. Their power is confined to matters of government.

Extraordinary representatives have whatever new powers it pleases the Nation to give them. Since a great nation cannot in real terms assemble every time that extraordinary circumstances may require, it has, on such occasions, to entrust the necessary powers to extraordinary representatives. If it really could assemble before your very eyes and express its will, would you dare to challenge that will simply because it was couched in one form rather than another? Here reality is everything and form nothing.

A body of extraordinary representatives is a surrogate for an assembly of that nation. Doubtless it does not need to be entrusted with the *plenitude* of the national will. All it needs is a special power and even this only in rare cases. But it is a surrogate for the Nation in its *independence* from all constitutional forms. Here it is not so necessary to take as many precautions against the abuse of power. Representatives of this kind are deputed to deal with a single matter for a limited time. I emphasize that they are not to be subject to the constitutional forms on which they have to decide. In the first place, this would be contradictory because these forms are in dispute, and it is up to them to settle them. Secondly, they have nothing to say about matters for which positive forms have been fixed. Thirdly, they have been put in the place of the Nation itself as if it was it that was settling the constitution. Like it they are independent. It is enough for them to will as an individual would will in the state of nature. Regardless of how they might have been deputed, how they assembled or deliberated, and provided that no one is ignorant that they are acting by virtue of an extraordinary commission from the people (and how could the nation that entrusted them ever be ignorant?), their common will has the same worth as that of the nation itself.

I do not mean to say that a nation cannot entrust its ordinary representatives with the type of new commission here in question. The same individuals can undoubtedly gather together to form several different bodies and, by virtue of special proxies, successively exercise powers that by nature should not be conflated with one another. But it is still the case that an extraordinary representation has no similarity to an ordinary legislature. Their powers are quite distinct. The movement of the one always accords with the procedural forms and conditions imposed upon it. The other is not subject to any particular form. It can assemble and deliberate as would the nation itself if, consisting of no more than a small number of individuals, it decided to give its government a constitution. These are not useless distinctions. All the principles just invoked are essential to the social order. That order would not be complete if it came up against a single case where it could not identify rules of conduct able to meet every eventuality.[31]

It is time to go back to the title of this chapter: *What should have been done* amidst the confusion and disputes over the forthcoming Estates-General? Summon the Notables? No. Allow the Nation and its affairs to languish? No. Negotiate with interested parties to get them all to give some ground? No. There should have been recourse to the great means of an extraordinary representation. It is the Nation that should have been consulted.

This means answering two further questions: Where is the Nation to be found? Who is entitled to consult it?

1. Where is the Nation? Where it is. In the forty thousand parishes covering the whole territory, in all the inhabitants and all the contributors to the public establishment—that is where the Nation is to be found. It ought to have been possible to make a territorial division able to produce an initial level of representation by means of the formation of circumscriptions, or *arrondissements,* made up twenty to thirty parishes. These circumscriptions could, following the same plan, have been grouped together to form provinces, and these latter could then have sent a number of genuinely extraordinary representatives to the capital with special powers to determine the constitution of the Estates-General.

You might say that this would have led to too many delays. No more, in truth, than the sequence of expedients that has served only to make

---

[31]These principles serve to settle the question presently in dispute between Mr Pitt and Mr Fox in England.[(*)] Mr Fox is wrong not to want the *Nation* to give the Regency to *whomever* and *however* it pleases. What the law does not enact, only the Nation can enact. Mr Pitt is mistaken in wanting to make Parliament decide the question. Parliament is incomplete and null, because the King, its third component part, is incapable of willing. The two Houses can certainly draft a statute, but they cannot *sanction* one. I use this term in keeping with contemporary usage. It should then have been necessary to call for extraordinary representatives from the nation. . . . But nothing of the kind will occur. This would have been the moment to establish a good constitution. But neither the opposition nor the ministry had any such desire. Preference was given to the established forms; however vicious they might be, they are preferred to the finest social order. But then, have you ever seen an infirm old man find solace for his own imminent death, however much the young man who he can see is ready to replace him might be fresh and full of life? It is natural for political bodies, like every living body, to put up as much resistance as they can against the final moment.

matters more muddled. Moreover, it is also a question of adopting the means appropriate to the ends, not simply of spinning out time. If anyone had wanted, or known how, to pay homage to true principles, it would have been possible to do more for the Nation in four months than, even though I take them to be very powerful, the course of enlightenment and public opinion could do in half a century.

But you might say, what would have become of privilege, what would have become of the distinction between the three orders, if the *majority* of citizens had nominated extraordinary representatives? The answer is that they would have become what they should be. The principles outlined here are absolutely certain. Either they have to be recognized or there will be no social order. The Nation is always the master of every reform to its constitution. Above all, it cannot avoid having to give itself one whose provisions are certain when its constitution is in dispute. Everyone can see that now. But you ought to be able to see too that it would be impossible to alter the constitution at all if the Nation was simply one side in the dispute. A body that is subject to constituted forms cannot do anything other than make its decisions according to its constitution. It cannot give itself another one. It ceases to exist as soon as it moves, speaks, or acts otherwise than in the forms imposed upon it. The Estates-General, even if it were assembled, would not therefore be competent to decide anything to do with the constitution. This is a right that belongs to the Nation alone, independently, as we keep repeating, of all forms and all conditions.

The privileged orders, as can be seen, have good reason for trying to muddle principles and ideas in this matter. They intrepidly proclaim now the opposite of what they set forth six months ago. Then there was but one cry in France: we have no constitution and demand that one be established. Now, we not only have a constitution, but, to believe the privileged orders, it also contains two excellent and inviolable provisions. The first is the *division* of the citizenry *into orders*. The second is the *equality of influence* of each order in the formation of the national will. We have already given enough proof of the reasons why, even if all these things really did form our constitution, the Nation would still be the master to change them. What more specifically still needs to be examined is the nature of that *equality* of influence over the national will that, it is said, ought to be attributed to each order. We will now proceed to show that this idea is the most absurd that there is and that no nation could ever put anything like this into its constitution.

A political society can never be anything other than the totality of its associate members. A nation cannot decide not to be the nation it is or choose to be itself in only one particular way, simply because this would amount to saying that it could not be a nation in any other way. In the same sense, a nation cannot stipulate that its common will should cease to be its common will. It is sad to have to spell out propositions like these, because they look so elementary until some thought is given to their consequences. Thus a nation could never have stipulated that the rights inherent in the common will, namely, the majority, could ever be transferred to the minority. The common will can never destroy itself. It cannot change the nature of things by making the opinion of the minority the opinion of the majority. It is obvious that instead of being a legal or moral act a stipulation like this would be an act of madness.

If it is claimed, therefore, that one of the properties of the French constitution is that two hundred thousand individuals out of a total number of twenty million citizens amounts to two-thirds of the common will; the only answer is that this amounts to claiming that two and two makes five.

Individual wills are the only elements of the common will. It is not possible to deprive the greatest number of individual wills of their right to contribute to its formation or decree that ten wills should have a value of one or that ten others should be worth thirty. To do so is a contradiction in terms and a manifest absurdity.

Reasoned argument is pointless if for a single moment one abandons the self-evident principle that the common will is the opinion of the majority, not the minority. By the latter token, one might just as well take the will of a single person to be the will of the majority, and then there would be no need for an Estates-General or a national will, etc. . . . If the will of a noble is worth ten, why not make the will of a minister worth a hundred, or a million, or twenty six million? With reasoning like that, one might as well send all the Nation's deputies home and impose silence on all popular protestation.

Is it still necessary to insist upon the natural consequences of such principles? It is patently obvious that in any national representation, either ordinary or extraordinary, influence should be in proportion to the number of individual heads that have a right to be represented. To do what it has to do, a representative body always has to stand in for the Nation itself. Influence within it ought to have the same *nature,* the same *proportions,* and the same *rules*.

The conclusion that must follow is that there is perfect agreement between all these principles and that they prove (1) that only an extraordinary representation can alter, or give us, a constitution, and (2) that this constituent representation should be formed without paying any attention to the distinction of orders.

2. Who is entitled to consult the Nation? If we had a constituted legislature, each of its parts would have a right to do so, because recourse to a judge is always open to a litigant or, rather, because anyone carrying out

someone else's will is obliged to consult the author of the initial delegation either to clarify the conditions of the trust or to communicate information about circumstances that call for new powers. But we have been without representatives for nearly two hundred years, always supposing that this is what they were. Since we have none, who can stand in their stead on behalf of the Nation? Who might be able to apprise the people of the need for extraordinary representatives? The answer to the question will be difficult only for those who give the word "convoke" a panoply of English connotations. Here it is not a matter of a royal *prerogative,* but of the natural and simple sense of the word "convoke." The word encompasses *notice* of a national need and an *indication* of a joint meeting place. Now, when great issues of public safety bear down on every citizen, is it likely that there will be much time wasted on finding out who has the *right* to convoke? It is surely rather a matter of asking who does not have the right? It is the sacred *duty* of everyone able to do anything. This is all the more reason why it ought to be open to the executive power to do so. It is much better placed than ordinary individuals to alert the generality of citizens, and it is also able to indicate a meeting place and eliminate all obstacles placed in its way by factional interest. It is also certain that, in his quality as First Citizen, the Prince is more interested in convoking the people than anyone else. If deciding upon the constitution is not within his competence, it cannot be said that he does not have the competence to bring such a decision about.

Thus there is no difficulty at all in answering the question, what should have been done? The Nation ought to have been convoked to depute a set of extraordinary representatives to the capital with a special mandate to draft the constitution of an ordinary National Assembly. I would not have wanted these representatives to have been given any power to become, under any other quality, an ordinary assembly, in keeping with the constitution that they themselves had established. I would have been fearful that instead of working solely for the national interest, they would have paid too much attention to the interest of the body that they were about to form. In politics, mixing up and conflating power is what constantly makes it impossible to establish social order on earth. Inversely, by separating what should be distinct, it will be possible finally to solve the great problem of establishing a human society arranged for the general advantage of those who compose it.

One might ask why I have taken so long to deal with *what should have been done*. The past, it will be said, is past. My answer is, firstly, that knowledge of what should have been done can lead to knowledge of what will be done. In the second place, it is always good to set out principles that are true, especially on a subject so new for most minds. Finally, the truths set out in this chapter will serve the better to explain those in the one to follow.

Chapter Six
What Remains to Be Done.
A Development of Some Principles

The time has passed when the three orders, thinking only of defending themselves against ministerial despotism, were ready to unite against the common enemy. Although it is clearly impossible for the Nation to draw any useful benefit from present circumstances or take a single step towards a genuinely social order unless the Third Estate is also a beneficiary, the mere sight of the call by the Kingdom's great municipalities for the least significant part of the political rights belonging to the people has inflamed the pride of the first two orders. Can the privileged orders really imagine that they can display so much ardor in defending rights that they have to the point of superfluity and yet be prepared to prevent the Third Estate from obtaining what, in this area, is simply bare necessity? Can they really believe that the prize of a long-promised regeneration should be theirs alone and that the long-suffering people are simply theirs to be used as no more than a blind instrument for extending and consolidating their own aristocracy?

What will future generations say when they learn of the kind of fury addressed by the second order of the state and the first order of the clergy to the demands of the towns? How will they be able to give any credence to the occult and open leagues, the feigned alarms[32] and the perfidy of the

---

[32]It is only too amusing to see the majority of nobles forcing themselves to travesty protests that at the bottom of their hearts they fear as being favourable to despotism, as an insurrection against royal authority. They are not at all afraid of depicting the unfortunate Third Estate, which they deny has any energy of its own and whose courage they explain in terms of maneuvers by the ministry itself, as a band of *rebels* against the king. Among themselves the nobles say that nothing is more dangerous to liberty than the language of the Third Estate, because it looks too much like the following: "Sire, do with us what you will, provided that you do not leave us to be devoured by the aristocrats." At the same time, they say to the king, "The people have their eyes on your throne; take care, they are aiming to overthrow the monarchy." With that kind of an attitude, why not simply undertake to excite a populace that is always blind and always superstitiously responsive to any movement it pleases the aristocracy to give it? At least it would spare them the trouble of having to say *"That is your Third Estate."* But honorable men everywhere will then be able to reply, "*Those are your aristocrats!"* How easy it would be for us to become the first nation in the world, namely the freest and most happy, if there were no aristocrats!

maneuvers in which the defenders of the people have been embroiled? Nothing will be forgotten in the authentic accounts now being prepared for posterity by patriotic writers. All will be revealed about the *noble* conduct shown by those magnates of France in conditions that were ready made for inspiring a measure of patriotic sentiment even among those most absorbed in their own egoism. How could the princes of the reigning house have decided to take part in a quarrel between the orders of the state? How could they have allowed a miserable group of hired pens to load the unbelievable memorandum published in their name with the mixture of atrocious and ridiculous calumnies that they have spewed out?(*)

There has been an outcry about the violence of some of those who have written on behalf of the Third Estate. But how much importance should be attached to the style adopted by an isolated individual? None. Legal, properly authenticated demands by the Third Estate are to be found in the petitions by the municipalities and some of the provinces with their own estates.(**) Compare them to the equally authenticated demands of the princes against a people that took the greatest possible care not to attack them. What modesty; what restraint by the latter! What violence; what profound iniquity by the former!

It is pointless for the Third Estate to expect joint action by the three orders to restore its *political* rights and all its *civil* rights in their full entirety. The fear of seeing abuse reformed has inspired more of a feeling of alarm than a desire for liberty among the aristocrats. Faced with a choice between liberty and a few odious privileges, they have opted for the latter. The privileged soul has aligned itself with the favors granted to servility. They are as afraid of the Estates-General today as they were once so vigorous in calling for them. As far as they are concerned, everything is fine. Their only cause for complaint is the spirit of innovation. Nothing, it seems, is now wanting. Fear has given them a constitution.

In the light of these changes in matters and moods, the Third Estate has to see that it has to rely solely upon its own vision and courage. Reason and justice are on its side. It ought to aim, at the least, to secure their full support. The time for working for conciliation between the parties is over. What hope of agreement can there be between the energy of the oppressed and the fury of the oppressor? It is they who now have dared to launch the word "secession" and use it as a threat against both the King and the People. Ah! Dear God, how happy a day it would be for the Nation if that great and desirable secession was to be accomplished and made final. How easy it would be to do without the privileged orders! How difficult it will be to induce them to become citizens!

Those aristocrats who were the first to attack do not seem to have realized how big a mistake they were making by raising certain questions.

Truth can be left to slumber among a people accustomed to servility. But once the attention has been awakened and a choice between truth and error has to be made, the mind turns as readily towards truth as healthy eyes turn naturally towards the light. In matters of morality, moreover, even a little light leads, like it or not, to equity, because truth, in matters of morality, is connected to rights. Knowledge of rights awakens a feeling for rights and a feeling for rights serves to revive, in the depths of the soul, that wellspring of liberty that, among European peoples, has never entirely run dry. One would have to be blind not to see how happily our Nation has grasped some of those fertile principles that lead to everything that is good, just, and useful. It is no longer possible to forget them or contemplate them with sterile indifference. In this new state of affairs, it is natural for the oppressed classes to have a more lively feeling for the need to restore good order. It is they who have the most interest in bringing men back to justice, the first of all the virtues, the virtue has been exiled for so long from earth. This means that it is the Third Estate that will have to make the greatest effort and almost all the initial outlay needed for the work of national restoration. Due warning must be given, moreover, that if things cannot be made better, there can be no question of simply leaving them as they are. Circumstances do not allow for that kind of cowardly calculation. The choice is either to advance or retreat. If you are not prepared to proscribe the mass of iniquitous and antisocial privileges, then you will have to choose to accept them and make them legal. But the blood boils at the mere thought that at the end of the eighteenth century it could be possible to give a *legal sanction* to the abominable fruit of feudal abomination. There once was a time (and, unhappily, it was a long time) when the impotence of the Third Estate would quite rightly have led patriots to shed a tear or heave a sigh. But if it were to seal its own misfortune now; if, at the very moment when it can do something, it were to subject itself voluntarily to abjection and opprobrium, with what sort of names and feelings would it not deserve to be castigated? If it is right to commiserate with the weak, it is also right to despise the coward. Better still to dismiss this image of a final misfortune that cannot now be conceived, presupposing as it does the most vile baseness among twenty-five million men.

While the aristocrats talk of their honor and attend to their interests, the Third Estate—namely, the Nation—will develop its virtue, since virtue is to the national interest what egoism is to the interest of a corporate institution. Nobles may be left to find some consolation for their dying vanity by taking pleasure in insulting the Third Estate with the most insolent terminology of the feudal language. But the more they repeat terms like *commoner, boor,* or *villein* the more they forget that, whatever they mean now, they are either foreign to the Third Estate as it is today or are common to all three orders, forgetting as they also do that when these terms really did mean something correct, ninety-nine out of a hundred nobles were indisputably *commoners, boors,* and *villeins,* while the others, necessarily, were brigands. Try as the privileged orders may want to close their eyes to the revolution produced by the force of circumstance and the passage of time, it is no less real. Once upon a time, the Third Estate consisted of serfs and the noble order was everything. Today, the Third Estate is everything and nobility is simply a word. But behind the word, and purely because of the influence of a false opinion, a new and intolerable aristocracy has insinuated itself illegally into its present position and the people have every reason not to want any aristocrats.[33]

In these circumstances, what does Third Estate need to do if it wishes to put itself in possession of its political rights in a way that is useful to the Nation? There are two possible courses of action.

In the first of these, the Third Estate should meet separately. It will not assemble with the clergy or the nobility and will not vote with them either by *order* or by *head*. It is vital to insist upon the enormous difference between an assembly of the Third Estate and those of the other two orders. The former represents twenty-five million individuals and is charged with deliberating upon the affairs of the Nation. The latter, even if they unite, have been entrusted with powers by about two hundred thousand individuals and are concerned solely with their privileges. The Third Estate, it is said, cannot form the *Estates-General* all by itself. Very

---

[33]NO ARISTOCRACY ought to be the rallying cry of all the Friends of the Nation and good order. The aristocrats might imagine that they can reply by calling for NO DEMOCRACY. But we too can call for no democracy against them. These gentlemen seem to be ignorant of the fact that representatives are not democrats and that since a genuine democracy is impossible among a numerous people, it is mad either to believe in it or appear to fear it. But a false democracy is, alas, only too real a possibility. It can be found among a caste that imagines that by right of birth or any other ridiculous title independent of the peoples' proxy it is entitled to all the *powers* exercised by the body of citizens in a genuine democracy. This false democracy and all the evils it brings in its wake are to be found in a country which is said and held to be a monarchy, but one in which a privileged caste has usurped the monopoly of government, place, and position. It is this feudal democracy that is the one to be feared, which never ceases to provoke vain terrors to preserve its great importance and which hides both its incapacity for the good under the guise of being an *intermediary body* and its power for harm under the imposing authority of the aristocrat Montesquieu. It will be obvious to anyone who can think that a caste of aristocrats, however much the most stupid of prejudices might decorate it, is as opposed to the authority of monarchy as it is to the interests of the people.

well! So much the better! It will form a *National Assembly*.[34] A recommendation of this importance needs to be justified with all the certain and clear reasons that true principle can supply.

I have emphasized that the deputies of the clergy and the nobility have nothing in common with the national representation, that no alliance is possible between the three orders in the Estates-General, and that, not being able to vote in *common,* they cannot vote either by *order* or by *head.* At the end of the third chapter an undertaking was given to prove that this was true, so that right-minded people could hasten to disseminate it publicly.

According to a maxim of universal law, there is *no greater deficiency than a deficiency of power.* It is clear enough that the nobility has not been mandated by the clergy or the Third Estate. The clergy does not carry a mandate from the nobility or the commons. It follows that each order is a distinct nation and is no more competent to interfere in the affairs of the other orders than, for example, the Dutch Estates-General or the Council of Venice might be entitled to vote in the proceedings of the English Parliament. Anyone acting with a power of attorney can bind no more than his principals, just as a representative has a right to speak only on behalf of those he represents.[35] If it is impossible to understand this, one might as well annihilate every principle and give up on reasoned argument.

---

[34]There are considerable advantages in having the legislative power exercised by three bodies or chambers rather than by a single chamber. But it would be an extreme folly to make up these three chambers of three *orders* that are enemies to one another. The correct solution is to separate the representatives of the Third Estate into three equal divisions. Under this arrangement, there would be the same mission, common interest, and objective. This comment is addressed to those who, captivated by the idea of *balancing the parts of the legislative power*, imagine that nothing is better suited for this purpose than the English Constitution. Is it impossible to welcome the good without adopting the bad? As has already been pointed out, the English have but one order, or rather have none, so that by making our legislative balance consist of different orders it would—and it cannot be emphasised too strongly—be infinitely more vicious than that of our neighbours. There is an important subject of research to be carried out in identifying the principles that ought to govern the formation of legislative chambers to enable them to avoid missing the *common* interest and instead secure it by way of a just balance between the great responsibilities that are its essence. It is a question we will deal with elsewhere.

[35]We should, nonetheless, refrain from calling for the unification of the three orders in every bailiwick (*bailliage*) in order to elect deputies in common. This proposition looks as if it is a solution to the problem raised here, but it needs to be seen as extremely dangerous for as long as no start is made in establishing equal *political* rights. It is essential for the Third Estate not to allow itself to countenance any move by which it might be made to recognise a *distinction* of orders and an absurd victory by the minority over the largest majority. Any such imprudent conduct would be as harmful to its interests, which are those of the Nation, as it would contradict the most simple rules of arithmetic and sound policy.

It should now be possible to see that according to the rules of ordinary logic it is perfectly useless to try to find a ratio or proportion by which each order should contribute to the formation of the general will. It cannot be a single, *unified* will as long as there are three orders and three sets of representatives. At the very most, the three assembles might be able to join together to express the same wish, just as three allied nations can form the same desire. But they can never be turned into *one* nation with *one* representation and *one* common will.

I can sense that these truths, however certain they might be, are likely to provoke something like embarrassment in a state which was not formed under the auspices of reason and political equity. Nothing, however, can be done about this. If the house that you built is held together by all sorts of artificial devices and supported by a forest of scaffolding put in place without any other taste or design than to prop up its various parts as and when they threaten to fall down, then you will either have to rebuild it or resign yourself to living, as they say, from one day to the next, constantly short of ease or comfort and perpetually anxious about being finally crushed under its debris. Everything in the social order is connected. If you neglect one part, the others will not be exempt. If you begin with disorder, you will soon necessarily experience its effects. These consequences are necessary. If it were as possible to gain as much from injustice and absurdity as from reason and equity, what would be the advantage of the latter?

You might well cry in triumph that if the Third Estate was to assemble separately to form a National Assembly, and not any so-called *General* version of the three estates, then it would be no more competent to vote for the clergy and the nobility than these two orders would be entitled to deliberate on behalf of the people. But take note, as has already been pointed out, that the representatives of the Third Estate will undoubtedly have been mandated by the twenty-five or twenty-six million individuals who make up the Nation, apart from some two hundred thousand nobles or priests. This is quite enough for them to able to give themselves the title of a National Assembly. They will, therefore, be able to deliberate without any difficulty on behalf of the whole Nation, minus two hundred thousand heads.

On the basis of this assumption, the clergy would still be able to assemble to discuss its voluntary fiscal donation to the royal treasury, and the nobility could adopt some sort of means to present its subsidy to the king. To ensure that arrangements peculiar to the two orders could never become a burden upon the Third Estate, it would begin its own proceedings by issuing a clear and firm declaration that it would not pay any tax that was not also born by the other two orders. It would agree to approve any subsidy only on this condition, and even after the amount had been fixed, it would not be levied on the people if it became apparent that the clergy and the nobility had found any possible pretext for exempting themselves.

Despite appearances, this arrangement might be as good as any other for gradually bringing the Nation back to social unity. At the least it might serve at once to lift the danger hanging over the country. How can the people not be panic-stricken at the sight of two privileged bodies, and perhaps part of a third, seeming to be disposed in the guise of the Estates-General to determine its future and subject it to a fate as immutable as it would be unhappy? It can never be too just to dispel the fears of twenty-five million individuals, and when there has been so much *talk* of constitutions, there ought to be some evidence, based on principle and conduct, of knowing and respecting their most basic elements.

It is certain that the deputies of the clergy and the nobility are not the representatives of the Nation. They are, therefore, incompetent to vote on its behalf.

If you were to allow them to debate on matters of general interest, what would be the result?

1. If votes were taken by *order,* it would mean that twenty-five million citizens could decide nothing for the general interest, because this might displease a hundred or two hundred thousand privileged individuals or, in other words, that the will of over a hundred individuals would be subject to a veto and could be blocked by the will of a single person.

2. If votes were taken by *head,* with each privileged and non-privileged vote having an equal weight, this would still mean that the will of two hundred thousand individuals would match those of twenty-five million, because they would have an equal number of representatives. But is it not monstrous to compose an assembly in such a way as to enable it to vote in favor of the interest of a minority? Surely this must be the *reverse* of an assembly?

In the previous chapter, we have already established the need to define the *common* will as the view of the majority alone. This maxim is indisputable. It follows that in France the representatives of the Third Estate are the true custodians of the national will. They alone can speak in the name of the whole Nation without error. Even if it is supposed that all the privileged votes were to be added together unanimously against the voice of the Third Estate, they would still be unable to match the majority produced by deliberations within that order itself. According to the proportions that have been fixed, each deputy of the Third Estate stands to vote in the place of about fifty thousand people. Thus, all that would be needed would be to stipulate that a majority would be half of the commons, plus five votes, for the unanimous votes of the two hundred thousand nobles or priests to be covered by these five votes and thus to become indifferent as far the outcome is concerned. Note that on this assumption no attention has been paid to the fact that the first two orders are not representatives of the Nation, although it is still assumed that if they were to sit in a proper National Assembly with an influence commensurate with their number, they would still vote consistently against the majority. Even here, it is still obvious that their view would be swallowed up in the minority.

This is quite enough to demonstrate why the Third Estate is obliged to form a National Assembly on its own and to authorize its claim in reason and equity to be able to deliberate and vote on behalf of the whole Nation without any exception.

I know that such principles will not be to the taste of even some of those members of the Third Estate who have been among the most resourceful in defending its interest. So be it—provided that it is agreed that I have begun with correct principles and have followed a proper logic as I have proceeded. It should be added that, by separating itself from the first two orders, the Third Estate cannot be accused of carrying out a *secession*. This imprudent expression and the sense it contains should be left to those who used it first. A majority cannot, as a matter of fact, separate itself off from the whole. This would be a contradiction in terms. To do so it would have to separate itself from itself. Only a minority has the property of being unwilling to subject itself to the will of the largest number and, as a result, of carrying out a secession.

But in showing the Third Estate the full extent of its resources or, rather, its rights, it is not our aim to exhort it to use them to the full.

I mentioned above that the Third Estate has two ways to put itself in possession of the place in the political order that is its due. If the first of these, as I have just described it, seems rather too abrupt; if it should seem that the public needs time to become accustomed to liberty; if it is believed that national rights, however obvious they may be, need, if challenged by even the tiniest number; to be given some sort of legal approval and, so to speak, be consecrated and made fixed by some ultimate sanction; then all this is entirely acceptable. What it implies is an appeal to the Nation, the only judge competent to hear disputes affecting the constitution. This is the second course of action open to the Third Estate.

Here we need to recall what was said in the previous chapter, both about the necessity to *constitute* the body of ordinary representatives and about the need to entrust this great work solely to an extraordinary deputation invested with ad hoc special powers.

It cannot be denied that in the forthcoming Estates-General the chamber of the Third Estate has full competence to convoke the kingdom by way of an *extraordinary representation.* It is its responsibility above all else, therefore, to expose the falsity of the existing French constitution to the generality of citizens. It is its responsibility to complain as loudly as possible that an Estates-General made up of several orders cannot be anything but a badly organized body, unable to perform its national functions. It is its responsibility at the same time to demonstrate the need to give special powers to an extraordinary deputation so that, through clearly defined laws, it can then draft the constitutional forms of its legislature.

Until then, the order of the Third Estate will suspend not its preparatory proceedings but the full exercise of its power. It will not enact anything definitively. It will wait until the Nation has pronounced its verdict in the great trial dividing the three orders. This, I acknowledge, is the course of action that is most in keeping with the dignity of the Third Estate. It is the most straightforward and the most magnanimous.

The Third Estate should, therefore, conceive of itself in two ways. Under the first of these conceptions it will think of itself as only an *order.* From this perspective there will be no point in entirely unsettling the prejudices of ancient barbarism. The Third Estate will continue to recognize two other orders in the State without, however, crediting them with any more influence than is compatible with the nature of things. It will show them every possible regard by agreeing to leave its own rights in doubt until the decision by the supreme judge.

Under the second conception the Third Estate is the *Nation.* In this quality its representatives will form the whole National Assembly and will have all of its powers. Since they are the *only* trustees of the general will, they do not need to consult those who mandated them about a disagreement that does not exist. If it is their responsibility to call for a constitution, they will do so with one accord. Doubtless they will always be willing to subject themselves to the laws it may please the Nation to give them. But they do not need to refer any possible question arising from the plurality of orders to the Nation. As far as they are concerned, there is but one, single order, or rather there are none, because there is only the Nation for the Nation.

Convening an *extraordinary* deputation to settle, above all else, the great matter of the constitution or, at the least, investing one deputation with a new, special power, as has been explained above, is therefore the surest way to put an end to present dissension and prevent the possibility of trouble within the Nation. Even if there were nothing to fear, it would still be a necessary measure to take because, whether or not we remain calm, it is impossible for us to continue without knowing and taking possession of our political rights. The need to do so will be seen to be all the more pressing if it is recognized that political rights are the only guarantee of civil rights and individual liberty. Readers are invited to give this proposition careful thought.

If I had undertaken solely to set out certain courses of action, I would end this memorandum on the Third Estate here. . . . But I also intended to examine certain principles. This involves pursuing the interests of the Third Estate up to the moment when public discussion of the true *composition* of a national assembly is likely to occur. In fixing the legislative constitution, should the extraordinary representatives pay any attention to the odious and impolitic *distinction* of orders? This is not a matter of issues or power but of the laws determining the composition of the individual membership of elected deputations. In addition to citizens, should any elected deputation contain nobles and priests by virtue of any other entitlement than that of ordinary citizenship? Should they above all be allowed to exercise separate, superior rights on the basis of this entitlement? These are important questions that should, at the least, be treated only after setting out true principle.

The first requirement is to have a clear idea of what the *object* or *goal* of the representative assembly of a nation should be. That *object* cannot be different from the one that the nation would have proposed to itself if it were able to gather and confer in a single place.

What is a nation's will? It is the product of individual wills, just as a nation itself is the result of individuals assembling together. It is impossible to conceive of a legitimate association whose objects are not common security, common liberty, and a public establishment. Doubtless, every individual also has individual goals and will say to himself, "I can go about my own affairs and find happiness in my own way under the protection of a common security, sure in the knowledge that the only legal limits to my desires will be those prescribed to me by society for a common interest in which I have a share and with which my own private interest has made so useful an alliance."

In the light of this, is it conceivable that any member of a general assembly could be mad enough to say, "You are not here to deliberate upon our common affairs, but to attend to mine in particular and those of a little clique that I have formed with some among you?"

Simply to say that members of an association gather together to decide how to deal with matters of *common* concern is all that needs to be said about why they decided to join it. It is so self-evident a truth that any further proof is tantamount to undermining it. The object of an assembly is simply this: common affairs.

At this particular juncture, however, it may be worth thinking about how all the members of a national assembly might be able to join their individual wills together to form a common will that should be synonymous with the public interest.

In the first instance, it is worth examining the mechanism or political process in question in the most favorable circumstances, namely, one in which the strength of public opinion makes it impossible for anyone in the assembly to exhibit anything other than the common interest. Prodigies of this kind have happened in different places, but none has lasted very long. It would be a grave misjudgment of human nature to entrust the destiny of societies to the endeavors of virtue. What is needed instead is for the nation's assembly to be constituted in such a way as to ensure that individual interests remain isolated and the will of the majority cleaves consistently to the public good even during those long periods when public manners are in a state of decadence and egoism seems to be the universal rule. This can be assured if the constitution is generally supported.

There are three types of interest to be found in the human heart: (1) The one by which citizens resemble one another—this is the measure of the common interest. (2) The one by which an individual allies himself with no more than a number of others—this amounts to factional interest. (3) The one by which each individual separates himself from the rest, thinking solely of himself—this is self-interest.

The interest that makes one man join together in concord with all his coassociates is, obviously, the *object* of the common will and the aim of the common association.

But each voter will also bring his other two interests to every assembly. This is unavoidable. Self-interest, however, is not to be feared. It is isolated. Everyone has his own. Its very variety is its own solution.

The real problem thus arises from that interest by which one citizen combines with no more than a small number of others. It is this interest that makes for combinations and leagues. It is the source of projects that are a danger to the community. It is the cradle of the most redoubtable public enemies. History is full of evidence of this sad truth.

It should not be surprising, therefore, that the social order should require such rigor in preventing private citizens from becoming members of corporate bodies and that it should even withhold eligibility for election to the legislature to those entrusted with public authority, because, by the nature of things, they alone will be members of collective bodies.

In this way and in no other can the common interest be sure to prevail over private interests.

These conditions—and these alone—suffice to explain what is needed to secure the possibility of founding human associations for the general advantage of their members and, as a result, to explain the *legitimacy* of political societies.

This is the way, and the only way, to find a solution to the problem outlined above, namely, how to ensure that *in a national assembly individual interests will be isolated, while the will of the majority will always cleave to the general good.*

Consideration of these principles shows how essential it is to organize or constitute the representative assembly in terms of a plan that leaves it with no room to develop a spirit of its own and degenerate into an aristocracy. Hence the importance of those fundamental maxims (outlined in sufficient detail elsewhere)[36] by which a third of the membership of the representative assembly should be renewed every year while those at the end of their term should not be eligible for reelection until a sufficient period of time has elapsed to enable the greatest possible number of citizens to take part in public affairs, something that would not occur if eligibility were ever to come to be seen as the property of a certain number of families, etc., etc.

But if, instead of respecting the basic notions enshrined in such clear and certain principles, a legislator himself were to create corporate bodies within the state and to recognize those that have been formed and underwrite their existence with his power; and if he were then to invite the greatest, most privileged, and, consequently, most harmful of these to become a part of the national representation under the name of an *order;* it would begin to look like there really is a principle of evil responsible for wrecking, ruining, and overturning everything in human affairs. All that would then be needed to crown and confirm this social disorder would be to give these ghastly *guilds* a real predominance over the great body of the Nation. But it is exactly this that it would be possible to accuse such a legislator of having done to France, even though it would be more natural to impute most of the evils to have befallen this proud kingdom to the blind course of events or to the ignorance and ferocity of our ancestors.

We know what the veritable *object* of a national assembly should be. It is not designed to be concerned with the private affairs of particular citizens but with the whole mass of citizens seen from the point of view of the *common* interest. The natural consequence of this proposition is that the right to be *represented* belongs to citizens only in respect to what they have in common and not to what serves to differentiate them.

Those assets and advantages that serve to differentiate citizens among themselves fall *beyond* the quality and character of citizenship. Inequalities of property and industry are like inequalities of age, sex, height, color, etc. These do not infringe upon civic *equality,* because rights of citizenship cannot be attached to such differences. Doubtless, *individual* advantages like these enjoy the protection of the law. But the legislator has no

---

[36]See the *Views of the executive means*, Section III.

part in creating differences of this nature or in conferring privileges on some and withholding them from others. The law confers nothing. It protects what is, up to the moment when what is becomes harmful to the common interest. Then and only then are there limits to individual liberty. I like to conceive of the law as if it is at the center of an immense globe. Every citizen, without exception, is at an equal distance from it on the circumference the globe, and each individual occupies an equal place. Everyone depends equally upon the law; everyone offers it his liberty and property to protect. This is what I mean by the *common rights* of citizens, insofar as it is this that makes them all resemble one another. These private individuals all have dealings with one another. They make their arrangements and engagements with each other, always under the common safeguard of the law. If, within this general activity, anyone were to wish to dominate his neighbor's person or usurp his property, the common law would repress the attempt. But it cannot prevent anyone from increasing his property with anything that favorable chance or rewarding labor might add to it, either according to his natural and acquired faculties or to the vagaries of fortune; nor, unless it involves overstepping legality, can it prevent anyone from aspiring to find or build a happiness that is in keeping with his taste and that is also the most to be envied. By protecting the common rights of every citizen, the law protects each citizen in all that he may want to be, up to the moment at which his actions infringe the rights of others.[37]

Perhaps I am returning to the same ideas a little too much. But I do not have time to reduce them to their most perfect simplicity, and in any event it is not a good idea to be too concise in dealing with notions that have been all-too-readily forgotten.

Those interests by which citizens resemble one another are therefore the only ones that they can treat in common, the only ones by which and in whose name they can demand political rights or an active part in the formation of the social law. They are therefore the only ones that make a citizen someone who can be *represented*.

It is not, therefore, because one is *privileged* but because one is a *citizen* that one has a right to elect deputies and to be eligible for election. Everything belonging to citizens, I repeat, whether it is a common or an

---

[37]I do not propose to make any effort to refute that miserable species of sometimes amusingly nonsensical but always despicably intended verbiage put about by little men and little women about that terrifying word *equality*. Such malevolent childishness may well have its moment, but once that moment has passed a writer would be very ashamed indeed to have turned his pen to refuting drivelling so pitiful as to astound even those who now repeat it, leading them then to say disdainfully, "But this writer must take us to be fools!"

individual advantage (provided that it does not offend the law), has a right to protection. But since the social union could have been formed only by the links between those points that its members had in common, it is this common quality alone that serves to give legislation its lawful character. It follows from this that any particular corporate body's interest, far from having an influence in the legislature, can only arouse its suspicion. It will always be as opposed to the object of a body of representatives as it will be alien to its purpose.

These principles become even more rigorous when it is a matter of dealing with *privileged orders*. I take "privileged" to mean anyone who falls outside the provisions of the common legal system either because he claims not to be subject to common legality *at all* or because he claims to have *exclusive* rights. We have provided sufficient proof of the fact that any privilege is by nature unjust, odious, and contrary to the social pact. A privileged class is to the Nation what individual advantages are to the citizen. Like them, it is not *something that can be represented*. But even this is not quite enough. A privileged class is to the Nation what *harmful* individual advantages are to the citizen. The legislator does his duty in suppressing them. The parallel also serves to reveal a final difference, which is that an individual advantage that is harmful to others is at least useful to its owner, while a privileged class is a pestilence upon the nation that is forced to suffer its existence. To make the comparison more exact, one would have to compare a privileged class in a nation to a frightful disease devouring the living flesh of the body of its unhappy victim. With this in mind, it is easy to see why a privileged class might feel a need to cloak itself in all the *honorable* distinctions it can find.

A privileged class is therefore harmful not only because of its corporate spirit but simply because it exists. The more it has been able to obtain of those favors that are necessarily opposed to common liberty, the more it is essential to exclude it from the National Assembly. Anyone privileged is entitled to be *represented* only on the basis of his quality as a citizen. But for him that quality has been destroyed. He is outside the civil order and an enemy of common legality.[38] To confer a right to be represented upon him would be a manifest legal contradiction. The Nation could have agreed to do so only as an act of servility, which is something that cannot be supposed.

Although it has been shown why anyone mandated to enforce the executive's active power should be neither an elector nor eligible for election to the legislative representation, this should not be taken to mean

---

[38]See the *Essay on privileges*.

that he should cease to be considered to be a true citizen. In terms of his personal rights he is as much of a citizen as anyone else, and, far from destroying his civic quality or affronting others' civic sense, those necessary and honorable functions that set him apart were established to serve those very qualities. If nonetheless it is necessary to suspend the exercise of his political rights, how much more so must it be for those who, scorning the provisions of common legality, consist of those for who the Nation is a foreign country, of those whose mere existence is tantamount to a continuous state of hostility towards the great body of the people? It is indisputable that these latter, having renounced the very character of citizenship, ought, more certainly than a foreigner, to be denied the right to elect or to be eligible. At least a foreigner's overt interest may well not be opposed to your own.

To sum up, it is a matter of principle that everything that falls outside the common attributes of citizenship cannot give rise to an entitlement to exercise political rights. A people's legislature can be charged only with providing for the general interest. But if privileged individuals enjoy an estate that makes them the enemy of the common order, not the beneficiaries of simple distinctions that are almost indifferent to the law, then they should be positively excluded. They can be neither electors nor eligible for election for as long as their odious privileges exist.

I know that such principles will seem *extravagant* to most readers. Truth must seem as strange to prejudice as prejudice must seem to truth. It all depends. If my principles are sure and my consequences correctly deduced, I am content.

But it might still be said that all these things are absolutely impracticable at the moment. In which case, I undertake not to practice them. My own role is that of every patriotic writer, namely, to publish the truth. Others, according to opportunity and their ability, will find ways to approach it or, by acting in bad faith, to stray from it, and then we will have to suffer what we cannot prevent. If everyone were to think *correctly,* even the greatest changes would not be difficult once it was obvious that they offered the prospect of some object of public utility. What better can I do than help with all my strength to disseminate what is true as the way to prepare the ground? Initially, this may not be well received. Gradually, however, it will come to be accepted; public opinion will take shape and principles that at first were taken to be wildly illusory will finally come to be felt to be entirely practicable. With almost every kind of prejudice, if writers were not at first willing to be described as *mad*, the world today would be very much the less *wise*.

It is not difficult to come across those who for reasons of moderation argue that the truth is best laid out *piecemeal* and that it is better to ration its availability. I am not sure whether they understand what they are saying. What is certain is that they do not give enough consideration to the difference between the duties required of an administrator and those required of a philosopher. The former proceeds as he can. Provided that he does not stray from the right path, he deserves nothing but praise. But the path itself has to be cleared right to the end by the philosopher. He has to get to the very end; otherwise he cannot be sure that it is truly the right path.

If he insists on stopping me when and where he pleases because it seems prudent, how can I be sure that he is guiding me properly? Should I simply take his word? But blind faith is not a part of any rational order.

To put matters bluntly, uttering no more than one word at a time looks more like wishing and hoping to lay a trap to surprise one's enemy. I have no inclination to discuss whether even among private individuals plain dealing is not also the most intelligent policy, but it is certain that the arts of dissimulation and any of those other kinds of sophisticated conduct held to be the fruit of human experience are the purest folly when it comes to national affairs that are being publicly discussed by so many real, well-informed interests. Here, the best way to make matters progress is not to hide what the enemy knows just as well as we do, but to convince the majority of citizens of the justice of their cause.

It is false to imagine that the truth can be divided up and separated into isolated parts to make it easier for it to enter the mind *piece by piece*. In point of fact, minds often need a sharp shock. Truth can never have too much light to make the kind of deep impression needed to engrave it forever in the depths of the soul, the kind of impression from which that passionate *interest* in what is true, beautiful, and useful is born. Note that in the physical world light is made by reflection, not by a direct ray, and in the moral world it consists of the relationships between, and the totality of, all the truths pertaining to a subject. In the absence of that totality, one is never likely to feel sufficiently illuminated and one often believes that one has found a truth which then has to be dropped once a subject has been given fuller thought.

It is a miserable idea of reason's progress to imagine that an entire people can remain blind to its real interests and that the most useful of truths, locked away in only a few thoughtful heads, should be made public only as and when a skillful administrator needs to reveal them to ensure the success of his operations! In the first place, it is a way of thinking that is false because it is one that is impossible to put into practice. It is also pernicious, because it ought to go without saying that truth can only gradually reach its appointed place in so enormous a mass as a nation. There is always too much time to lose. Is it not better to give those who may be unsettled by truth the time to become accustomed to it, and better too to give the young who receive it so avidly the time to become something, and better also to give the old the time to pass away? Is it necessary, in short, to wait for the harvest before starting to sow?

Reason, moreover, is not at ease with secrecy. Only when it is spread most widely is it able to perform its powerful work. Only when it is able to strike everywhere is it able to strike true, because it is then that public opinion comes to be formed, and it is to public opinion that the majority of those changes that have been genuinely advantageous to peoples everywhere should probably be attributed, and it is why it alone has the property of being useful to a free people.

You might yet say that minds are still not ready to understand you and that you are bound to offend a large number of people. So be it. The truth that it is most useful to publicize will not be the one that is already almost visible and almost ready to be accepted. On the contrary, it is precisely a truth that offends the most prejudices and the most personal interests that is the one that it is most essential to spread.

Not enough attention is paid to the fact that the prejudice which should be handled with the greatest care is one that is joined to good faith and that the most dangerous personal interest to arouse is one reinforced by a feeling that, in good faith, one has right on one's side. It is essential to deprive the Nation's enemies of that resource. It is essential to condemn them to a *debilitating* awareness of acting in bad faith by disseminating the light of reason.

Those inclined to moderation, to whom these remarks are addressed, will cease to feel apprehension about the fate of truths that they call premature once they cease to confuse the measured and prudent conduct of the administrator who is capable of spoiling everything unless he can foresee the obstacles with the freedom and imagination of the philosopher whose ardor is excited yet further at the sight of every difficulty. It is not his task to compromise with these. The more that minds are encrusted with feudal barbarism, the more he is obliged to lay out true social principles.

When the philosopher clears a path, his sole concern is with *error.* To proceed he has to eliminate it without mercy. The administrator comes later. He has to confront *interests.* These, I acknowledge, are more difficult to face. They call for a new kind of talent and a rarer species of science, quite different from the simple meditations of the studious man. But let there be no mistake—they are even more different from the artifice of a certain kind of minister who takes himself to be an administrator simply because he is not a philosopher.

To be just, it should also be acknowledged, on the other hand, that the speculations of the philosopher do not always deserve to be dismissed scornfully as mere chimeras. If public opinion finally comes to dictate the law even to the legislator, then it cannot be doubted that he who is able to exercise influence over the formation of public opinion is not as useless or inactive as is claimed by so many people who have influenced nothing.

Peddlers of verbiage—and there are some—endlessly make vacuous pronouncements about what they call the importance of practice and the uselessness and danger of theory. There is only one thing to say on this. Imagine any sequence of the most useful, excellent, and considered facts that you possibly can. Can you imagine that the theoretical order does not contain a sequence of ideas and truths that corresponds exactly to your practical chain? Unless you have entirely lost your reason, you will see that the one follows from the other or, better, precedes it. What, pray, is theory unless it is that connected sequence of truths that you might not be able to see until it has been made *real* but which someone has to have seen, unless of course everyone proceeds on the basis of not knowing what they are doing? Those who usually wear out conversation with the nonsense I have just described are in truth no better at practice than theory. Might it not be better for them to opt for the wiser, more *practical* choice, and if they are capable, try a little theory, or if not, try taking advantage of those produced by others while keeping silent on questions that at bottom they can have the consolation of not being able to understand? But to continue. . .

It might in the end be said that even if the privileged orders have no right to interest the *common will* in their privileges, they ought nonetheless to be able, as citizens, to enjoy their political right to representation together with the rest of the society.

But I have already said that by adopting the mantle of privilege, they have become the real enemies of the common interest. They cannot therefore be entrusted with the task of providing for it.

I would add that they are, of course, free to rejoin the veritable Nation whenever they wish, simply by purging themselves of their unjust privileges. Their exclusion from exercising their political rights is therefore entirely voluntary. In any event, since their true rights, those that are the object of the National Assembly, are held in common with those deputed to be its members, they can take comfort from the thought that these latter would be harming themselves if they were to make any attempt to infringe them.

It is certain, therefore, that only the non-privileged members of society are entitled to be electors and deputies to the National Assembly. The will of the Third Estate will always be right for the generality of citizens, while that of the privileged orders will always be wrong, unless by neglecting their private interest they vote like ordinary citizens or like the

Third Estate itself. Thus the Third Estate contains everything to be hoped for of a national assembly. It alone is capable of producing all the advantages that one is entitled to expect of the Estates-General.

It might perhaps be thought that the privileged orders still have one last resort in considering themselves to be a nation apart and in demanding a distinct and independent representation. I myself once made this assumption. But it is unacceptable. It has already been shown in the first chapter of this work that the privileged orders are not and cannot be a people apart. They can be so and can only be so at the expense of a veritable nation. But what sort of nation would voluntarily agree to such a burden?

Reason and justice cannot bend to suit your preferences. In the end it is not worth asking what kind of place there should be for privileged classes in the social order. It is like asking what kind of place a malignant tumor should have in the body of someone who is ill, as it devours and ruins its health. It simply has to be *neutralized*. It is essential to restore every organ to health and activity so that any malign combination able to vitiate the most essential principles of life can no longer occur. But you seem to have been told that you are not yet ready for good health, and you accept this pearl of aristocratic wisdom with all the docility with which peoples in the Orient accept the consolations of fatalism. Keep, then, ill!

THE DEBATE BETWEEN SIEYÈS AND TOM PAINE

The exchange between Sieyès and Tom Paine that took place in the pages of the Parisian Moniteur *early in July 1791 was translated into English and published in the August 1791 issue of* The European Magazine and London Review. *This is the version published here. In an immediate sense, the debate was a product of Louis XVI's flight to Varennes in June 1791 and the glaring question mark that it raised about the future of the French monarchy. One of the first Parisian reactions to the news that the king had secretly left Paris on 21 June leaving a note disowning almost everything that he had sanctioned since the fall of the Bastille only to be arrested two days later in the little town of Varennes, was the publication of a new Parisian daily paper entitled* Le Républicain. *In its first issue it published a letter from Paine arguing that France should have a republican government. It is not clear why Sieyès chose to reply to him and why he did so in the* Moniteur *rather than the* Républicain, *publishing an open letter in the former's 6 July 1791 issue in which he stated that it was his conviction that more people enjoyed more liberty under a monarchy than a republic and inviting "all true republicans" to discuss the respective merits of monarchical and republican forms of government. One obvious reason is that the* Moniteur *had a much bigger circulation than the* Républicain *and that Sieyès wanted to get his message across to as many readers as possible. But it is also possible that his real target was not Paine's letter to the* Républicain *at all. On the eve of the flight to Varennes, Sieyès had been on the receiving end of a fierce attack in the Parisian Jacobin club, first on 19 June, by Maximilien Robespierre and then a day later by Georges Danton, when he had tried unsuccessfully to win support there for a voluntary declaration of allegiance to the principles of equality, a unitary legislature, and lawful political activity to be signed by patriots in all the French departments as a prelude to the forthcoming elections to the new Legislative Assembly. The wording of the second clause however made it clear that Sieyès was still committed to the idea of a single legislature made up of two chambers, but voting in common. Robespierre pointedly interrupted an attempt to initiate a debate on the declaration and proposed instead that the Jacobin club should circulate a very radical set of instructions to voters in the forthcoming elections including a recommendation that voters with little or no property should be paid an indemnity from public funds to make up for the loss of time and money that their participation in electoral assemblies would necessarily entail (a recommendation that Robespierre was to succeed in making a reality some two years later, in September 1793). This was a much more democratic version of a republic than anything advocated by Paine. It is possible, therefore, that Sieyès had more than Paine in mind when he initiated the debate in the pages of the* Moniteur *in July 1791 and that, as some of those best placed to know commented, the exchange was somewhat stage managed. (Whether Paine, who did not speak French, was entirely aware of this is another question).[1] The text of the exchange between Paine and Sieyès has been reproduced from* The European Magazine and London Review, *vol. 20 (1791), pp. 229–33.*

---

[1]On the exchanges between Sieyès, Robespierre, and Danton in the Jacobin club, see F-A Aulard (ed.), *La Société des Jacobins. Receuil de documents pour l'histoire des Jacobins de Paris,* 3 vols. (Paris, 1891), vol. 2, pp. 516–31. The claim that the debate was stage managed was made by Sieyès' friend Joseph Lakanal in the *Journal des patriotes de 1789* (11 Ventôse IV), a claim which, as Pierre Samuel Dupont de Nemours' *L' Historien* pointed out (14 and 23 Ventôse IV), was entirely compatible with the two men having different motives for doing so. On this, see Alfred Owen Aldridge, "Condorcet et Paine. Leurs rapports intellectuels," *Revue de littérature comparée,* 32 (1958), pp. 47–65 (p. 55) and his *Man of Reason. The Life of Thomas Paine* (London, 1959), ch. 10. See also Jean Martin, "Achille Du Chastellet et le premier mouvement républicain en France d'après des lettres inédites (1791–1792)," *La Révolution française,* 80 (1927), pp. 104–32 (p. 108).

Controversy between Mr. Paine and M. Emanuel Syeyes

From Mr Thomas Paine to M. Emanuel Syeyes
Paris, 8 July 1791

Sir,

During my preparation for a journey to England, I read in the *Moniteur* of Wednesday last a letter, in which you give to all true Republicans a challenge upon the subject of Government, and offer yourself for the defence of what is called "Monarchic Opinion" against the "Republican System."

I accept your challenge with pleasure, and have such confidence in the superiority of the Republican System over that nullity of a System called Monarchy, that I engage myself not to exceed the extent of fifty pages in my part of the controversy, though I leave to you the liberty of taking whatever latitude you please.

My respect for your moral and literary character will be a sufficient assurance to you for my candour in our discussion; but, though I propose to conduct myself in it with as much seriousness as good faith, I ought to mention, that I do not preclude myself from the liberty of ridiculing, as they deserve, any monarchical absurdities which may occasionally present themselves to my mind.

I do not mean by Republicanism that which bears the name in Holland, or in some Italian States. I consider it simply as a Government by Representation; a Government founded upon the principles of the "Declaration of Rights;" principles with which many parts of the French Constitution are at variance. The French and the American Declarations of Rights are but one and the same thing in principles, and almost in expressions; and this is the republicanism which I undertake to defend against what is called Monarchy and Aristocracy.

I observe with pleasure, that we are already agreed upon one point—*the extreme danger of a Civil List of thirty millions*. I cannot conceive the reason why one part of the Government should be supported with such extravagant profusion, while the other receives scarcely sufficient for its plainest wants.

This disproportion, at once dangerous and dishonourable, furnishes to one the means of corruption, and places the other in a situation to be corrupted. In America, we make but little difference, in this respect, between the legislative and the executive parts of Government; but the first is much better treated than in France.

But, however I may consider the subject, of which you, Sir, have proposed the discussion, I am anxious that you should have no doubt of my entire respect for yourself. I should also add, that I am not the personal enemy of Kings; on the contrary, no person can be more sincere than myself, in wishing to see them in the happy and honourable state of plain individuals. But I am the declared, open, and intrepid enemy of that which is called Monarchy, and I am so on account of principles which nothing can alter or corrupt;—my predilection for humanity, my anxiety for the dignity and honour of the human species, my disgust at seeing men directed by infants and governed by brutes, and the horror inspired by all the evils which Monarchy has scattered over the earth; and by the misery, the exactions, the wars and the massacres with which it has wounded humanity.

In short, it is against the *whole hell of Monarchy* that I have declared war.

Thomas Paine

The Explanatory Note of M. Syeyes, in Answer to the Letter Of Mr. Paine, and to Several Other Provocations of the Same Sort

Mr. Thomas Paine is one of those men who have contributed the most to establish the liberty of America. His ardent love of humanity and his hatred of every sort of tyranny, have induced him to take up in England the defence of the French Revolution, against the *amphigorical* declamation of Mr. Burke. His work has been translated into our language, under the title of "*Des Droits de l' Homme*" and is universally known.

What French Patriot is there, who has not already, from the bottom of his heart, thanked this foreigner for having strengthened our cause by all the powers of his reason and his reputation? It is with pleasure that I observe an opportunity of offering him the tribute of my gratitude and my profound esteem for the truly philosophical application of talents so distinguished as his own.

Mr. Paine supposed that I have given him a challenge, and he accepts it. I have not given any challenge; but I shall be very glad to afford to so able an author an opportunity of giving the world some further truths.

Mr. Paine declares himself to be the open enemy of Monarchical Government. I merely say, that a Republican form of Government appears to me to be insufficient for liberty. After an avowal so positive on both sides, nothing seems to remain for us but to produce our proofs, the public being entirely ready to decide between us. But unfortunately abstract questions, those especially that relate to a science, the very language of which is scarcely yet fixed, require to be prepared for investigation by a sort of preliminary convention. Before we begin a contest, to be carried on at least under the standard of philosophy, it is necessary that we should be understood. Mr. Paine is so conscious of this necessity, that he begins by giving definitions. "I do not understand," says he, "by Republicanism that which bears the name in Holland, and some States of Italy"

When he wrote thus, this author was, no doubt, aware that I, on my part, do not undertake to defend either the Ottoman or the —— Monarchy. In order to be reasonable in this discussion, and certainly we both desire to be so, we ought to begin by rejecting all examples. In point of social order, Mr. Paine cannot be less[2] pleased than I am with the models which history offers us. The question between us then depends upon simple theory. Mr. Paine defends his Republic, such as he understands it; I defend Monarchy, such as I have conceived it.

"In short," says Mr. Paine, "it is against the whole HELL of Monarchy that I have declared war." I intreat him to believe, that, in this undertaking, I would be his second, and not his adversary. I do not adopt the interest of the whole Hell of Republics. The one is as real as the other, and avails just as much. It is impossible that either Mr. Paine or myself should ever take the part of any sort of Hell.

"By Republicanism," says Mr. Paine, "I understand merely a Government by Representation." I have had some difficulty in conceiving, why

[2]Here we have presumed, upon the sense of the context, to make an alternation in the original, which appears to have been misprinted (note by the *European Magazine*).

it should be endeavoured to confound two notions so distinct as those of a representative system and republicanism; and I hope for some attention to my answer.

It is only since the event of the 21st of June last, that this Republican Party has been perceived. What is their object? Can they be ignorant, that the plan of representation which the National Assembly has presented to France, though imperfect in some of its parts, is, notwithstanding, the purest and the best which has hitherto appeared in the world? What then is the object of those who desire a Republic, when they define it to be simply a Government by Representation?—What! does this Party, so lately formed, already endeavour to array itself with the honour of demanding, representative administration against the National Assembly itself? Will they seriously undertake to persuade men, that in all this there are but two opinions, that of the Republicans, who wish for a representation, and that of the National Assembly, who do not? It is impossible to impute to M. M. the new Republicans such a chimera; or, that they should hope for such a blind docility on the part of the public and posterity.

When I speak of political representation, I go further than Mr. Paine. I maintain that every social constitution of which representation is not the essence, is a false constitution. Whether a Monarchy or not, every association, the members of which do not all at once vacate their common administration, has but to chuse between representatives and masters, between despotism and a legitimate Government. There may be varieties in the manner of classing the representatives, and in their internal regulations; and none of the different forms may be able to attribute to itself exclusively the true, essential, and distinctive character of all good government. We are not to imitate those who say—Observe, I understand by a Republic a good Government; and by Monarchy, a bad one: take that ground, and defend yourself. It is not to a man of abilities, like Mr. Paine, that it is necessary to give a caution against such language.

Whatever dispute may arise upon the different sorts of representations; however it may be enquired, for instance, whether it is wise to employ exactly the same method in the executive and the legislative order; or whatever other questions of this sort may be produced; it does not follow, that upon these gradations and shades depends the difference between Republicans and Monarchicans.

All these debates are, or will be, common to partisans of both systems, and they will be equally so in either hypothesis of a good or a bad representation. In fact, whether our established proxies shall be well or ill chosen, or well or ill established, it will remain to be known what shall be their correlation, and how you will dispose them amongst themselves for the best distribution and greatest facility of public operation.

In one word, it will still remain to be known, whether you will have a Republic or a Monarchy; because, of themselves, the republican and monarchic forms will apply either to a good or bad constitution, to a good or bad government. It is not, therefore, the character of a true representation that it must bear the distinguishing attributes which mark republicans.

Here, in my opinion, are the two principal points, by which the difference of the two systems may be recognized.

Make all political action, that which you please to call the Executive Power, center in a Council of Execution appointed by the people or by the National Assembly, and you have formed a Republic.

Place, on the contrary, at the head of the departments which you call ministerial, and which ought to be better divided, responsible chiefs, independent of one another, but depending, as to their ministerial existence, upon an individual of superior rank, in whom is represented the stable unity of Government, or, what is the same, of National Monarchy; let this individual be authorized to chuse and dismiss, in the name of the people, these first executive chiefs, and to exercise some other functions useful to the public interest, but his irresponsibility for which cannot be dangerous, and you have formed a Monarchy.

It appears that the question depends entirely upon the manner of *crowning* the Government. What the Monarchists would do by individual unity, the Republicans would do by a collective body. I do not accuse the last of failing to perceive the necessity of unity in action, and I do not deny that it may be possible to establish this unity in a Senate, or superior Council of Execution, But I believe, that it would be ill-constituted under a multitude of Reports of Committees; and that in order to preserve all the advantages of which the unity of action is capable, it should not be separated from individual unity.

Thus, in our system, the Government is composed of a first Monarch, the Elector and irresponsible, in whose name act six Monarchs, named by him and responsible. After these are the Directories of the Departments.

In the other, a Senate or Council, named by the Departments or by the Legislative Assembly, would be in the first degree of execution; then the Administration of the Departments.

Those who aim at investing an image with abstract notions, may figure a monarchical Government as ending in a point, and a republican Government in a platform. But the advantages which we attribute to one form rather than the other, are so important, that they cannot be conveyed by a simple image. I do not give the exposition of them; this is not the place; but I am not unwilling to repeat, that in the two points here mentioned consist the distinctive characters of the two systems; that is to say, the difference which there is between an individual responsible decision, withheld by an irresponsible electing will, and a decision by a majority discharged of all legal responsibility. The consequences will be deduced elsewhere.

The Republicans and we may, moreover, differ upon many great questions referring to social regulation, though there may be no reason to acknowledge any new difference between Republicanism and Monarchism. For example: several combinations may be imagined in the election of the Council or Senate of Execution, with the design of extending them more or less to the deliberating administrative bodies. So may we also admit that there may be more than one method proper to regulate what is called the succession to the throne; for there is a latitude of opinion to be either a Republican or a Monarchist, according to several varieties.

It is to be enquired, and I have no doubt that the enquiry will be made, what is my opinion with respect to the hereditary right of the Monarch Elector. I answer, without hesitation, that, in good theory, an hereditary transmission of office, whatever it is, can never accord with the laws of a true representation. Hereditaryship, in this sense, is as much an attaint upon principle, as an outrage upon society. But let us refer to the history of all Elective Monarchies or Principalities. Is there one in which the elective mode is not still worse than the hereditary succession? Is any man so insensible as to intend any blame upon the National Assembly, or to reproach them with want of courage?

What more than they have done could have been performed in the two years past by men, at bottom, like others; that is to say, who can judge only by that which they know, and who, for the most part, know that only to be possible which has already been done? And, if they had thought themselves able to enter into the examination of this question, would it have been for them to balance against an absurd, but peaceable, hereditaryship, the equally absurd custom of election, which is also sometimes accompanied with a civil war? At present, indeed, we are habituated to an elective mode, and have sufficiently reflected to believe, that there may exist a great variety of combinations in that respect.

There is certainly one very applicable to the first public function. It appears to me to unite all the advantages attributed to *hereditary*, without any of its inconveniences; and all the advantages of election, without its dangers. Nevertheless, I am far from thinking that circumstances are favourable for producing a change in this respect of the decreed Constitution, and I am very glad to deliver my opinion strongly upon this subject. The obstacles, I admit, are no longer the same; but have they therefore all disappeared, and have not some new ones arisen? Would an interior division be an indifferent transaction, at the æra in which we are placed? The National Assembly is secure of the union of all parts of France for the Constitution, as already known.

An universal wish appears for the completion and the confirmation of it throughout with uniformity, and with a force capable of giving empire to the law. Would it be reasonable to take this moment for throwing an apple of discord in the midst of the departments, and of hazarding incongruities in the decrees, to which it be hereafter so difficult to place limits? If the Nation will one day explain itself by a constituent Assembly as to the place of the Monarch, whether it shall become elective, or remain hereditary, we need not, on that account, lose Monarchy, since there will always remain what is its essence, an individual decision, as well on the part of acting Monarchs as of the Monarch elector. In short, I hope, that as the public opinion is simplifying more and more in political matters, the *triangle* Monarchy will be generally perceived to be more suitable than the republican *platform* to that division of powers, which is the true bulwark of public liberty.

"*I understand by a Republic,*" says Mr. Paine, "*a government founded upon the principles of the 'Declaration of Rights.'*" I do not see why this government should not be a Monarchy.

"Principles," says he, "with which many parts of the *French* constitution are in contradiction." This is possible; and it is probable, that if it was proposed to form a Republic, offences might be committed against the Declaration of Rights. But who does not see that these contradictions may be remedied without an abolition of the Monarchy? Mr. Paine will permit me to tell him a second time, that, since I do not require him to support any particular Republican form, it is right that he should allow me the same liberty with respect to Monarchy.

I desire, that our discussion, if it takes place, may not depart from the *spheres of theory*. The truths which we shall establish may descend too slowly, or too fast, to be applicable to facts. But I have already said enough to make it understood, that, at present, I feel much more powerfully the instant necessity of establishing the decreed Constitution, than of reforming it.

The Declaration of Rights of France and America are only one and the same thing in principles, and nearly so in words. So much the worse. I could wish that ours might be the best, and it would not be difficult to make it so.

And that is the Republicanism which I have undertaken to defend against what is called Monarchy and Aristocracy. A man who lives in France, or any other part of Europe, will allow, that if we are to take the words *Republic* and *Monarchy* only in their common acceptation, we shall be sufficiently disgusted by the mere mention of them. Have I not an opportunity, if I was to follow the example given me by Mr. Paine, to cast some discredit upon that which is called Republic and Aristocracy? Would a Senate of Execution be less aristocratical, than Ministers acting under the free and irresponsible choice of a Monarch, whose evident and palpable interest would be always inseparable from that of the majority?

I have, perhaps, done wrong in making so early a discovery of my doubts as to the excellence of the Republican system. How far are those from understanding me, who reproach me with not adopting a Republic, and believe, that not to proceed so far is to stop upon the road! Neither the ideas nor the sentiments which are called Republican are unknown to me; but, in my design of advancing always towards the *maximum* of social liberty, I ought to pass the Republic, to leave it far behind, and to arrive at *true Monarchy!* If I am in error, I declare, that is neither for want of time or attention; for my researches and results preceded the Revolution.

I acknowledge, that, for a note, this is become very long; but I was desirous of providing, that if our discussion took place, it would not degenerate into a dispute of words. It will result, I believe, from the perusal of the above, that men who are willing to speak in precise terms will not permit themselves to suppose that Republicanism is the opposite of Monarchism. The correlative of *one* is *many*. Our adversaries are *Poliarchists—Policrates*; those are their true titles. When they call themselves Republicans, it should not be by opposition to Monarchy: they are Republicans, because they are for the public interest, and certainly we are so too.

The public interest, it is true, has been for a long time sacrificed to private views; but has not this evil been common to all known States, without regard to their denominations? If, instead of adopting clear notions, happily suggested by etymology itself, it is determined to persist in a confusion of words which can be useful to no possible end, without doubt I shall not obstinately oppose it. I will permit the word "Republic" to be taken as synonymous to "Representative Constitution"; but I declare, that, after having taken it in this sense, I shall feel a necessity of enquiring, after all, whether they would wish that our Republic should be Monarchic or Poliarchic. Let us then, if we can, establish the question in these terms—"In a good Republic, is it better that the government should be Monarchic or Poliarchic"?

I finish this Letter by a remark with which I ought to have begun it. My Letter inserted in the *Moniteur* of the 6th of July does not announce "that I have leisure to enter into the controversy with the Republican *Policrates.*" My words are these: "I shall, perhaps, soon have time to develope this question." Why *soon*? Because I am persuaded that the National Assembly will, in a short time, put the last hand to their work, and that it is upon the very point of being finished.

Until then, it is impossible for me to leave my daily occupations to fill the Journals with any sort of discussion. I may be told, that this question is the *order of the day*, but I do not perceive that it is. Besides, a friend of liberty does not chuse to discuss questions of right under the empire of questions of fact. This enquiry into principles, and the publication of them, has been already so sufficiently laborious, to a man left to his own individual powers, that he should not expose himself to the regret of having wished to speak reason, at a time when the most decided determinations deprive many of the possibility of attending to it, and leave only the resolution of serving, in spite of him, the one or the other party.

EM. SYEYES

Notes on French Terms

Everything that Sieyès published was connected to a topical political issue of one kind or another. As a result, many of his more abstract arguments were embedded in descriptions or evaluations of contemporary institutions, administrative divisions, or choices of policy that may be unfamiliar to non-specialists in eighteenth-century French history. In the case of the pamphlets published here, these centered mainly upon the French monarchy, its institutions and administrative divisions, on the one hand and on the sequence of events preceding the meeting of the Estates-General of the kingdom on 1 May 1789 on the other. These relatively unfamiliar terms are indicated in the text by one or more bracketed asterisks (*) and are listed below in the order of the page numbers on which they occur.

4 (*)The ministry in question was headed by Etienne Charles Loménie de Brienne (1727–1794), archbishop of Toulouse and, later, of Sens. Brienne was appointed principal minister on 30 April 1787 and resigned on 24 August 1788. As Sieyès' preliminary notice indicates, this means that the *Views of the executive means* was written before this date.

4 (**) Jacques Necker (1732–1804) was born in Geneva and became a member of a large Parisian (and international) banking house, Thellusson, Necker et Cie, and one of the directors of the French *Compagnie des Indes*. He was appointed director general of finance in 1776 and resigned in 1781. He was reappointed on 26 August 1788 and resigned from office two years later, in August 1790.

4 (***) The three orders of the kingdom were the clergy (the First Estate), the nobility (the Second Estate) and the commoners (the Third Estate). During the fifteenth and sixteenth centuries representatives of the three orders were summoned from to time to meet as the Estates-General of the kingdom. The last of these assemblies to meet before 1789 took place in 1614.

6 (*) The Estates-General was summoned to meet at Versailles on 1 May 1789. But the ministry did not specify whether the number of representatives of the clergy, nobility, and the Third Estate would remain the same as they had been in 1614 or, irrespective of whether the number of representatives of the Third Estate would be double those of 1614 and equal to those of the two other orders together, whether the three sets of representatives would meet and vote separately (thus voting by order) or would meet and vote as a single body (thus voting by head). These issues became matters of intense conflict before and after the Estates-General convened. The question as to whether voting was to be carried out by order or by head resulted in deadlock until unilateral action by the representatives of the Third Estate proclaiming themselves a national assembly on 17 June

1789 brought matters to a head and set in motion the sequence of events that led to the fall of the Bastille on 14 July 1789.

6 (**) Assemblies of Notables (nominated by the royal government) were also a feature of the government of the kingdom before the seventeenth century. The practice was revived in the spring of 1787 by Brienne's predecessor, Charles Alexandre de Calonne, partly to avoid presenting his proposals to raise additional funds to meet the royal government's financial needs for ratification by the parlements. The thirteen parlements of the kingdom (of which the largest was the Parlement of Paris) were high courts of appeal in affairs involving the civil or criminal law and, more controversially, were also responsible for registering royal legislation. In this latter role, the parlements were frequently involved in conflict with the royal government during the reign of Louis XV. It was partly to prevent a revival of conflict of this kind that Calonne had recourse to the Notables in 1787. After his dismissal in April 1787 and his replacement by Brienne, conflict between the ministry and the magistracy led in August 1788 to the decision to convene the Estates-General in May 1789. A second Assembly of Notables was held between October and December 1788 to discuss the composition and procedures to be followed by the Estates-General. Until the autumn of 1788, both the notables and the parlements were broadly hostile to the ministry and broadly favorable to the proposal to convene an assembly of the Estates-General. In December 1788, however, both came out against doubling the number of representatives of the Third Estate and in favor of voting by order rather than by head. These developments led Sieyès to produce his *Essay on privileges* and *What is the Third Estate?*

6 (***) "Bankruptcy" is used here in a more active sense than is usually assumed by modern historiography. It meant a voluntary default on interest payments on the public debt. Claims that the royal government was planning to do so were most widespread in the fall of 1787, at the time of the conflict between the parlements on one side and Brienne and the royal chancellor Chrétien François de Lamoignon on the other over the latter's proposal to replace the parlements by a plenary court. One of the main burdens of Sieyès' pamphlet was to argue against the possibility of a voluntary default carried out with the approval of the Estates-General as a way of cutting the deficit and, as could be claimed, of reducing the tax-burden on the poor.

8 (*) The deficit in the royal finances was the issue that had led first to the Assembly of Notables in the spring of 1787 and then to the royal government's decision in 1788 to convoke the Estates-General of the kingdom.

8 (**) A list of grievances (*cahier de doléances*) to be redressed by the king was a part of the old system of royal government by way of estates. The Estates-General, as indicated here, was responsible for drawing up a general list of grievances from the various lists drafted in the various parish and *bailliage* assemblies involved in the election of the representatives of the three estates of the kingdom. As before, electors to the Estates-General in 1789 were invited to draw up these *cahiers de doléances* when they met to elect their representatives. This raised the question as to whether those elected to the Estates-General were bound by the mandates

contained in the *cahiers de doléances* that they brought with them. Sieyès' theory of representation was fundamentally incompatible with this idea.

18 (*) On the contemporary meanings of these terms, see the notes at p. 99, below.

35 (*) The allusions here are to the assemblies of some of the various provincial estates, like those of the provinces of Brittany and the Artois, which remained in active existence in the eighteenth century. The clergy, too, met regularly in a general assembly, although it was represented by the bishops, not by the parish clergy. As Sieyès indicates, the officers presiding over these assemblies were usually royal officeholders rather than elected members of the assemblies themselves.

37 (*) The Assembly of Notables recommended by Charles Alexandre de Calonne, *contrôleur général des finances,* as the body most suitable for agreeing to the royal government's fiscal solution to avert its projected financial deficit, convened on 22 February 1787 and was dissolved on 25 May 1787.

37 (**) The *bailliages* (or bailiwicks) were a set of royal judicial and administrative divisions established in the second half of the sixteenth century.

50 (*) As noted above (6**), the parlements were responsible for registering royal legislation and were entitled (as they rather more consistently than royal ministers claimed) to present legal remonstrations to the royal government if they deemed that the provisions of royal legislation were incompatible with the (sometimes tendentious) fundamental laws of the kingdom. This gave rise to many confrontations between ministers and magistrates during the eighteenth century. The most serious of these was, arguably, the Brittany affair of the 1760s, which led to the abolition of the parlements in 1771. They were reinstated when Louis XVI became king in 1774.

52 (*) The allusion here is to the state of education in France in the aftermath of the expulsion of the Jesuit order in 1763.

53 (*) Municipal officers were to be found in even the smallest villages of southern France during the eighteenth century. In more northerly regions, municipal government was usually part of parish government. In both cases, officers were either elected, appointed by the owner of the local seigneurial court or, at times, required to purchase their offices from the crown.

69 (*) The source of the quotation has not been identified. In Diderot and d'Alembert's *Encyclopédie* the entry under "Privilege" defines it as "a useful or honorable distinction enjoyed by certain members of society and which the others do not."

77, note 5 (*) Cherin was the royal genealogist and, in this capacity, was responsible for the verification of titles of nobility.

87 (*) Before 1787 France was divided into *pays d'états,* meaning regions in which there were provincial estates, made up of representatives of the three estates, and *pays d'élections,* or regions that were subject directly to the royal government and, for fiscal purposes, were divided into *élections*. These divisions had a particular bearing on fiscal matters insofar as the amounts to be raised by royal taxes were al-

located directly in the latter but were allocated by the provincial estates in the former. These divisions were superseded by the provincial administrations, first established by Necker in a small number of provinces in 1778 and extended to the whole kingdom first by Calonne and then under Brienne's Ministry in 1787. Their composition was initially intended to be based on the ownership of different kinds of property but, under Brienne, reverted to representation based upon the division by orders.

87 (**) The Intendants were a body of royal officials established in the late seventeenth century who were responsible for the administration of each of the thirty-two *généralités* into which the kingdom was divided for administrative and some fiscal purposes, notably the collection of a tax called the *capitation*. Unlike almost every other royal office, the office of Intendant was revocable by the crown and could not be owned by its incumbent.

91 (*) The passage in question is actually in Livy, Bk. 4, ch. 3, § 8 (vol. 2, p. 265 of the Loeb Classical Library edition, translated by B. O. Forster, Harvard University Press, Cambridge, Mass. 1922). It can be translated as: "Have you any conception of the contempt in which you are held? Were it possible, they would take from you a portion of the very daylight. That you breathe, that you speak, that you have the shape of men, fills them with resentment." (Thanks to Richard Bourke for the translation and to John Henderson for locating the passage.)

96, note 2 (*) The reference here is to Guillaume François Raynal, *Histoire philosophique et politique des établissements et du commerce des Européens dans les Deux Indes* (Paris, 1770). The third edition of this work, famously including a large number of passages written by Denis Diderot, was published in 1781.

98, note 6 (*) The allusion here is to the pamphlet by the Protestant pastor Jean Paul Rabaut Saint-Etienne, *Considérations sur les intérêts du Tiers Etat, adressées au peuple des provinces par un propriétaire foncier* (n. p.1788).

99 (*) The allusion here is to the longstanding argument about the origins of the French monarchy and the claim, mainly associated with the work of the early eighteenth-century writer, Henri, comte de Boulainvilliers, that the Germanic peoples who invaded Roman Gaul were genuine conquerors of the country they invaded, rather than, as Boulainvilliers' opponents argued, nations whose leaders who had been invited to play a part in the government of Gaul by the Romans themselves before the Roman Empire finally fell. On Boulainvilliers' construction, the invaders, headed by the Germanic Franks, established a new system of government based upon the principles underlying the aristocratic Frankish system. On his critics' construction, the Franks simply inherited and modified an existing system of Roman rule. Sieyès, like Voltaire earlier, had no patience with either kind of historical justification of the existing system of rule. For more information, see Harold A. Ellis, *Boulainvilliers and the French Monarchy* (Ithaca, Cornell University Press, 1988) and Robin Briggs, "From the German Forest to Civil Society: The Frankish Myth and the Ancient Constitution in France," in *Civil Histories: Essays Presented to Sir Keith Thomas* (Oxford, Oxford University Press, 2000), pp. 231–49.

99 (**) The Sicambrians were a Germanic people. The word "Welche" (meaning "what") was a term said to have been used by these Germanic peoples to refer to the indigenous inhabitants of the territories occupied by the Romans. It was picked up and used by Voltaire to refer, disparagingly, to the continuing survival of the beliefs and values of these barbarous nations in modern times. For more information, see the works referred to in the preceding note.

100 (*) The practice remained a feature of representation to the surviving provincial estates. In the estates of the Languedoc, for example, representatives of the Third Estate were drawn exclusively from those holding an office in the municipal governments of the major cities of the province.

100 (**) This concern with noble lineage became a feature of royal legislation during the latter half of reign of Louis XV, beginning with the foundation of the *Ecole militaire* in 1751.

100, note 7 (***) As indicated (at p. 87* above), until 1789 the kingdom was divided into *pays d'états* (mainly south of the river Loire, but including the Artois, on the northwestern frontier) and *pays d'élections* (mainly north of the Loire). As this passage indicates, the elections to the Estates-General in 1789 gave rise to widespread argument about the status of different kinds of nobles and, in particular, about the question as to whether nobles of relatively recent origin were entitled to membership of the nobility in electing representatives of the second estate to the Estates-General. As Sieyès noted, nobles in southern France initially excluded recently ennobled nobles from their electoral assemblies, but the tactic misfired when patriot nobles like the comte de Mirabeau were then elected, controversially, by the Third Estate. Hence the greater flexibility shown by nobles in the *bailliage* assemblies, mainly in northern France.

101, note 8 (*) A *présidial* court was a court attached to a *bailliage* or *sénéchaussée.* Procurators (*procureurs*) were responsible for drawing up the legal documentation presented in civil or criminal cases to the courts by barristers (*avocats*).

102 (*) It has been estimated that there were some 60,000 venal offices (and officeholders) in eighteenth-century France. Some of these offices (notoriously the office of King's Secretary) gave rights of nobility to the grandchildren of their owners. Although many others also gave privileges of one kind or another to their owners during their tenure of office (usually a fiscal or legal immunity), they did not confer any right to nobility for the descendants of the officeholder. These officials were, therefore, still members of the Third Estate. Among the exemptions enjoyed by the owners of privilege of one kind or another was exemption from going into the ballot from which those required to serve in the provincial militia were drawn.

102, note 10 (**) The reference here is to the pamphlet by Joachim Cérutti, *Mémoire pour le peuple français* (n. p. 1788), p. 28. It was a reply to the *Mémoire* published by the Princes of the Blood on 12 December 1788 in which they announced that in keeping with the earlier blood sacrifices made by their ancestors they would give up their fiscal immunities.

103 (*) The reference here is to the *Délibération des six corps de la municipalité de*

Paris, the six great corporations responsible for providing the majority of members of the municipal government of Paris, and its call for doubling the number of representatives of the Third Estate so that it had a number of representatives equal to the combined number of representatives of the clergy and nobility.

104, note 11 (*) By the ruling of the Royal Council of State of 27 December 1788, the Third Estate was granted a number of representatives equal to those of the other two orders. But the ruling rejected the call for voting by head and sanctioned the election of either clergy or nobles as representatives of the Third Estate.

105 (*) Elections to the Estates-General by the Third Estate were indirect, not direct. At the initial level, electors met in parish or municipal (or, in large cities, district) assemblies to elect delegates to *bailliage* assemblies, which, in turn, elected representatives of the *bailliage* or, in the south of France, the *sénéchaussée* to the Estates-General itself.

106 (*) Magistrates in both the parlements and the *bailliage* courts were usually known as the robe nobility (*noblesse de robe*), while nobles serving as officers in the army or navy (or those belonging to grand court families able to claim a long tradition of such service) were known as the sword nobility (*noblesse d'épée*).

107 (*) See the note at 105 (*). In mainly rural *bailliages*, the primary assemblies looked as if they might be dominated by officials of the local owner of the seigneurial court and the, mainly-nominated, members of the municipal or village government.

108 (*) In the autumn of 1788, the province of the Dauphiné in southeastern France initiated a series of declarations that were imitated widely in other parts of the kingdom. Among their provisions was a declaration excluding royal or seigneurial officers from representing the Third Estate.

109, note 15 (*) The allusion is to the celebrated early eighteenth-century highwayman, Louis Dominique Bourguignon, known as Cartouche, who had been executed in 1721.

111 (*) The *bailliage* of Gex was said to have 10,000 inhabitants, while that of Poitiers, over 600,000.

112 (*) In eighteenth-century France, derogation from nobility was held to occur whenever a noble was involved in trade. In Brittany, this did not apply to large-scale wholesale trade. Nobles who invested in trade of this kind were said to belong to the category of "dormant" nobility. As Sieyès also indicates, nobles in Brittany had a strong incentive to reside in the province, because the Breton nobility continued to participate directly in the provincial estates.

113, note 17 (*) In 1781, the magistrates of the Parlement of Paris stipulated that anyone purchasing a magisterial office in one of the high courts of appeal was required to show proof of noble lineage stretching back four generations. The ordinance "requiring proof to enter the army" (as Sieyès put it, rather tendentiously) was the Ségur ordinance of May 1781, requiring all army officers of the rank of captain and above to show proof of four quarters of nobility.

114 (*) The *bonnes villes*, a term which corresponds to the English term "borough," were towns that were granted the liberty to elect representatives to the Estates-General by Philip the Fair.

116 (*) Charles Alexandre de Calonne, was *contrôleur général des finances* from 1783 to 1787. His proposal for the provincial assemblies was presented to the first Assembly of Notables in February 1787 as part of the more general program of fiscal reform that he planned to introduce.

117 (*) The allusion here is to Calonne's successor, Brienne (see the note at p. 4).

118 (*) The reference is to the pamphlet by Joachim Cérutti (see the note at p. 102, note 10**).

119 (*) The reference is to the outcome of the second Assembly of Notables of December 1788 and its decision to reject Necker's proposal to double the number of representatives of the Third Estate in the forthcoming Estates-General.

123 (*) In France, as in most European countries, nobles convicted of a capital offence were taken to have fallen from their rank (*déchéance*).

125 (*) This applied to the *taille*, or hearth tax, in those parts of France in which the tax fell on the person, not his or her property. Nobles were exempt from paying the *taille personnelle*, even if they might still pay the *taille réelle*.

128 (*) The barons, by virtue of their titles, were hereditarily entitled to sit in the Estates of the Languedoc.

130 (*) This plenary court, or *cour plénière*, was proposed, to considerable (and ultimately successful) opposition, by the King's Chancellor, Lamoignon, in 1787.

130, note 26 (**) The reference is to the *Examen du gouvernement d'Angleterre comparé aux constitutions des Etats-Unis, ou l' on réfute quelques assertions contenues dans l'ouvrage de M. Adams, intitulé Apologie des constitutions des Etats-Unis d'Amérique, et dans celui de M. Delolme, intitulé De la constitution d'Angleterre. Par un cultivateur de New Jersey* (Paris, 1789). This was a translation of the pamphlet by the American John Stevens, with notes by Condorcet, Gauvin Gallois, and Pierre Samuel Dupont de Nemours.

140, note 31 (*) In Britain, George III went mad in November 1788. What then became an issue was the question of the terms on which the Prince of Wales should become Regent and, were such terms to be applied, whether Parliament could approve them without the royal consent. Pitt and his supporters, fearing for the future of their ministry under a Regency, argued that it could, thus restricting the Regent's freedom of action. Fox and his supporters argued that the Prince of Wales should simply assume all the powers of the Monarchy (including the power to dismiss the ministry).

145 (*) The allusion is to the *Mémoire* by the Princes of the royal blood of 12 December 1788. It called for voting by order, not by head, and rejected double representation for the Third Estate.

145 (**) See the note at p. 103.

Bibliographical Note on Sieyès' Works and on Further Reading

Full bibliographies of works by and on Sieyès can be found in Christine Fauré, Jacques Guilhaumou, and Jacques Valier (eds.), *Des Manuscrits de Sieyès* (Paris, Honoré Champion, 1999) and in Eberhard Schmitt and Rolf Reichardt (eds.), *Emmanuel Joseph Sieyès, Politische Schriften 1788–1790 mit Glossar und kritscher Sieyès-Bibliographie* (Munich, Oldenbourg, 1981). The best and also the most recent political biography of Sieyès is by Jean-Denis Bredin, *Sieyès: La clé de la Révolution française* (Paris, Editions de Fallois, 1988).

Only one of Sieyès' publications has been given a proper scholarly edition in the language in which it was written. This is *Qu'est ce que le tiers état*, edited by Roberto Zapperi (Geneva, Droz, 1970). There is also an edition of the *Essai sur les privilèges* with textual variants, edited by Edmé Champion (Paris, 1888). A facsimile edition of all Sieyès' pamphlets, with introductory notes by Marcel Dorigny, was published under the general title of *Œuvres de Sieyès*, (3 vols. Paris, Editions d' Histoire Sociale, 1989). The texts of his speeches on the draft constitution of 1795 were reprinted in Paul Bastid, *Les discours de Sieyès dans les débats constitutionnels de l'an III* (Paris, Hachette, 1939). A description of Sieyès' version of what was to become the Constitution of the Year VIII can be found in Antoine Jacques Claude Joseph Boulay de la Meurthe, *Théorie constitutionnelle de Sieyès. Constitution de l'an VIII* (Paris, 1836).

Sieyès' papers and unpublished manuscripts are housed in the Archives Nationales de France in Paris. Selections from these can be found in Christine Fauré, Jacques Guilhaumou, and Jacques Valier (eds.), *Des Manuscrits de Sieyès* (Paris, Honoré Champion, 1999) and in Roberto Zapperi (ed.), *Emmanuel-Joseph Sieyès, Ecrits politiques* (Montreux, Editions des archives contemporaines, 1989). Further extracts can be found in Christine Fauré (ed.), *Les Déclarations des droits de l'homme de 1789* (Paris, Payot, 1988); Murray Forsyth, *Reason and Revolution: The Political Thought of the abbé Sieyes* (Leicester, Leicester University Press, 1987); Thomas Hafen, *Staat, Gesellschaft und Burger im Denken von Emmanuel Joseph Sieyès* (Berne, Haupt, 1994); Stefano Mannoni, *Une et indivisible: storia dell'accentramento amministrativo in Francia* (Milan, Giuffré 1994); and Pasquale Pasquino, *Sieyès et l'invention de la constitution en France* (Paris, Editions Odile Jacob, 1998).

The best English language starting points for understanding Sieyès' political thought are to be found in Istvan Hont, "The Permanent Crisis of a Divided Mankind: 'Contemporary Crisis of the Nation State' in Historical Perspective" in John Dunn (ed.), *Contemporary Crisis of the Nation State?* (Oxford, Blackwell, 1995), pp. 166–231 (originally published in *Political Studies*, vol. 42, 1994, pp. 166–231) and Richard Tuck, *The Laws of War and Peace* (Oxford, Oxford University Press, 1999). Istvan Hont's forthcoming *Jealousy of Trade* (Harvard University

Press, 2004) will be an examination of several of the political and analytical problems which had the most bearing on Sieyès' political thought. The French context is described most broadly in Nannerl O. Keohane, *Philosophy and the State in France: From the Renaissance to the Enlightenment* (Princeton, Princeton University Press, 1980). The more immediate intellectual context is described most fully in Keith Michael Baker, *Inventing the French Revolution: Essays on French Political Culture in the 18th Century* (Cambridge, U.K., Cambridge University Press, 1990). The political setting in which Sieyès published the pamphlets translated in this edition is described in William Doyle, *The Oxford History of the French Revolution* (Oxford, Oxford University Press, 1989) and particularly vividly in Munro Price, *The Fall of the French Monarchy* (London, Macmillan, 2002). The relationship between that political setting and the questions which Sieyès addressed is outlined in Michael Sonenscher, "The Nation's Debt and the Birth of the Modern Republic," *History of Political Thought*, 18 (1997), pp. 64–103, 267–325.

Valuable additional analytical or historical information can be found in Terence Ball, James Farr, and Russell L. Hanson (eds.), *Political Innovation and Conceptual Change* (Cambridge, U.K., Cambridge University Press, 1989); François Furet, *Interpreting the French Revolution* (Cambridge, U.K., Cambridge University Press, 1981); François Furet and Mona Ozouf (eds.), *A Historical Dictionary of the French Revolution* (Cambridge, Massachusetts, Harvard University Press, 1989); Bernard Manin, *Principles of Representative Government* (Cambridge, U.K., Cambridge University Press, 1994); Robert R. Palmer, *The Age of the Democratic Revolution*, 2 vols. (Princeton, Princeton University Press, 1959); Hanna Fenichel Pitkin, *The Concept of Representation* (Berkeley, University of California Press, 1967); Dale Van Kley (ed.), *The French Idea of Freedom* (Palo Alto, Stanford University Press 1994); Franco Venturi, *The End of the Old Regime in Europe,* 3 vols. (Princeton, Princeton University Press, 1989 and 1991); and David Wootton (ed.), *Republicanism, Liberty and Commercial Society 1649–1776* (Palo Alto, Stanford University Press, 1994).

The best English language account of Sieyès' political thought is to be found in Murray Forsyth, *Reason and Revolution: The Political Thought of the abbé Sieyes* (Leicester, Leicester University Press, 1987). A more summary account can be found in the same author's "Emmanuel Sieyes: *What is the Third Estate?*" in *The Political Classics: Hamilton to Mill*, ed. Murray Forsyth, Maurice Keens-Soper, and John Hoffman (Oxford, Oxford University Press, 1993). Readers of French will find much of value in Pasquale Pasquino, *Sieyès et l'invention de la constitution en France* (Paris, Editions Odile Jacob, 1998). Additional information can be found in Marcelle Adler-Bresse, *Sieyès et le monde allemand* (Lille, 1977); Paul Bastid, *Sieyès et sa pensée* (2d ed. Paris, Hachette, 1970); Jean-Pierre Cotten, Robert Damien, and André Tosel (eds.), *La Représentation et ses crises*, Annales Littéraires de l' Université de Franche-Comté, 709 (2001); Marcel Gauchet, *La Révolution des pouvoirs: la souveraineté, le peuple et la représentation (1789–1799)* (Paris, Gallimard, 1995); and Lucien Jaume, *Echec au Libéralisme* (Paris, Editions Kimé, 1990).

Index

Unless they have been qualified in a significant sense, generic terms that encompass much of the subject-matter of Sieyès' pamphlets (such as France *or* Estates-General*) have been omitted from this index. Italicized entries refer to French language words.*